'... excellent work by Kenneth Williford and David Rudrauf. ... The new translators have left the division of the text as the author intended. They have also included Maurice Merleau-Ponty's 1936 review of the book, as an appendix. ... [The] editorial notes are exemplary of the care with which a work of some importance has been made available to us once again.'

— *Santiago Ramos*, Continental Philosophy Review

The Imagination

'Every theory of imagination must satisfy two requirements. It must account for the spontaneous discrimination that the mind makes between its images and its perceptions, and it must explain the role that the image plays in the operation of thought. Whatever form it has taken, the classical conception of the image could not fulfil these two essential tasks.'

—*Jean-Paul Sartre*

Jean-Paul Sartre's *L'Imagination* was published in 1936 when he was thirty years old. *The Imagination* is Sartre's first full philosophical work, presenting some of the basic arguments concerning phenomenology, consciousness, and intentionality that were to mark his philosophy as a whole and be so influential in the course of twentieth-century philosophy.

Sartre begins by criticizing philosophical theories of the imagination, particularly those of Descartes, Leibniz, and Hume, before establishing his central thesis. Imagination does not involve the perception of 'mental images' in any literal sense, Sartre argues, yet reveals some of the fundamental capacities of consciousness. He then reviews psychological theories of the imagination, including a fascinating discussion of the work of Henri Bergson.

Sartre argues that the 'classical conception' is fundamentally flawed because it begins by conceiving of the imagination as being like perception and then seeks, in vain, to re-establish the difference between the two. Sartre concludes with an important chapter on Husserl's theory of the imagination which, despite sharing the flaws of earlier approaches, signals a new phenomenological way forward in understanding the imagination.

The Imagination is essential reading for anyone interested in the philosophy of Jean-Paul Sartre, phenomenology, and the history of twentieth-century philosophy. The translation has been revised throughout for this Routledge Classics edition. There is also a revised Translators' Introduction and a new Foreword, both by Kenneth Williford and David Rudrauf. Also included is Maurice Merleau-Ponty's important review of *L'Imagination* upon its publication in French in 1936.

Translated by Kenneth Williford and David Rudrauf.

Jean-Paul Sartre (1905–1980) was one of the great philosophers of the twentieth century and a renowned novelist, dramatist, and political activist. He passed the agrégation in philosophy at the École Normale Supérieure in Paris in 1929. His first novel, *La Nausée*, which Sartre considered one of his best works, was published in 1938. Sartre served as a meteorologist in the French army before being captured by German troops in 1940, spending nine months as a prisoner of war. He continued to write during his captivity, and, after his release, he published his great trilogy of novels, *Les Chemins de la Liberté* and his classic of existential phenomenology, *L'Être et le Néant*. In 1964, Sartre was awarded the Nobel Prize in Literature but declined it. During the events of 1968 he was arrested for civil disobedience but swiftly released by President Charles de Gaulle, who allegedly said 'one does not arrest Voltaire'. He died on 15 April 1980 in Paris, his funeral attracting an enormous crowd of up to 50,000 mourners. He is buried in the Cimetière du Montparnasse in Paris.

"Routledge Classics is more than just a collection of texts ... it embodies and circulates challenging ideas and keeps vital debates current and alive." – *Hilary Mantel*

The Routledge Classics series contains the very best of Routledge's publishing over the past century or so, books that have, by popular consent, become established as classics in their field. Drawing on a fantastic heritage of innovative writing published by Routledge and its associated imprints, this series makes available in attractive, affordable form some of the most important works of modern times.

For a complete list of titles visit:
https://www.routledge.com/Routledge-Classics/book-series/SE0585

Jean-Paul

Sartre

The Imagination

Translated by Kenneth Williford and David Rudrauf

With a new Foreword by Kenneth Williford and David Rudrauf

London and New York

Designed cover image: *Cafe chairs.* Courtesy of Getty Images

First published in Routledge Classics 2026
by Routledge
4 Park Square, Milton Park, Abingdon, Oxon OX14 4RN

and by Routledge
605 Third Avenue, New York, NY 10158

Routledge is an imprint of the Taylor & Francis Group, an informa business

This translation first published in 2012 by Routledge

British Library Cataloguing-in-Publication Data
A catalogue record for this book is available from the British Library

ISBN: 978-1-041-10912-9 (hbk)
ISBN: 978-1-032-93330-6 (pbk)
ISBN: 978-1-003-65740-8 (ebk)

DOI: 10.4324/9781003657408

Typeset in Joanna
by codeMantra

CONTENTS

ACKNOWLEDGEMENTS

FOR THE ROUTLEDGE CLASSICS EDITION

We would like to thank Alex Moino for his thoughtful suggestions on improving this translation. KW would like to thank Anya, Lydia, Peter, and Sasha for putting up with him while he worked endlessly on Sartrean matters and to thank The University of Texas at Arlington (and specifically Miriam Byrd, Elizabeth Newman, and Tamara Brown) for a post-Chairing teaching leave in the spring of 2025 that enabled concentration on this and related work. DR would like to thank Dominique, Valérie, and Joseph.

FOR THE FIRST EDITION

We would like to thank Jonathan Webber for his very useful feedback on an early draft of the translation, and Adam Johnson and Tony Bruce for their good nature and patience with us. Sometimes it felt like our promises about the completion of the work were like so many predictions of the end of the world: it doesn't matter that the vast majority of them turn out to be false; someday, some prophet of doom will turn out to be right. And that, apparently, is motive enough for them to keep making the forecast.

We'd also like to thank Andrea Swenson for letting us take over and 'trash' her apartment for a translation frenzy early in the process.

As is customary, the translators blame each other for any flaws remaining in this translation.

I (KW) would like to dedicate this work to the memory of Denny Bradshaw, who first showed me the importance of Sartre's early phenomenological works, and to Panayot Butchvarov, Denny's mentor and then my own, whose course on Sartre at The University of Iowa was the stuff of academic legend and whose philosophical breadth and depth continue to astound.

I (DR) would like to dedicate this work to my father, Jacques Rudrauf, to whom I owe an understanding of a certain French intellectual tradition and discourse that was pivotal in the making of this translation.

FOREWORD TO THE ROUTLEDGE CLASSICS EDITION

Kenneth Williford and David Rudrauf

Sartre's *The Imagination* was published by the Librairie Félix Alcan in 1936. It was Sartre's first philosophical book, and it concerned a topic that he had been researching and then teaching on for about a decade. The book has its origins in the thesis Sartre wrote during 1926 and 1927 for his *Diplôme d'Études Supérieures de Philosophie* under the direction of Henri Delacroix, who had once been a student of Henri Bergson and was at the time and until his death in 1937 a very well-known, well-respected, and wide-ranging psychologist. Sartre's thesis, around 150 pages in length and entitled *L'Image dans la vie psychologique: rôle et nature*, has only recently been published in French (see Sartre 2018). In it one can find embryonic and 'pre-phenomenological' versions of many of the arguments and themes he would present in a much more refined form in *The Imagination* and *The Imaginary*. And one can see from it that by 1927 he had already acquired a broad and deep knowledge of the late nineteenth- and early twentieth-century French and German psychological, philosophical, and even some neurological literature on images and imagination and their relation to thought, perception, and affectivity.

On the strength of this thesis, which received a mark of 'excellent', Delacroix had invited Sartre to write a book to be published in Alcan's *Nouvelle Encyclopédie philosophique* series under the editorship of Delacroix himself. Sartre turned in a long book entitled *L'Image* which comprised versions of both *The Imagination* and *The Imaginary*. Alcan accepted only the former, historico-critical part of the work. The more original part, *The Imaginary*, would have to wait for full publication until 1940 with Gallimard, only the very first portion of the work being published as an article in 1938 in the *Revue de Métaphysique et de Morale*.

Given that Sartre devoted a decade to the topic of the imagination, not only mastering much of the existing literature, but teaching on the topic to *lycée* students, involving them in experiments, experimenting himself and on himself (including, famously, with mescaline—on this see, esp., Dassonneville 2023), and enriching his approach, on the theoretical side, via the study of Husserl's Phenomenology beginning in the early 1930s, it should come as no surprise that Sartre's two books on the imagination constitute his most academically rigorous and, arguably, most penetrating philosophical work. On the strength of these books, Sartre could have, if he had wanted to and if literary fame had not intervened, pursued what no doubt would have been a luminous academic career within the French university system.

The general consensus is that *The Imaginary* is the more original of Sartre's two texts on the imagination. Up to now, it is safe to say that this 85-year-old book, *The Imaginary*, ought to be read by every psychologist, cognitive scientist, neuroscientist, literary theorist, aesthetician, or philosopher interested in the imagination. It has not ceased to spur original and excellent critical, historical, and expository work from a variety of orientations (see, e.g., McGinn 2004, Elpidorou 2011, Stawarska 2013, Windt 2015, Kriegel 2016, Smith 2016, Hopkins 2018, Kind 2018, Godelier 2020, Webber 2020, Warmbier 2022). Even if it does not satisfactorily answer all the questions it raises, and even if it makes crucial mistakes, it delineates the *Problematik* of the imagination in such a lucid and forceful way, and explodes so many of the errors we naïvely tend to make when first reflecting on images and our capacity to form them, that those who do not master the contents of the work are in much greater danger of winding up in one of the conceptual dead ends the book exposes than they would be had they done so.

But why, then, one might ask, should we also read the supposedly merely propaedeutic work, *The Imagination*? Why not bypass it and head straight for the philosopher's gold? There are, in our view, essentially three main reasons with historical and systematic dimensions.

First, *The Imagination* amounts to a kind of summative document that preserves a transitional period in the development of psychology from the late nineteenth century to the first third of the twentieth. This period was of crucial importance in the progress of the discipline away from rather procrustean forms of Associationism and from a reliance upon sometimes naïve forms of introspection towards a great deal more conceptual, explanatory, and phenomenological sophistication. On the European continent, the scourge of Behaviourism never really took hold as it did in the United States, and cruder forms of Positivism in Psychology were always held in check by significant counter-tendencies. The resulting plurality of inter-related approaches in psychological theory created a much richer universe of thought than was to be found, with some exceptions (William James, above all), in Britain or North America.

On the one hand, there is the work of Brentano's and Wundt's heretical 'offspring', notably the Würzburg School, the Gestalt School, and the Psychoanalytic tradition. On the other, there is the development of France's autochthonous (but, characteristically, also cosmopolitan) psychological, psychiatric, and neurological traditions from Paul Broca, Hippolyte Taine, Théodule-Armand Ribot, and Alfred Binet to Édouard Claparède, Pierre Janet, and Henri Delacroix himself, among others. And, of course, there are the philosophical interventions interacting with all of these sub-traditions to consider—above all those of Henri Bergson (*The Imagination* contains Sartre's most extensive discussion of his work) and Edmund Husserl, but the lesser-known intervention of Albert Spaier should not be forgotten (which it might have been were it not for Sartre).

That *The Imagination* culminates in a discussion of Husserl is, of course, no accident, since Husserl's Phenomenology, which Sartre had studied intensively in Berlin in 1933 and 1934, had been a philosophical revelation to him and his chosen vehicle for developing a philosophy that put one back in touch with concrete reality, with 'the matters themselves'. For Sartre, this meant, above all, treating Husserl's doctrine of intentionality, even as it was developed in Husserl's *Ideas*, in the realist manner in which it was first articulated in the *Logical Investigations*. Consequently, one finds a very favourable discussion of Husserl's famous critique of psychologism as well as a discussion of Husserl's *noema* doctrine that ought to be of interest to anyone trying to come to grips with what exactly that doctrine was. Those familiar with the 'East Coast' vs 'West Coast' interpretive controversies that have grown up around Husserl's *noema* doctrine will find much food for thought and may find it worth considering which side of the controversy the Sartre of 1936 would have come down on. Sartre will make good, if implicitly critical, use of Husserl's *noesis–noema* distinction up through *Being and Nothingness*, where it is finally subjected to more explicit scrutiny, though, we might argue, never exactly abandoned. In fact, to speak anachronistically, we might argue that Sartre thinks that the Husserl of the *Ideas* has a more 'West Coast' or 'Fregean' interpretation of his own doctrine, whereas Sartre maintains that a more 'East Coast' version is the phenomenologically and ontologically correct one.

The Imagination, one might say, provides a kind of 'history in amber' of this segment of the development of core Continental European psychology and philosophy, seen from the angle of the questions that drove Sartre in this work: What is it to imagine? What is it, generally speaking, *that* we imagine? How does imagination differ from perception? How does imagination relate to thought? How do all of these modalities relate to consciousness as such?

None of these questions is today fully resolved, of course, but one can find that what was written on them in the period Sartre covers sometimes rivals if not betters what is written today. Our lack of historical depth and the ever-increasing mass output of scholarly articles and books on these deep and seductive topics all but guarantee that many of us will simply re-invent ultimately useless wheels, instead of wheels we might have made roll if only we had stood on the shoulders of past giants (to mix metaphors).

A second reason for reading *The Imagination* has to do with the development of Sartre's own philosophy. In *The Imagination*, one can already find the elements of Sartre's radical conception of consciousness as both an empty, self-transparent, insubstantial revelator of objects other than itself and yet a kind of self-determining spontaneity or 'absolute' that can only act on itself and that no object can literally act on in a causal way. 'We call spontaneous', Sartre says, 'an existence that by itself determines itself to exist. ... [T]o exist spontaneously is to exist for itself and by itself. One reality alone ... merits the name spontaneous, and that is consciousness.' Sartre equates this with 'the great ontological law of consciousness ...: '*The sole manner of existing for a consciousness is in having consciousness that it exists.*' Readers familiar with *The Transcendence of the Ego* and *Being and Nothingness* will recognize this as a statement of what we might call Sartre's 'Central Dogma' (as the expression is used in the sciences) concerning consciousness, namely, the thesis that consciousness always involves an immediate, pre-reflective, and non-representational self-consciousness or self-acquaintance. This is the *pour soi*, the *for-itself*; and Sartre uses this term, made so famous in *Being in Nothingness*, already in the very first paragraph of *The Imagination*.

Arguably, Sartre conflates this claim, which many of us agree captures a, if not *the*, definitive feature of consciousness, with the much more suspect claim that consciousness has immediate and complete access to all of its intrinsic or essential features. Because of that conflation, Sartre is able to infer, as he says after enunciating his Dogma, 'that consciousness can determine itself to exist but cannot act upon something other than itself'. One might balk at this apparent *non sequitur*, but once one realizes that Sartre regards inertia and opacity as definitive of the physical and required by any objects in physical interaction, and regards consciousness *qua* self-transparent spontaneity as essentially non-inertial and, via the epistemic side of the Central Dogma, known to itself to be so, one can understand his inference.

As it happens, this conflation of pre-reflective self-consciousness (which, we could argue, is indeed an essential feature of consciousness) and complete and immediate epistemic self-access (which is completely implausible) functions as a kind of dialectical engine powering the entire development of Sartre's philosophy—indeed, well beyond *Being and Nothingness*, as the epistemic claim gets progressively attenuated. In the early Phenomenological works, Sartre's Central Dogma is on full display.

On the one hand, especially as coupled with his realist interpretation of Husserl's intentionality thesis, the Dogma provides a powerful tool for re-articulating, in a highly satisfying and plausible way, our understanding of imagination, emotion, and egological experience. To take the case at hand, the images we create in acts of imagination are not little simulacra literally living inside of consciousness. No, the image is a way of intentionally aiming at an absent object or state of affairs and using our bodily movements, knowledge, and affective responses to engender in ourselves a present analogue (or 'analogon' as he will say in *The Imaginary*) of what is absent. And there is no possibility of conflating these images with perceptions because they have a fundamentally different intentional structure.

Moreover, perceptual 'surfaces', if you like, are no more little impressions or ideas inside consciousness than are imagined scenes. Perception is just our way of intentionally aiming at what is indeed present in our immediate environment; and what is present is not a 'Veil of Ideas' but the very objects themselves. For perception, we might say, the object aimed at intentionally is, by essential norm, supposed to be the object given in the flesh via the sensory channels. For imagination, we know in advance that the object intentionally aimed at is not so given; it is absent or given otherwise than we imagine it to be. Negation thus enters into imagination in a way that goes beyond the intentional transcendence-negation inherent in the consciousness of any object via any modality. To take Sartre's very first example in the opening pages of *The Imaginary*, when you see a piece of paper, it is present before you, and you *ipso facto* know that it is *not* you. But when you imagine the same paper, it remains not-you, but it is also no longer present in the flesh—there is another layer of negation involved.

On the other hand, the epistemic completeness thesis Sartre builds into his Central Dogma leads him into difficulty after difficulty. This is less obvious in *The Imagination*, but in *The Imaginary* it will manifest when he tries to make sense of hypnagogic images, dreams, and drug-induced hallucinations as acts of imagination. If mescaline does not, in some very definite sense, and even if in a highly mediated way, 'act on' consciousness, then, we suppose, indeed, nothing does! What drives Sartre here is the idea that if consciousness is acted on by something outside of its immediate access, then, in the end, it is not really spontaneous, not really free. As much as he may have appreciated Freud's *The Interpretation of Dreams*, Sartre, in this period, absolutely rejected the idea of some unconscious processes somehow creating contents which they then presented on the 'screen' of consciousness. Accordingly, Sartre tries to convince us that in hallucination and in dream, it is in terms of consciousness fascinating, hypnotizing, transfixing, or spellbinding *itself* via its own imaginative acts that we can understand these phenomena.

And he tells a similar story about 'passion' and 'being overcome with emotion' in his *Sketch for a Theory of the Emotions*. If emotion is but a modality of consciousness, and consciousness is intrinsically self-transparent, spontaneous, and free, we cannot say that we were literally overcome by an emotion, blinded by rage, carried away by desire, or crushed by grief or trauma. Situations and bodily reactions do not *make us* emote, he thinks. Rather, we choose to 'descend' to the magico-emotional way of relating to the world, and we remain fully responsible and free throughout. It is no wonder that Sartre, despite his own explicit disavowals, is sometimes classed as a neo-Stoic of sorts, especially as it touches his early works (see, e.g., D'Jeranian 2020).

We have no space here to trace the dialectic of Sartre's Central Dogma into *Being and Nothingness*. Suffice it to say that the aporias it produces are many and worth considering carefully. One might, as was customary in both post-Sartrean French philosophy and in much anglophone analytic philosophy, simply dismiss the Sartrean conception of consciousness as 'warmed-over Cartesianism'. But this would be a grave mistake. For one thing, conceptions of consciousness that incorporate, in one way or another, Sartre's epistemic completeness thesis (sometimes called the 'Revelation' thesis) are far from dead in contemporary philosophy of mind (e.g., Russellian monism, panpsychism, Chalmersian neo-dualism), though the proponents of these views tend to be less consistent and cognizant of the actual consequences of this position (see, e.g., Williford 2020). Sartre, by contrast, is well aware of these consequences and, as it were, bites every bullet. Moreover, Sartre, due to his realist conception of perceptual intentionality and his 'intentionalism' or 'externalism', is not willing to make consciousness into the very substance of reality as some of these positions have it. In fact, because of its perceptual intentionality, according to Sartre, consciousness is *ipso facto* metaphysically (though not causally) dependent on the World, on something other than itself; it is as far from being substantial, categorially speaking, as anything can be. Consequently, Sartre finds himself with an essentially 'Mysterian' position on the mind–body problem, which, we could argue, is certainly more plausible, all things considered, than some reversion to consciousness 'fundamentalism'.

Thus, studying the early Sartre is not merely a matter of developing an understanding of his philosophical development, something only of interest to the student of 'classical' Phenomenology or the history of French philosophy. No, by studying

Sartre's early phenomenological works, from *The Imagination* to *Being and Nothingness*, the serious student of the philosophy of mind, and of the theory of consciousness, in particular, can acquire a very deep and vivid understanding of both the power and the potential pitfalls of taking the phenomenology of consciousness seriously, which is what any such student, whatever their theoretical inclination, ought to do. And this study ought to begin with Sartre's *The Imagination*.

One final reason for reading *The Imagination* ought also to be considered. This reason, too, is of both historical and systematic interest. Sartre begins *The Imagination* with a discussion of Descartes, Spinoza, Leibniz, Locke, Berkeley, and Hume. His claim is that these Early Modern greats, with their 'Way of Ideas', set the stage for the *Problematik* of the image in philosophy and psychology as it developed up to the early twentieth century. While these philosophers had different conceptions of the relationship between thought and imagination, and had different ideas about how we are able to distinguish perception from imagination (e.g. Hume's distinction between vivid 'impressions' vs fainter 'ideas'), what they had in common was an understanding of the nature of images, be they perceptual, imaginary, memorial, or hallucinatory. According to that understanding, images are like things that are somehow 'in the mind' or 'in consciousness'. In *The Imaginary* he will call this the 'illusion of immanence'. The more familiar Lockean 'Veil of Ideas' is a version of this illusion.

According to Sartre, this thesis is at the root of nearly all evils in this domain. It makes it impossible to explain the intuitive ease with which we distinguish imagination from perception. It entails the denial of the spontaneity of consciousness because, by introducing essentially a whole inert world into consciousness, it transfers to consciousness that very inertia. Consciousness would then be as passive as a rock being crushed by a hammer. But, Sartre believes, we know it is not like that: it is active; it is always able to transcend its situation. And its imaginative capacity, its ability to consider and make the absent *as if present* to itself is the key expression of its freedom from the chains of the immediate, the constraints of the current situation or impasse. It is because we can imagine the world differently that we can set about to change it.

Moreover, this 'thingist' conception of the image creates insuperable problems for understanding the relation between imagination and thought. If thought requires images, and images are no different really from perceptual *things*, then thinking with images would be as clunky as trying to speak with things—recall the Balnibarbians of Swift's *Gulliver's Travels* who try to lay aside words altogether and express their thoughts with things and are thus obliged to carry around great packs on their backs full of the sundry items they might wish to talk about. If our perception of things is already penetrated by conceptual thought or, so to say, 'renderable' by such thought, and yet thing-images are required to deploy such thought, are we not in danger of an infinite regress? Sartre thinks we are.

As Sartre summarizes the situation:

> Every theory of imagination must ... account for the spontaneous discrimination that the mind makes between its images and its perceptions, and it must explain the role that the image plays in the operation of thought. Whatever form it has taken, the classical conception of the image could not fulfil these two essential tasks.

Following Husserl's clues, Sartre, in *The Imaginary*, will elaborate an alternative conception of the image that aims at satisfying these desiderata. And it is not hard to argue that he succeeds admirably. His modal-intentional or noetico-noematic characterization of imagination still rings true after nearly a century. And his phenomenological descriptions of how thought and imagination interact are some of the most penetrating and subtle he ever wrote—and that says a great deal.

The systematic import of Sartre's refutation of the Early Modern 'Way of Ideas' remains of interest because that conception of consciousness has certainly not gone away. Even if, like Bergson and James and his followers (e.g. Ralph Barton Perry), we want to massage the distinction between conscious image and perceived thing, loosen the two up, breathe life and movement into them all, and blur their differences in an effort to find a 'neutral monism'—a position Sartre attacks in *The Imagination* under the name of 'American Neo-Realism'—we will only succeed in making consciousness into a kind of inert thing and making the apparent inertia of things vis-à-vis consciousness unintelligible or, at best, a surface illusion hiding a truly magical, even carnivalesque world. For Sartre, the root of the problem here can be found in the denial of the intentionality of consciousness and in a corresponding denial of its immediate, non-representational self-consciousness. In *The Transcendence of the Ego*, published one year after *The Imagination*, the intentionality thesis is more explicitly incorporated into what we have called Sartre's Central Dogma. As he puts it there: 'the type of existence of consciousness is to be consciousness of itself. And consciousness is aware of itself *in so far as it is consciousness of a transcendent object.*'

To suggest that consciousness (and the World) could consist in a set of images, with neither the subjectivity afforded by self-presence nor the object-directedness afforded by intentionality, is really to offer no account of consciousness at all. It is both phenomenologically crass and explanatorily bankrupt. And, sadly, one should not suppose that this way of thinking about consciousness has disappeared. Any theory of consciousness that attempts to reduce it to the realization of monadic phenomenal property instances or qualia tropes fits into this category—as if by fusing or synthesizing a bunch of independent qualitative instances (or creating a 'bundle' of Humean ideas) one could arrive at consciousness as we know it, with its perspectival, self-manifesting, and temporal supra-modal structures and its capacity to intentionally aim at highly articulated objects via multiple modalities at once.

The same can be said of many so-called enactivist conceptions of consciousness that, once again, make the self-presence and intentional-negational structure of consciousness dissolve into a dynamical system of worldy objects and Gibsonian affordances. It is no wonder, we might add here, that Merleau-Ponty, in his review of *The Imagination* included in this volume, suggested that Sartre missed the 'deeper' meaning of Bergson's version of something quite like 'neutral monism' (Bergson did not use the term himself). Merleau-Ponty was headed precisely in that sort of direction. And perhaps this is why Sartre later said of Merleau-Ponty's position on the Consciousness–World relation that it is fundamentally obscure. Of course, as we have noted, Sartre's own position, much clearer on the surface, leads to an entirely different set of obscurities.

Be this as it may, for Sartre, many evils in the theory of consciousness begin to grow from the Early Modern forgetting of (or, at best, deep confusion about) intentionality. The 'Way of Ideas' indeed prevented a proper conception of consciousness and its modalities, in spite of the rare but lucid protestations by the likes of Antoine Arnauld and Thomas Reid. It was not until the work of Brentano and Husserl that genuine progress could once again be made.

We can imagine that Sartre may have taken himself to be bringing Phenomenology to its radical and far-reaching culmination. As with all great philosophical efforts, Sartre's reach exceeded his grasp. But there is so much to be learned by entering into the spirit of his ambition and trying to reach with him and as he did. Perhaps some lucky reader will succeed in grasping what Sartre could not. And a good place to begin that effort is with the very work that began Sartre's own—*The Imagination*.

Kenneth Williford and David Rudrauf
Arlington, Texas and Saclay, France, 2025

*
* *

The Routledge Classics Edition of *The Imagination* is based on an updated, corrected, and slightly revised version of the text of the 2012 Routledge edition of the Williford–Rudrauf translation. The Translators' Introduction has also been revised and expanded.

REFERENCES

Dassonneville, G. 2023. 'Mescaline, between Psychopathology and Phenomenology: Sartre and Experimentation in 1930s France'. In E. Dyck and C. Elcock (eds) *Expanding Mindscapes: A Global History of Psychedelics*. Cambridge, MA: MIT Press, pp. 51–73.

D'Jeranian, O. 2020. 'Sartre, Stoicism, and the Problem of Moral Responsibility (from 1939 to 1948)'. In K. Lampe and J. Sholtz (eds) *French and Italian Stoicisms: From Sartre to Agamben*. London: Bloomsbury, pp. 15–34.

Elpidorou, A. 2011. 'Imagination in Non-Representational Painting'. In J. Webber (ed.) *Reading Sartre: On Phenomenology and Existentialism*. London: Routledge, pp. 15–30.

Godelier, M. 2020. *The Imagined, the Imaginary and the Symbolic*, trans. Nora Scott. London: Verso Books.

Hopkins, R. 2018. 'Imagining the Past: On the Nature of Episodic Memory'. In F. Macpherson and F. Dorsch (eds) *Perceptual*

Imagination and Perceptual Memory. Oxford: Oxford University Press, pp. 46–71.

Kind, A. 2018. 'How Imagination Gives Rise to Knowledge'. In F. Macpherson and F. Dorsch (eds) *Perceptual Imagination and Perceptual Memory*. Oxford: Oxford University Press, pp. 227–246.

Kriegel, U. 2016. 'Perception and Imagination: A Sartrean Account'. In S. Miguens, G. Preyer, and C.B. Morando (eds) *Pre-Reflective Consciousness: Sartre and Contemporary Philosophy of Mind*. London: Routledge, pp. 245–276.

McGinn, C. 2004. *Mindsight: Image, Dream, Meaning*. Cambridge, MA: Harvard University Press.

Sartre, J.-P. 2018. *L'Image dans la vie psychologique: rôle et nature*. In *Études Sartriennes, 22, Sartre inédit: le mémoire de fin d'études (1927)*, edited and annotated by G. Dassonneville.

Smith, J. 2016. *Experiencing Phenomenology: An Introduction*. London: Routledge, Ch. 6.

Stawarska, B. 2013. 'Sartre and Husserl's *Ideen*: Phenomenology and Imagination'. In S. Churchill and J. Reynolds (eds) *Jean-Paul Sartre: Key Concepts*. Durham: Acumen, pp. 12–31.

Warmbier, A. 2022. 'Emotional Affectivity and the Question of Appraisal, Viewed in the Light of a Phenomenological Account of Pre-Reflective Affective Consciousness'. *Forum Philosophicum*, 27(2), pp. 163–177.

Webber, J. 2020. 'Sartre's Phenomenological Psychology of Imagination'. In M.C. Eshleman and C.L. Mui (eds) *The Sartrean Mind*. London: Routledge, pp. 104–116.

Williford, K. 2020. 'Headlessness without Illusions: Phenomenological Undecidability and Materialism'. *Journal of Consciousness Studies*, 27(5–6), pp. 190–200.

Windt, J.M. 2015. *Dreaming: A Conceptual Framework for Philosophy of Mind and Empirical Research*. Cambridge, MA: MIT Press.

TRANSLATORS' INTRODUCTION

Kenneth Williford and David Rudrauf

SARTRE'S EARLY *ANNI MIRABILES*

Duly acknowledging the element of arbitrariness in all such claims, it is still fairly safe to say that the thirteen-year period stretching from September 1933, when Sartre began his nine-month residency at the Institut français de Berlin, to the publication of 'Existentialism is a Humanism' and *Anti-Semite and Jew* in 1946 stands as a truly remarkable period of productivity in the annals of philosophical *and* literary biography. During this period Sartre wrote and published (though not always in the order written) no less than five philosophical classics: *The Imagination* (1936), *The Transcendence of the Ego* (1937), *Sketch for a Theory of the Emotions* (1939), *The Imaginary* (1940), and *Being and Nothingness* (1943). Remarkable as that is, in the same period he wrote (or rewrote) and published (or premiered) no less than seven literary classics: *Nausea* (1938), *The Wall* (1939), *The Flies* (1943), *No Exit* (1944–45), *The Age of Reason* (1945), *The Reprieve* (1945), and *The Respectful Prostitute* (1946). If one thinks of other significant works published right after 1946, like *The Chips Are Down* (1947) and *Baudelaire* (1947), this should serve as a reminder of the arbitrariness just mentioned.

And if one thinks of smaller, but not unimportant pieces, like 'Intentionality: a fundamental idea of Husserl's phenomenology' (1939) and 'Consciousness of self and knowledge of self' (1948), one will gain a still better sense of the fecundity of this period and its long afterglow. Sartre's perceived importance as a philosopher and writer has continued to wax and wane inside and outside of France, but no one who has spent careful time in the pages from his early *anni mirabiles* can deny the power his overall vision or seriously doubt his philosophical breadth and depth, the occasional interpretive or argumentative lapse notwithstanding.

THE UNFORESEEN SIGNIFICANCE OF SARTRE'S EARLY PHENOMENOLOGICAL WORKS

As academic years go by and old ideological obstructions melt into the past, we continue to witness a deepening appreciation of Sartre's early phenomenological works on the part of philosophers from many different intellectual orientations and micro-traditions inside and outside of France. Outside the home country, this development has been encouraged by new and better translations and scholarship. The interest in these works on the part of recent anglophone philosophers of mind we find particularly notable, though Sartre has always had some presence in even the most 'analytic' sectors of twentieth-century Anglo-American philosophy.[1] For example, one finds him cited or engaged by Roderick Chisholm, Jay Rosenberg, Panayot Butchvarov, and Daniel Dennett, to name only four.[2]

In the late 1980s Bryan Magee, chatting with Hubert Dreyfus, once quipped that he found it 'difficult to believe that Sartre will survive as a philosopher'. One can perhaps forgive Magee, but Dreyfus, whose love for Merleau-Ponty should have taught him better but whose even greater love of Heidegger evidently obstructed his vision, should have been able to foresee that the great resurgence of interest in the problems of consciousness, already well underway at the time in anglophone philosophy of mind, would eventually lead to the rediscovery and re-appropriation of these Sartrean gems.[3]

When philosophers as responsible, rigorous, and stolidly 'analytic' as Colin McGinn and Joseph Levine can freely acknowledge a deep debt to Sartre's phenomenological works, we can feel as if Anglo-American philosophy has reached a new level of maturity and has, almost in spite of itself, understood something of lasting value, something that faddish ideological preoccupations had perhaps prevented others, indeed both 'analytic' and 'Continental'—though for different reasons, from seeing.[4] The mention of Colin McGinn, whose 2004 book *Mindsight* was heavily influenced by Sartre's *The Imaginary*, brings us closer to our present concern.[5]

THE IMAGINATION AND THE IMAGINARY

Critics as widely separated in general orientation as Daniel Lagache and Roland Barthes have well understood the significance and originality of Sartre's *The Imaginary*.[6] It is not too unknown that forty years after its publication, Barthes, in the very year of his tragic death—which was also the year of Sartre's death—dedicated his 1980 *Camera Lucida* (*La chambre claire*) 'In Homage to *L'Imaginaire* by Jean-Paul Sartre'. But it has largely been forgotten that in a 1941 review of *The Imaginary*, Lagache summarized these matters lucidly:

> The interest of M. Sartre in the problems of the imagination is not new. It's not just that this writer has already revealed himself to the philosophical public through a penetrating and sometimes acerbic historico-critical study of the imagination. Already nearly fifteen years ago Sartre completed his first dissertation on images, a dissertation that remains unpublished and that has probably passed in part into his subsequent works. But that was only a point of departure. Since then, the thought and orientation of the author have been enriched and strengthened. The essential change has been his intimate contact with phenomenology and existential philosophy. On the other hand, Sartre has continued to affirm himself not only as a philosopher but also as a poet and more precisely as a novelist. *Nausea*, his principal literary work, nourished on existential philosophy, treats precisely 'of the nauseous disgust that characterizes the realizing consciousness' in an autobiographical form. This formula, borrowed from the end of *The Imaginary*, is a significant reminder of the ties that can unite poetic work with philosophical and scientific work. Need we recall further that the hero and narrator of *Nausea*, in whom it is difficult not to see an imaginary Sartre, gives up writing a historical work, that is to say, a work about existing things, to undertake a novel, that is to say, to produce an irreal? Even the moral recovery within which this decision takes place is an authentically Sartrean trait. In truth, the imagination is indeed 'the problem' for Jean-Paul Sartre.7

Philosophically and psychologica lly, that problem, for Sartre, is fundamentally about the proper characterization of the difference between imagination and perception and their respective objects. The difference is phenomenologically manifest, and we all make the distinction as a matter of common sense. But how do we characterize this difference in a rigorous and philosophically responsible way? Moreover, what are the implications, both ontological and practical, of the imaginative type of 'negating activity'—our relating imaginatively to objects and states of affairs that *do not exist* or *are not present* or *are not thus*—for our understanding of consciousness? The imagination is the vehicle of our relation to nothingness *par excellence*. Readers of *Being and Nothingness* will recall the centrality of the 'negating' capacity of consciousness in that work. *The Imagination* and *The Imaginary* are thus, of course, essential reading for those who wish to gain a full understanding of Sartre's early *magnum opus*.

Lagache goes on to write a review of *The Imaginary* that rewards close scrutiny. But our theme is not *The Imaginary*, which English readers can now enjoy in Jonathan Webber's translation. Nor is it Sartre's 1926–27 dissertation 'The Image in Psychological Life', written under the direction of the philosopher and psychologist Henri Delacroix for the *Diplôme d'Études Supérieures* and alluded to here by Lagache, who was Sartre's friend and classmate at the École Normale Supérieure at the time of its writing. It is, rather, that 'penetrating and sometimes acerbic historico-critical study' known as *The Imagination*.

According to Simone de Beauvoir's *The Prime of Life*, Henri Delacroix commissioned Sartre to write a book on the problematic of the image and the imagination for publication in a series, *Nouvelle Encyclopédie philosophique*, then being brought out by the F. Alcan publishing house. Sartre produced one book, *L'Image*, but Alcan accepted only the first part, which was published as *L'Imagination*. The second part, which was to become *L'Imaginaire*, interested Sartre far more, as its highly original, constructive account went well beyond history and criticism.[8] But despite the fact that *The Imagination* has, rightly, been eclipsed by *The Imaginary*, the former merits careful study for a significant number of reasons.

THE IMPORTANCE OF *THE IMAGINATION*

To begin with, there is the fact that Sartre himself conceived of *The Imagination* as a historical and critical propaedeutic to *The Imaginary*. On the historical side, Sartre displays his *normalien* sweep and penetration with considerable fluidity, if occasional diffuseness. His references, all of them on target, range from Aristotle and the Epicureans and Stoics, through the Early Moderns and Kant, right up to Bergson, Alain (Émile Chartier), William James, and, of course, Husserl. His discussions of Descartes, Spinoza, Leibniz, and Hume are illuminating not only for the light they shed on Sartre's own appropriation of the tradition but also for the possible insights into the thinking of the 'greats' themselves that they contain.

Sartre's discussion of the problematic of the image, with its primary but not exclusive emphasis on nineteenth- and early twentieth-century French contributions, is, again, not merely of interest to historians of French philosophy and psychology and to Sartre scholars, it is of intrinsic philosophical value. The theoretical temptations and confusions, the muddled acceptance of a sloppy and undisciplined sort of introspection—half descriptive and half driven by *a priori* assumptions—all unearthed in great detail by Sartre, have not entirely disappeared from today's cognitive science and its own attempts at self-understanding and methodological clarity, though things have been improving. But, indeed, for the historian and the Sartre scholar there is much to glean. In particular, *The Imagination* contains some of Sartre's fullest discussions of the French philosophers, notably Henri Bergson and Alain, whose role in Sartre's philosophical development has often been obscured by the impact of Husserl and Heidegger. And like *The Imaginary* and the *Sketch for a Theory of the Emotions*, *The Imagination* indicates beyond any doubt that Sartre possessed an extremely impressive grasp of not only the relevant philosophical works but also of the relevant empirical psychology of his day, French, German, and, to some extent, English as well.[9]

After the publication of the sprawling *Being and Nothingness*, and after his literary fame and accession to the politico-public sphere, it became easy to forget that Sartre's first four, smaller phenomenological works were disciplined, scholarly, and generally tightly argued pieces of philosophy. This is, after all, not that surprising given that at the time of their writing it seemed, as likely as not, that Sartre would make his living as a *lycée* professor or in higher academia. But it has also become too easy to forget the foundational role the pieces play in the intellectual house, or houses, that Sartre built.

SYNOPSIS OF THE IMAGINATION

The Imagination is divided into four chapters prefaced by a short introduction and finished off with a short conclusion. There are some subdivisions within the chapters,[10] but most of them are untitled and indicated by a triangle of asterisks (which we have retained). In Chapter III there are properly titled subsections. Generally, the historical narrative and critical dialectic run in parallel, leading up to the stage setting for Sartre's own constructive account (to be presented in *The Imaginary*), which then appears as both a logical and historical next step.

Sartre's introduction to *The Imagination* contains as concise, forceful and clear a statement of his conception of the two heterogeneous modes of being—the spontaneous *for-itself*, intrinsically conscious of its own existence, and the essentially inert world of objects, the world of being *in-itself*—as any he ever made. And it offers a brief but very evocative description of the phenomenologically intuitive distinction between perception and imagination, which sets the stage.

In Chapter I, 'The Great Metaphysical Systems', Sartre argues that the Early Modern greats, Descartes, Leibniz, and Hume, had already exhausted the space of logically possible solutions to the problem of the image *relative to the assumption* that the image is, in itself, on a par with the objects of perception and is thus like a *thing*, a view of images he refers to as a type of 'thingism' (*chosisme*). The Early Modern tradition of thinking on the problematic of the image *begins*, according to Sartre, with the assumption that imagination is not essentially different from perception. The problem then becomes recovering the spontaneous distinction between the two, a distinction we, and the philosophers in question, have no trouble making pre-theoretically. Under normal conditions, at any rate, no one is in danger of confusing, say, a centaur imagined with a centaur perceived. And putting to the side for the moment the problematic cases he will discuss in detail in *The Imaginary* (dream, delusion, hallucination), one would have a hard time not granting him this.

As Sartre tells the tale, Descartes tried to solve the problem by claiming that the exercise of the pure intellect is the necessary and sufficient basis for distinguishing 'true images', images that correspond to real objects in the world beyond the mind, from 'false images', the images making up the world of dream, delusion, and pure fancy. The 'true images', the theory goes, display a coherence and order that the 'false images' lack; and one must infer, on the basis of the intellectual grasp of this coherence, or its lack, which set of one's images is which.

For Sartre's Leibniz, who wished to treat thought and images as, in a certain sense, continuous, the distinction comes down to that between the clear and confused 'expression' of an object. Relative to the intellectual capacity of the mind in question, a particular 'expression' of an object will seem either clear or confused; the greater the intellect, the greater the scope of clarity. The Leibnizian ontology, Sartre maintains, intellectualizes the perceptual image, robbing it of its genuinely 'non-conceptual' character as containing some brutely given data. From there, Leibniz attempts to recover the intuitive phenomenological distinction between thought and the image (be it perceptual, oneiric, hallucinatory, or imaginative) in quasi-mathematical terms. Thoughts constitute our 'clear ideas', and images our 'confused' ones. The confusion for a particular finite mind derives from the fact that the image conceals within itself an infinite and therefore fundamentally intellectually impenetrable set of relations. What we call thought involves 'object expressions' that are finitely articulable and thus seem transparent to us, devoid of resistance or opaque givenness. What we call an image, on the other hand, involves 'object expressions' that contain a plenitude of constituents, thereby outstripping our finite powers of analysis and thus appearing to us as brute, irrational data. But to an infinite intellect, it would all appear as clear as pure thought. To put it in contemporary terms, the phenomenology of God is entirely cognitive. God experiences all things the way we experience, say, the thought that two plus two is four. If our capacities were but expanded, the taste of coffee, say, would no longer be a matter of apparent acquaintance with that brutely given flavour; it would become a matter of something generically similar to the experience of mathematical insight. At the level of metaphysics, for Leibniz, there are, strictly speaking, only monads and their thoughts (some involving clear and others confused ideas); images are, so to say, 'upwardly' reducible to thoughts. Their 'irrational' appearance is a function of the finitude of our minds. God, being infinite, has no such problem. But Sartre maintains that no distinction in mere quantity, even if the quantity involved is infinite, can amount to a genuinely qualitative or noetic distinction. Imagining involves an attitude different from that of perception, on the one hand, and thought, on the other; and these differences are not accounted for by the finitude or infinitude of the intentional correlates of these attitudes.

In stark contrast to Leibniz's thoughts, Hume's thoughts are 'downwardly' reducible to images. Strictly speaking, in Hume's view, we are aware only of images; and images are conceived of as being like things. The distinction between ideas and impressions, ideas being the less vivid copies of the latter, is the sole, and, according to Sartre, manifestly inadequate, tool Hume has at his disposal for attempting to recapture the distinction between perception and imagination. But thought itself, on the Humean model, is just the quasi-mechanical play of ideas governed by the laws of association. These laws correspond to a set of fundamentally external relations between image-things, and thus the synthetic power of thought, which appears to traffic in the grasp of intrinsic relations and essences, is revealed to be a sort of illusion. Hence, there is here no real hope of distinguishing between the world of delusive images and the world of 'true' ones by an appeal to pure thought in the manner of Descartes. But doing so on the basis of degrees of vivacity proves to be likewise theoretically intractable and, further, phenomenologically quite implausible, Sartre argues. We experience dimly or faintly perceived objects all the time, and we occasionally engender in ourselves very vivid images; but we are, he maintains, never in danger of confusing the two. Were it otherwise, our daily experience would be a veritable and perhaps menacing psychological 'fun house' in which we constantly confused imagining and perceiving.

The theories of Descartes, Leibniz, and Hume represent, for Sartre, the three possible *types* of solution to the problem of the image open to one once one assumes that images are fundamentally like the objects of perception, or things. The Cartesian solution will make a radical distinction between image and thought and make it the purely theoretical job of the latter to distinguish between the perception of reality and the world of dream and fantasy. Leibnizian panlogicism will reduce image to thought at the metaphysical level and make the phenomenological distinction between the two into a function of our finitude. Humean panpsychologism, on the other hand, will reduce thought to the play of images and try, dismally, to capture the difference between perception and imagination with the distinction between vivid impressions and their fainter copies. All of these solution types Sartre will find again and again throughout the nineteenth and early twentieth centuries. And all of them, he will argue, are fundamentally unsatisfactory. The assumption upon which they all rest, that the image is at bottom just like a perceived thing, must be rejected. We must start over.

Chapter II, 'The Problem of the Image and the Effort of Psychologists to Find a Positive Method', traces the historical and dialectical development of these possible positions through the nineteenth and early twentieth centuries. J.S. Mill, Sir Francis Galton, Paul Broca, Charcot, Hippolyte Taine, Théodule-Armand Ribot, William James, Alfred Binet (the inventor of what would become known as the IQ test), Edward Titchener, Henri Bergson, the psychologists of the Würzburg School, as well as lesser-known figures such as Victor Brochard, Luigi Ferri, Albert Spaier, and Ignace Meyerson (not to be confused with the better-known Émile Meyerson), all enter the sustained discussion. The range of positions on the image here represented is seen to move within the tripolar framework already mapped out in the seventeenth and eighteenth centuries. But two main highlights of the chapter readily offer themselves.

First, Sartre presents a sustained discussion of Bergson, whose *Essai sur les données immédiates de la conscience* (or *Time and Free Will*, as many English-speaking readers know it) had, years before, been instrumental in drawing Sartre into philosophy. While

Bergson's attempt to inject fluidity, temporality, synthetic elements, and a certain organicism into his conception of the image could be viewed as a step in the right direction, Sartre concludes that Bergson's account still makes the fundamental and disastrous assumption of 'thingism'. No matter how imbued with spontaneity the images are made out to be, their mode of being remains essentially that of things.

The second highlight is Sartre's discussion of the work of the Würzburg School of psychology (which included Oswald Külpe, Narziß Ach, Karl Bühler, Karl Marbe, and Henry Jackson Watt), the heretical descendants of Wilhelm Wundt who, in violation of Wundt's views about what was amenable to study on the basis of introspective methods, had claimed to find through these very methods, once again, the old radical Cartesian distinction between pure, imageless higher thought processes and the image.[11] The works of Bühler, Ach, Marbe, and Watt all come in for discussion by Sartre, as does the relation of the School to Husserl and his *Logical Investigations*. Sartre's main contention with the Würzburg School is not their acceptance of Husserl's anti-psychologism, since he, of course, accepts it as well. It is rather with the way that they oppose an essentially Cartesian conception of pure thought, a conception, he suggests, that may well not actually correspond to Husserl's own, to an essentially Associationist conception of the image. Even if the Würzburg School had succeeded in demonstrating empirically the existence of pure thought, their conception of the image remained mired in 'thingism' and thus prevented them from understanding the proper relationship between imagination and thinking.

In Chapter III, 'The Contradictions of the Classical Conception', Sartre forcefully spells out the impasses that, he argues, necessarily issue from the assumption that the image is fundamentally like a perceived thing. The problem of distinguishing the real, perceived world from a world of imagination becomes theoretically insoluble on this assumption, which is in direct contrast to our immediate, pre-theoretical grasp of the distinction. Equally intractable is, once again, the problem of clearly articulating the relationship between images and thought. Along the way, Sartre provides interesting analyses of the work of Albert Spaier and Alain on the image, relates the discussion to the philosophical motives behind the denial of the very existence of the image on the part of J.B. Watson and the behaviourists as well as neurologists like François Moutier, and alludes to Lagache's 1934 *Les hallucinations verbales et la parole*, which will come to play an important role in the section of *The Imaginary* entitled 'Pathology of the Imagination'.[12] The chapter ends with a call for a new approach to the image, an approach that is firmly rooted in our pre-reflective grasp of the radical distinction between perception and imagination and yet is not merely inductive but eidetic as well. It is, of course, in Husserl that Sartre finds the sought-after method.

Chapter IV, 'Husserl', contains some of Sartre's first published (if not first written) interpretations and appropriations of key elements of the fundamental concepts of Husserlian phenomenology: intentionality, empty vs filled intendings, the noetico-noematic correlation, the positional characters of different act types, active vs passive syntheses, time-consciousness, reflection-in-memory, the Husserlian *epochē*, the foundational eidetic function of phenomenology vis-à-vis empirical psychology, intentional *Erlebnisse*, the notion of antepredicative (or prepredicative) evidence, and the distinction between hyletic data or matter and animating intentional form. Along with a reading of *The Imaginary*, one can gain from a study of Sartre's discussion a much fuller sense of his understanding of these essential, technical phenomenological concepts, an understanding of which he tends to presuppose in other works. Indeed, as

Lagache hints in his review, the very titles of the two books can be seen in a Husserlian light: if the word 'imagination' suggests the noetic, the psychological acts of imaginative consciousness as such, the word 'imaginary', in addition to its rich set of other connotations in French, suggests, in this context, the noematic, the irreal, intentional correlates or objects of all such acts of consciousness.[13]

Centred around a discussion of Husserl's famous treatment of Albrecht Dürer's engraving *The Knight, Death, and the Devil*, Sartre broaches the topic, which will become of central importance in *The Imaginary*, of the relation between the matter or *hylē* of an image, and the intentional form or *morphē* through which we 'animate' the matter and, in the case of the image properly so called, aim at what is not perceptually present. The discussion of the intentional animation of Dürer's engraving also leads naturally to questions about what Sartre will come to call the 'image family'. In the case of photographs, paintings, mimicry, etc., the matter of the image is clearly distinguishable from the irreal or absent objects intentionally aimed at through that matter. The matter, with which we are acquainted is literally present and is what provides acts of imagination with their quasi-presentational aspect. We use what is literally present to consciousness to aim at what is not present. And this partly accounts for the tendency to think of imagination as akin to perception. But we can easily shift our attitude and view the reproduction of the engraving as lines printed on paper and ignore the *objects* depicted, or focus on the perceived movements of the mimic as such, and forget about the person mimicked, the *object* of the mimicry. But in the case of acts of imagination that rest upon no such clearly sensorily mediated hyletic data, or, if one prefers, purely mental images as such, the matter is elusive. It seems to disappear along with the shift out of the imaginative attitude. Thus, Sartre maintains, we may well have to leave the field of eidetic phenomenological investigation and limit ourselves to formulating empirical hypotheses about the identity of the matter of these purely mental images. Readers of *The Imaginary* will recognize this new problematic immediately.

Returning to Husserl, Sartre does not imagine that the Phenomenologist has provided a complete theory of the image in his published works. Sartre was well aware that Husserl's published work represented only a fraction of his total oeuvre, and he suggests, rightly, that Husserl had probably developed his ideas on image-consciousness at much greater depth in his courses and unpublished writings.[14] Nonetheless, he notes that there is a *prima facie* problem here already facing Husserl's notion of the 'neutrality modification' or suspension operative in the *epochē* and 'phenomenological reduction'. If, according to that method, we are to suspend the natural and spontaneous positing of the existence of the objects of perception, do we thereby lose the pre-theoretical, intrinsic distinction between imagining and perceiving? That is, does this methodology, quite self-consciously reminiscent of Descartes' Method of Doubt, implicitly assume the very Cartesian conception of the image that Sartre has set out to undermine? Moreover, to the extent that he does not find a clearly drawn distinction in Husserl between the matter of purely mental images and the 'bi-stable' matter of images projected on the basis of photographs, paintings, and the like, Sartre is unsatisfied and sees the necessity of blazing a new trail, a trail he will blaze in *The Imaginary*.

MERLEAU-PONTY'S REVIEW OF *THE IMAGINATION*

We have included in this volume a new translation of Merleau-Ponty's generally favourable review of *The Imagination*, which appeared in 1936 in the *Journal de Psychologie normale et pathologique*. The review can itself serve as an excellent introduction to *The Imagination*, but it is also of interest in that it gives some sense of Merleau-Ponty's attitude towards Sartre *the philosopher* at the time. So much has been written on the relationship between Sartre and Merleau-Ponty. And though we do not wish to articulate a position on the relationship at present and would never dream of detracting from Merleau-Ponty's achievement, we do believe that some of this literature has been rather unfair to Sartre. Perhaps the time is right for a reassessment of their philosophical interaction.[15] One notable point: Merleau-Ponty is much more favourably disposed to Bergson's philosophy than Sartre is, and indicates as much towards the end of this review. One can speculate that this was because Merleau-Ponty saw in Bergson an inchoate effort towards a view like his own, one in which, so to speak, mind and body are so 'massaged' and 'loosened up' that the mind–body problem dissolves in a conceptual acid bath of obscurity. That Sartre saw Merleau-Ponty's overall position on consciousness as ultimately deeply obscure is fairly well known. Sartre himself retained a kernel of Cartesian 'clarity and distinctness' on this matter to the end.[16] It is not implausible to suggest that it was the same sort of 'obscurity' that Sartre saw and objected to in Bergson (and in neutral monism), an 'obscurity' that Merleau-Ponty, by contrast, found philosophically inspiring.

NOTES ON THE TRANSLATION

> The translation [*Die Legenden des Nā-ro-pa*] is a faithful picture of the translator's tragic illness. Part of it is what a psychiatrist calls 'word-salad' and unintelligible even to a German-speaking person; the remainder is intelligible nonsense.
>
> Herbert V. Guenther

Generalities

The text we used for this translation is that of the sixth ('Quadrige') edition published by the Presses Universitaires de France in 2003. The text was corrected by Arlette Elkaïm-Sartre, Sartre's adopted daughter and literary executor.

We took a quasi-'archaeological' approach to this translation. Of course, we wanted the text to read as smoothly as possible, but our main aim was not simply to make it easy for the contemporary reader to understand the text. Rather, our main aim was to render the text so that it reads to the English reader the way it reads to the French reader, insofar as this is possible. This does not always mean a preference for literal translation or word-for-word translation but a serious effort to find the closest possible English expressions that capture not only the basic meaning but also the style and the multiple threads of connotations and historico-critical elements that are buried in the text and its 'inter-text'. These are apparent to and even pivotal for the French scholar reading Sartre. This was all the more a duty for us since Sartre was more than a philosopher (in the narrow sense of the term), as we all know. He was also a writer and a leftward-thinking intellectual[17] in the Continental, and, in particular, French sense of the terms. The text is full of parallel threads, involving the expression of critical views that have an ideological and political dimension. For instance, the spite Sartre directs at certain theories of the image is as much directed towards their 'spiritualist' (read 'bourgeois idealist' in the Marxist pejorative sense) undertone. And some of his historico-critical hermeneutic, as he tells the tale of theories of the image, employs a quasi-Marxist sociological analytic methodology to pinpoint the biases driving some philosophical rationales. Moreover, much of this text is, evidently, a direct reflection of Sartre's time and his assumptions, conscious or unconscious, about his likely audience and a certain academic milieu and type of discourse he implicitly endorses as normative. In some ways this is Sartre's most standardly 'scholarly' philosophical text, and this marks it, historically and geographically, in a rather pronounced way.

We wanted to deliver Sartre, and not just what would amount to a paraphrase of his ideas served up for academics and students. Sartre is not easily reduced to a type, as a writer. Hence our effort included trying to achieve the almost impossible goal of conveying the oddities of the text, including the choices of analogies and metaphors and specific paradigmatic choices (syntactic and lexical) that are at times quite puzzling for the French reader as well. These can leave the reader either with a sigh directed against Sartre's elitist mannerisms or with the humorous feeling of being tricked by Sartre into making sense of something quite strange and almost surrealistic, coupled with a noticeable departure from the almost narrowly academic and tedious style of the work that one finds in many places. Given the rigour and depth of Sartre's thinking and writing, we felt that these elements should not be discarded as the mere result of a lousy or undisciplined sense of expression. Thus, we attempted to preserve some of the academic stiffness of the work and some of its pretentiousness. Sometimes this is reflected in our preference for constructions once fairly common in English academic writing (e.g. frequent use of the passive voice, use of the narrative present tense) but now long on the wane. Moreover, it is certainly not the role of the translator just to smooth over a writer's failures of form or content. In any case, we tried to preserve as much of Sartre's style as possible, including some of his (at times inconsistent) punctuation and capitalization choices.

On the more linguistic side, we note that we were guided by a sort of 'post-Saussurean' assumption that specific paradigmatic word choices from a set of semantically related and equally employable words carry important information, as much by exclusion as by inclusion. And we thought that this should be reflected, as much as possible, in our translation. In other words, the translator should bear in mind what was excluded by the choices the author made. This generates tighter constraints on the translation. And while this did not mean we adopted a policy of rigidly uniform translation for a given word or phrase, it does mean that deviations from uniform translation had to be justified by contextual considerations, where this included both macro-contextual frames (e.g. *'the' French language in the early twentieth century* vs *'the' English language in the early twenty-first century*) and micro-contextual ones (e.g. *French academic philosophy in the early 1930s* vs *anglophone philosophy ('analytic' and 'Continental') in the early 2000s*), or by overwhelming aesthetic considerations—if it just sounded too odd in English, we would go against our preference.

PARTICULARITIES

There are many lengthy quotations in this work. For many of them there are English translations (e.g. for Taine). However, we found that many of these translations contain what we regard to be infelicities. Thus we decided simply to retain our own translations. We should also note that the quotations from Husserl's *Ideen I* are our translations of what are presumably Sartre's translations of Husserl's German. Given that Sartre could read German, that he had spent time in Berlin studying Husserl, that he does not simply take translated passages from Levinas' 1930

The Theory of Intuition in Husserl's Phenomenology (the first book Sartre read on Phenomenology), and that Husserl's *Ideen I* was not published in French until 1950 in Paul Ricoeur's translation, we think it is safe to assume that Sartre translated these passages himself. We thus thought it important to try as best we could to render Sartre's apprehension of Husserl's texts into English for the light it might shed on his appropriation of Husserlian concepts. We note that, for scholarly and comparative purposes, we have given references to the most recent Husserl translations and to the English translations of other texts where these exist. We tried as well to correct and fill out Sartre's bibliographical references, and we have added a complete bibliography of these. Often, he quotes without giving a page number. And in some cases, he quotes without any citation at all. In most cases we were able to find this information, and we added notes in the relevant places. The text in all such notes is in brackets. And bibliographical information or other text *not* in brackets is Sartre's own.

We note that we have generally left the titles of works in the language in which Sartre cites those works, but we have offered English translations of his own French translations of the titles of works originally in German, unless the German title is very well known. Thus Husserl's *Ideas* is sometimes referred to as *Ideen*, and where it is, we have left this in the text. The same goes for Husserl's *Logical Investigations*, which is referred to by the original German title, *Logische Untersuchungen*. However, Sartre refers to Husserl's 1928 *Vorlesungen zur Phänomenologie des inneren Zeitbewusstseins* as *Leçons sur la conscience interne du temps*, and we have referred to it under the title of the older English version as *Phenomenology of Internal Time-Consciousness*. We have made this choice simply because the older Churchill translation contains only what the 1928 volume contained, whereas Brough's translation of Volume X of the *Husserliana* series (*On the Phenomenology of the Consciousness of Internal Time* (1893–1917)) contains much else besides.[18]

It remains then simply to discuss the choices we have made about certain words and phrases. In the cases in which we thought it important, we put the French word or phrase in parentheses following the word or phrase we chose. When we have done so, we have, of course, retained the number of nouns, the number and gender of adjectives, and the number, tense, and mood of verbs. In the case of some technical philosophical terms we consulted with much profit the justly famous *Vocabulaire technique et critique de la philosophie* (second 'Quadrige' edition, published in 2006—making for a total of twenty editions) edited by André Lalande. The work was first published in 1926. It is an indispensable resource for any student of twentieth-century French philosophy and, indeed, for any student of philosophy. It should be remembered that many of the luminaries of early twentieth-century French academic philosophy, who formed the milieu in which Sartre's formal philosophical education was carried out, constructed this unique dictionary.

When, at the beginning of Chapter I, Sartre speaks of 'species' (**les espèces**) conceived of in the Scholastic tradition as being 'half-material, half-mental entities', he has in mind the doctrine according to which immediate sensory contents are, as it were, emitted by objects, which they resemble, and yet capable of being taken up into the intellect, conceptually articulated and thereby rendered 'thinkable'. See the discussion in Lalande (p. 300).

When Sartre speaks of a 'positive method', as in the title of Chapter II ('... the Effort of Psychologists to find a Positive Method'), he almost certainly has in mind the sense of **positif** operative in but not narrowly limited to Auguste Comte's notion of 'Positivism'. In this sense, a 'positive method' is just a method that, as it is put in Lalande (p. 793), 'constantly maintains contact with experience and renounces all *a priori* preconceptions'. (See the articles in Lalande for **Positif** and **Positivisme**.) Sartre's chapter has to do with the (ultimately failed) attempts psychologists made in the nineteenth century up to the early twentieth century to develop a psychology (of the image, *inter alia*) that was empirically driven, empirically adequate, and not hobbled by the metaphysical assumptions about the image operative in the Rationalist and Empiricist traditions.

In Chapter I, Sartre speaks of 'American Neorealism' (**néo-réalisme américain**) and refers to its adherents as **néo-réalistes** elsewhere in the book. He has in mind a philosophical research programme most notably articulated by Ralph Barton Perry and collaborators and trumpeted in a 1912 collaborative book entitled *The New Realism: Cooperative Studies in Philosophy*.[19] The overall position on the mind defended by the New Realists was very similar to what has come to be called, after Bertrand Russell, 'Neutral Monism' and was influenced by (though also different from and critical of) positions defended by William James and Henri Bergson. Roughly, the idea is that what we call consciousness is not some special substance, property, or mode of being but just a matter of intrinsically 'neutral' (i.e. not inherently mental or physical) things entering into certain mundane relations with one another.[20]

We have rendered **en face de** variously as 'in front of', 'facing', or 'before' (in the non-temporal sense of 'before') as context demanded. The phrase is, strictly speaking, empty of mentalistic or agonistic connotations or connotations of agency.

We have, as is common, systematically rendered **âme** by 'soul' but have noted its use in cases where it may have seemed odd.

We have generally rendered **esprit** by 'mind' but obviously not in phrases like 'esprit d'analyse', 'spirit of analysis'. We have generally rendered the cognate words **spirituel**, and **spiritualité** by 'mental' and 'mentality', but we have always noted the original French when we have done so. The matter is somewhat complicated by the fact that the various contexts at play tend to privilege different connotations. In English one tends to take the word 'spiritual' in a quasi-religious sense. But in French the primary connotation is that of the mental (vs the material or corporeal). However, the religious connotation need not be entirely absent. For the cognate, **spiritualisme**, we have uniformly kept 'spiritualism'. This is because the term is essentially a historico-technical term in French philosophy often associated with the philosophy of Félix Ravaisson (1813–1900) and Charles Renouvier (1815–1903). Ravaisson traced his spiritualism back to Maine de Biran (1766–1824) and was a teacher of Lachelier and Boutroux and exerted a major influence on Bergson, all of whom form part of Sartre's immediate French academic philosophical context. (Lachelier and Boutroux were instrumental in bringing Kant to greater prominence in French philosophy. Lachelier is briefly mentioned in the second chapter of this text as the 'champion' of Kantianism in France, and Boutroux's interpretation of Kant is favourably referred to in the opening section of *The Transcendence of the Ego*.[21]) To put it roughly, spiritualism, in this sense, is the view that the higher mental functions cannot be explained in terms of lower mental functions (e.g. the Empiricists' 'laws of association' operating over perceptual 'ideas'). Rather, intelligence and teleological activity must be seen as explanatory principles in their own right. The orientation combines a certain type of phenomenological sensibility with a tendency towards intellectualism and even idealism. See the first chapter of Gutting's *French Philosophy in the Twentieth Century* for a useful overview of the philosophy of Renouvier, Ravaisson, Lachelier, and Boutroux, and see the entries on **spiritualisme, spiritualité**, and **spirituel** in Lalande.[22] It should be noted that in certain contexts, in which his analysis flirts with historico-criticism of a sociological type, Sartre uses the term 'spiritualism' in a highly pejorative manner to pinpoint and criticize suspicious ulterior motives of a quasi-religious nature behind certain arguments, currents of thoughts and publications, and to implicitly suggest their dismissal on this basis.

We have rendered **durer** and **la durée** as 'to endure' and 'duration', respectively. And we have generally put the French in parentheses in the cases of its use. It is important to note this term in the present context because it is effectively a Bergsonian technical term. For Bergson **la durée** indicates our sense of lived duration and is opposed to **le temps** ('time'), which indicates time understood abstractly via the essentially geometrical analogy we use to reconceptualize and thereby distort the concrete experience of lived time.[23]

In some cases we have rendered **ensemble** as 'ensemble'. *The Oxford English Dictionary* will tell you that the sense in which we are using it only occurs in English 'as French', but we beg to differ. For example, in a phrase like 'ensemble de représentations', where the context concerns the idea of 'reducing', in a phenomenalistic or idealistic manner, physical objects to representations, it seems that the word 'ensemble' is a better choice than 'collection' or 'set' or 'totality' or any other of the available options. The word, in French and in English, immediately connotes a unified or interconnected multiplicity, like a musical ensemble, and not a mere aggregation (even if it is the standard French word for mathematical sets). Depending on the exact context, either the unity or the multiplicity will be emphasized.

We have systematically rendered **en image** by 'as imaged'. This is Sartre's way of describing the objects of imaginative consciousness given as such. That is, such objects are given *as imaged* as opposed to *as perceived* (**en perception**). And the phrase is certainly not meant to imply that such objects are literally, spatially *in* an image conceived of as a sort of thing. To imagine a centaur is not, on the Sartrean view, to 'see' (with the mind's 'eye') a little centaur inside of an image, which is conceived of as a little simulacrum literally located in consciousness. But it should be noted that his use of the phrase in this work tends to be neutral with respect to different theories of the imagination and of the nature of the image. So, one can think of it as a piece of Sartrean quasi-technical phenomenological vocabulary. We have marked its use by putting it in parentheses after our 'as imaged'.

We have systematically rendered **psychique** by 'psychic' rather than 'psychical'. In English both can have paranormal connotations, as can the French word, but 'psychical' has a decidedly quaint and archaic flavour. In any case, the word 'psychic' here should be totally divorced from these connotations. In this context and in Sartre's use, it is just another term for, roughly, mental or psychological (as in 'mental states', 'psychological phenomena', etc.). This may sound a bit strange to the contemporary English ear, but we thought 'psychological' would be misleading in other ways, ways that are not as easily eliminated from the mind as are any paranormal connotations. Evidently, Sartre is not talking about telepathy and precognition, but 'psychological' might suggest the accretions that years of psychological research in the twentieth century (from Behaviourism to Cognitive Science) have given to the term. We also avoided 'mental' because Sartre and some of the authors he quotes do sometimes use the French **mental** and we wished to reflect this difference. When it seemed important we indicated his use of **mental** in parentheses.

In a couple of quotations from Hippolyte Taine and in discussion centred around them, the phrase **sensation consécutive** is used. We have rendered it by 'consecutive sensation' indicating the French word **consécutive** in parentheses, but it must be understood that this is actually a technical term. It refers to a sort of sensation that persists after the stimulus that provoked it has ceased to act on the perceiver, where there can be a considerable amount of time between the cessation of the stimulus and the presence of the 'consecutive sensation'. In English this has sometimes been rendered as 'after-effect' or 'after-sensation'. See the corresponding entry in Lalande (p. 176).

In one case Sartre speaks of **l'individualisme Berkeleyen**, which we have rendered 'Berkeleyan particularism' placing **individualisme** in parentheses directly thereafter. Particularism is the view that, strictly speaking, only particulars exist, and Berkeley certainly subscribes to this thesis. (Berkeley also, of course, rejects the existence of abstract particulars, though that is not ruled out by many uses of the appellation 'particularism'.) It will be recalled that Berkeley argues strenuously against the existence of Lockean abstract general ideas (and he tends just to assume that there could be no universals as such), which Berkeley thinks of as ideas that would be indeterminate or general in their very nature. As Sartre notes in *The Imaginary* (p. 15), 'Berkeley and Hume … declared general images, indeterminate images, impossible'. In place of such images or ideas, Berkeley (and Hume) held the view that single, particular ideas can function generally by denoting indifferently other particular ideas that they resemble in certain key respects. (See Berkeley's *Principles of Human Knowledge*, 'Introduction' §§12–18 and Hume's *A Treatise of Human Nature*, 1.1.7.) This use of the term **individualisme** in French philosophy is, as it says in the relevant entry in Lalande (p. 500), very rare, though Renouvier, for example, did use it in that sense in an article on Duns Scotus. The context of Sartre's use, however, clearly indicates that he had this sense in mind.

We have systematically rendered **sensible** by 'sensible' with the meaning 'can be perceived via the senses', as in 'sensible qualities'. This is the meaning the term often has in Berkeley and Hume, so the uses should not be completely unfamiliar to anglophone students of philosophy. And though this use of the term has not completely disappeared from contemporary philosophical parlance, it has generally been supplanted by 'sensory', which we find unfortunate in certain ways. We reserve 'sensory' for the translation of **sensoriel** and **sensori-** (as in **sensori-moteur**, 'sensory-motor').

Though it sounds slightly odd, our choice to render **sentiment** by 'sentiment' is not without historical foundation. It is used only in a passage quoted from Ribot, and it there means, more or less, 'feeling' or 'affective nuance'.

We have rendered **chosisme** by the equally odd 'thingism'. In the very brief entry in Lalande (p. 140) for this word, it is said that it is sometimes used as a synonym for 'naïve realism'. However, in this case, we do not think that this is exactly what Sartre has in mind. Nor does he have exactly in mind something like the reism of Brentano or Kotarbiński. Rather, in the context of this text he means, generally, the tendency to treat mental phenomena as if they were just like concrete physical things; and, more particularly, he means the tendency to treat images as if they were such things.

We have rendered the word **contenu** uniformly by 'content'. Though Sartre will eventually argue that the intentionality of consciousness implies that consciousness 'has no "content"' (*Being and Nothingness*, 'Introduction', §III), and though there is good reason to believe that he *already* held this view at the time of his writing of *The Imagination*, he still sometimes uses the term without explicitly critical comment. At some point in the development of Anglo-American philosophy, the word 'content' came to be used in a theory-neutral sort of way so that one can, without any perceived countersense, speak of internalist and externalist theories of content. Using this terminology, one would say that Sartre espouses a non-naturalistic sort of externalist theory of the intentional content of consciousness, a sort of externalist 'representationalism' (without the naturalistic appeal to causal co-variation or evolutionary history often appended to such theories today). Sartre expresses this view sometimes by *denying* that consciousness has any content. In such cases, one must bear in mind that Sartre is placing emphasis on the spatial connotation of **contenu** (or its German equivalent, *Inhalt*)—a content is, literally, 'something spatially *contained in* something else'. Sartre emphatically rejects the idea that anything could literally be contained spatially *in* consciousness. In this work, however, he sometimes uses **contenu** in a more or less theory-neutral sense, a sense that does not necessarily imply that the contents are literally inside or contained within the mind or consciousness, a sense that also exists in French philosophical usage (again, see the entry in Lalande (p. 180)). One can see this in the opening sentences of the 'Introduction' where he speaks neutrally of **contenu sensible** and explicitly puts to the side idealist and phenomenalist theories of the perceived object. However, his dissatisfaction with the term can also be seen in his discussion of Alain towards the end of Chapter III where he speaks condescendingly of 'this famous re-emerging "sensible content"' (his quotation marks). His ultimate rejection of this terminology, even in its possibly neutral use, had to do, we think, both with the literal sense of the term that has a potentially misleading tendency to make one think of consciousness in certain spatial terms (cf. what he calls 'the illusion of immanence' in *The Imaginary* (see, e.g., p. 5)), though he still sometimes uses the term in *The Imaginary* to refer to the matter of, for example, a photograph through which one intentionally aims at an object) and with the fact that many theories of consciousness, in both French philosophy and psychology and, on his interpretation, the Husserl of *Ideen I* and after, in some sense just reify and enshrine this misleading metaphor. But he will deal with these issues more directly in *The Transcendence of the Ego, The Imaginary*, and *Being and Nothingness*.[24]

We have generally translated **constituer** (and its relatives) by 'to constitute' (and its relatives). In some cases Sartre uses this word in the usual senses (more or less the same in English and French) of 'to make', 'to make up', 'to form', etc. But in many cases, certainly in the chapter on Husserl, but earlier in the book as well, Sartre is using the term in more or less the sense of Husserl's *Konstitution* and *konstituieren*, about which entire books have been and no doubt will continue to be written.[25] In such uses, the important thing to realize is that 'constituting' an object of consciousness is not a matter of literally creating the object. It is rather a matter of a correlation between intentionally aiming at an object in different ways (on the noetic side) and thus having the object presented to one in different ways (on the noematic side). For example, in fearing a face, the face appears to one as frightening or horrible. So, one might say, in fear, one *constitutes* the face as horrible. The phenomenological investigation of constitution, in this sense, has to do with spelling out the essential features of the noetico-noematic correlation for different types of lived experience (e.g. perceptual, emotional, imaginative). For example, on the noetic side, perception and emotion involve an affirmative doxastic positing attitude; one, so to say, spontaneously, if temporarily, *believes that* the objects experienced literally have the properties they are experienced as having. But on the noematic side, there is a difference. In the natural perceptual attitude, objects are given in the 'practico-inert' mode as being governed by purely causal relationships. But the objects of emotional consciousness are often given in the 'magical' mode in an almost animistic way such that they transcend causal relationships.[26] In the case of the imagination, on the noetic side, the affirmative doxastic attitude is either suspended or it becomes a negating doxastic attitude. One either knows that one is imagining something that is not the case or is otherwise, or, for all one knows, what one is imagining is not the case, and so one suspends one's judgement. (See *The Imaginary*, pp. 11–14.) In either case, it will be true to say that, strictly speaking, one does not *believe* what one only imagines insofar as one only imagines. Extremely paranoid people might come to believe what they imagine, but, on the Sartrean view, the believing and the imagining are still two different sorts of 'acts'. One does *not believe* that there literally is a centaur in the room when one imagines a centaur in the room; indeed, in this instance, one *does believe* that *it is not the case* that there is a centaur in the room. The full treatment of the 'irrealities' that make up the noematic side of imaginative consciousness is contained in *The Imaginary*. The present work limits itself to refuting the view that the objects of imaginative consciousness are 'image-things'. In a couple of cases, it was unclear to us if Sartre was using **constituer** in a Husserlian sense or not. In those two cases we have put the word in parentheses after our translation.

We rendered **constater** (and its relatives) variously as 'to witness' or 'to bear witness to' and 'to observe' (and their relatives) depending on the context. When it seemed important, as in Sartre's discussion of Albert Spaier, we indicated the use of the word by putting it in parentheses.

In his discussion of Alain towards the end of Chapter III, Sartre briefly mentions **le donné cœnaesthésique**, which we have rendered by 'the cœnaesthetic given'. The *Oxford English Dictionary* defines 'cœnaesthesis' as 'The general sense or feeling of existence arising from the sum of bodily impressions, as distinct from the definite sensations of the special senses; the vital sense'. This is the sense it has in the text. The term derives ultimately from the *koinē aisthēsis* of Aristotle. In the entry in Lalande (p. 144) for **cœnaesthésie** it is noted that Ribot held that cœnaesthesis was the essential basis for the sense of being an individual self or ego.

We have uniformly translated Sartre's use of **sens intime**, which apparently originated with Maine de Biran, as simply 'intimate sense'. This takes a little getting used to for the English reader, but we find that it is better than the alternatives like 'inner sense' or 'internal sense' (as Hallie translates it in one of the few studies in English devoted to Maine de Biran[27]) because it has less of a tendency to reinforce the 'inner vs outer' or 'internal vs external' analogy that, if reified and taken very literally, is problematic with respect to consciousness—from a Sartrean point of view and from other points of view as well. Note, however, that on one occasion, in the Introduction, Sartre does speak of 'internal intuition' (**intuition interne**) and, in Chapter III, once of 'internal experience' (**expérience interne**). And there is one usage of the hybrid phrase **expérience intime**. The Biranian phrase, which is predominant in the text, is just meant to denote the immediate, non-representational self-knowledge of consciousness that grounds our explicit reflective knowledge and cannot be identified with or reduced to the knowledge acquired from our sensory organs. It is of interest that in the discussion of **sens intime** in Lalande (pp. 533–34), it is noted that 'Today this expression has fallen almost completely into desuetude'. If this is so, perhaps Sartre made a very conscious choice to use it.

We have uniformly translated **entendement** as 'understanding', even though, in the context of Sartre's discussion of Spinoza, one familiar with the dominant English-language translations of the latter might think 'intellect' would be better. Historically influential French translators (e.g. Saisset for Spinoza, Coste for Locke, and Jean Bernard Mérian for Hume) chose **entendement** both for Locke's and Hume's 'understanding' and for Spinoza's 'intellectus'.

Speaking of Spinoza, at one point Sartre uses the phrase **l'expérience vague**, which is a standard French rendering of Spinoza's 'experientia vaga' and which we have translated, directly but in a sense misleadingly, as 'vague experience'. In Part II, Proposition XL, Scholium 2 of the *Ethics*, where Spinoza introduces this expression, he has in mind not 'vague' in the sense of 'unclear', 'indeterminate', 'fuzzy', and the like, but the original Latin sense of 'vagus', that is 'wandering', 'roaming', 'inconstant', 'diffuse', 'aimless'. Thus English translators (with the exception of White) have indicated this variously as 'random experience' (Curley), 'casual experience' (Shirley), and 'suggestions of experience' (Elwes).

In his discussion of Leibniz, Sartre uses the expression **proposition identique**, which we have rendered as 'analytic proposition' just because the Kantian terminology, which has survived well in Anglo-American philosophy, is likely to be much more familiar to the English reader than is the Leibnizian (which was also adopted by Condillac). A true 'identical proposition' in the Leibnizian context is a necessarily true proposition (the negation of which is a contradiction) that can, in some cases, be seen to be true by 'analysis', which is a rational procedure for drawing out the content of the subject term (of a proposition in subject-predicate form) in such a way that one can see that the content of the predicate term is, in some sense, 'contained within' the content of the subject term. For Leibniz, humans are limited to employing finite analysis, but God, who can perform 'supertasks' according to Leibniz, is not and so can see certain propositions to be necessarily true—relative, that is, to God's free choice to actualize the best of all possible worlds—that we can only perceive as contingently true.[28]

We have translated Sartre's **en droit** and **de droit** generally as 'by right' and 'of right', respectively, though in one case we resorted to Forrest Williams' choice of '*de jure*' for **de droit**. The general opposition is with **en fait** and **de fait**, which we have generally rendered as 'in fact' and 'of fact', respectively, with, again, the exception of one case in which we used '*de facto*'. In one sense, the opposition is between what is and what ought to be. But **droit** here is not at all limited to an essentially moral connotation, and in fact in this work moral normativity is not at all what is intended. Rather, Sartre has in mind epistemic and logical normativity or rationality conceived of in a roughly Kantian way, but where this bleeds over into the sense of 'in principle'. Though we have used 'in principle' on a few occasions when this seemed innocuous, the English 'in principle' is not quite right because that expression tends to underemphasize the connotation of 'norms of rationality' that is pronounced in this use of **droit**. So, in this use, if A is said to be reducible 'by right' to B, what is meant is, more or less, that it is rational to believe that A can in principle be reduced to B.

We have translated Sartre's **reviviscence** as the somewhat rare English 'reviviscence' because it seemed better to us, all things considered, than 'revival' and other possibilities.

We have translated **renaissant** as either 'reborn' or 're-emerging' or 're-emergent' according to context.

In a brief discussion of Husserl's relation to the Würzburg School in Chapter II, Sartre mentions the Husserlian contrast between empty and filled (or fulfilled) intentions. One can aim at or intend an object emptily without any perceptual or imagistic 'fulfilment' of the intention. It is one thing to converse and think about your sister's new pair of shoes, it is quite another to literally see them or imagine them. In the former case we intend the shoes emptily; in the latter two we have filled (or fulfilled) perceptual or imaginative intentions of them (which differ intrinsically from one another on the Sartrean view). In this context Sartre uses **plein** which we simply render by 'full', though arguably one could, in this context, render it by 'filled' or even 'fulfilled'.

We have translated Sartre's **virtuel** as either 'virtual' or 'potential', as context dictated, often indicating the French word by placing it in parentheses in the latter case. It is important to realize that in French philosophical usage **virtuel** is sometimes used to indicate a contrast with the actual and sometimes a contrast with the fully real or genuine, for example a simulation vs the original or authentic item. The English 'virtual' has generally lost the former contrast so that no one would think of 'virtual reality' as meaning 'potential reality'. However, the second sense of **virtuel** at play in this text should not be too rigidly interpreted on the model of 'virtual reality' or 'virtual interface', for it is not exactly simulation that is at issue. Rather, in some cases it means something like 'existing in degraded or lesser way'. More vaguely still, it can also mean something like 'existing' in imagination or thought, or, more generally, in another 'world', but in a way in which the question of the possibility of the existence of the 'virtual' entity remains suspended or unaddressed. In this sense, one is a bit reminded of Meinongian 'objects' that, on some interpretations of his doctrine, in some sense 'have being' even if they do not, strictly speaking, exist, and even if they are impossible.[29] Finally, in his discussion of Valéry and lexical meanings in Chapter II, it means something like 'existing in a socially distributed way'.

We have translated Sartre's **en acte** as 'in act'. This reads oddly until one realizes that Sartre is using the phrase essentially in its Scholastic sense of *actus*, which derives ultimately from the Aristotelian's ἐνέργεια ('activity'). The contrast is with being merely potential and also with being past or accomplished (see Lalande, p. 17). For Sartre, consciousness is activity, through and through. As he writes in Chapter II, 'There is no "potentiality" ["*virtualité*"] or "possibility" that would hold here; consciousness is act and everything that exists in consciousness exists in act (*en acte*)'.

Relatedly, his use of **actuel** often does not merely mean 'current' or 'present', as it usually does in French (see Lalande, pp. 24–25). It often carries the connotation of **en acte** in addition to this usual meaning. We have often translated his **actuel** by 'occurrent' because in contemporary anglophone philosophical usage 'occurrent' arguably gets somewhat closer, at least in this technical usage, to this combination of senses. In this context one routinely distinguishes between occurrent thoughts vs dispositional beliefs; occurrent thoughts are what constitute one's presently lived mental activity (e.g. currently thinking that Paris is in France versus knowing it but not thinking about it at the moment). This is not a perfect translation, however, because 'to occur' can also often connote a certain passivity, even in mentalistic contexts (e.g. 'It just occurred to me that I left my keys in the car'). And though 'I am going to occur' is not ungrammatical, it would, in addition to being a rather droll thing to say, not carry anything like the connotation of 'I am going to act'.

We have usually translated the word **signification** as 'meaning' because in most contexts what is intended is the propositional, logical, or semantic content of a thought (or other mental act) and not the mental act of signification itself. In instances in which it was unclear whether it was the content or the act that was intended by the word, we translated it as 'signification', which is similarly ambiguous in English.

In his discussions of Kant, Bergson, and others, Sartre speaks of **le schème** and **le schéma**. English and French both have the two closely related (indeed, ultimately etymologically identical) words 'scheme' and 'schema'. Somewhat disadvantageously we chose the English 'schema' to translate both terms, because it sounded better in all contexts to us than to use 'scheme', but also because in English psychological discussions of the same matters Sartre is concerned with, it is 'schema' that is the usually used term; and the same goes for translations of the relevant parts of Kant's *Critique of Pure Reason* (esp. the notorious 'Transcendental Schematism' section of the Transcendental Analytic). Consequently, we have had to indicate which French word was being used in many cases. The interested reader should consult the detailed discussions of **schème**, **schéma**, and **schèmatisme** as well as the discussion of Bergson's **schéma dynamique** in Lalande (see pp. 950–953). In some cases, **schème** and **schéma** are used synonymously; but in a note Lachelier (p. 951) opines that **schéma** ought to be used to mean 'drawing or schematic figure' and **schème** for 'the rule we follow in tracing that figure and that exists in a state of pure tendency in our imagination'. The notion of a scheme or schema in these contexts can, on the one hand, be that of a rule that allows one to relate conceptually to images and thereby render them intelligible to thought, with its abstraction and generality—whether this is a matter of 'decoding' an image or producing one (e.g. drawing an object). On the other hand, it can also sometimes be the notion of a specified but diagrammatic image that one uses in a general way. In either case, in the present context, schemes or schemas are supposed to mediate between images and thought in some way. But their status is difficult to understand, and there is the concern that the notion will collapse back either into that of particular images used as exemplars and governed by mechanical association (in the manner of Berkeley and Hume) or into that of abstract, general objects of pure thought (in the manner of Descartes and Plato). In the first case, rational conceptual thought (as applied to perception and imagination) seems to be rendered illusory, and the account possibly invites a vicious explanatory regress. In the latter case, empirically applied rational conceptual thought is rendered well-nigh 'magical' and incomprehensible.

On a couple of occasions Sartre refers to Leibniz's response to Locke in the *Nouveaux Essais* II.i: *Nihil est in intellectu quod non prius fuerit in sensu nisi ipse intellectus.* ('Nothing is in the intellect that was not first in sense, except for the intellect itself.') It is worth remembering the context of this passage:

> Someone will confront me with this accepted philosophical axiom, that there is nothing in the soul that does not come from the senses. But an exception must be made of the soul itself and its states. *Nihil est in intellectu quod non prius fuerit in sensu nisi ipse intellectus.* Now the soul includes being, substance, one, same, cause, perception, reasoning, and many other notions which the senses cannot provide.[30]

Note, incidentally, that Sartre is making an innocuous historical error when he speaks, in Chapter II, of 'the time when Leibniz published his *Nouveaux Essais* in response to Locke'. The *Nouveaux Essais* were not published in Leibniz's lifetime; they were first published in 1765, nearly 50 years after Leibniz's death.

We have left Sartre's use of Greek phrases intact, though we have either placed a transliteration in brackets afterwards or provided a translation. In the case of his reproduction of a sentence from Aristotle's *De Anima* in a note, we used an old (1902) translation (that of William Alexander Hammond) but one that we think captures that particular sentence very clearly.

It is worth noting, however, that Sartre quotes the passage in a note before quoting from Émile Peillaube's 1910 *Les Images: Essai sur la mémoire et l'imagination* (pp. 470–471) where the exact passage from Aristotle is also reproduced in Greek. Sartre does not note this fact.

We remind the reader that the **ἐποχή** (*epochē*) (suspension of judgement) derives from the Greek Sceptics (not Stoics, as it erroneously says in Sartre's discussion of Alain) and was given a new sense by Husserl (bracketing or putting out of play the positing and reifying attitude we naturally have towards the world so as to bring the ways in which the world is given to consciousness into better focus for purposes of eidetic phenomenological description).

The notion of the **λεκτόν** (*lekton*) is, indeed, of Stoic origin; a *lekton* is, roughly, a signification or, as some translate it, a 'sayable' and even 'content' in the theory-neutral contemporary sense. According to Benson Mates it is what questions, propositions, subject terms, and predicate terms all have in common.[31] As it bears on this text, it is the abstract ideality of *lekta* that Sartre finds relevant to understanding the status of the Husserlian noema.

Finally, in a quote from Spaier we find yet another Stoic term, **φαντασία καταληπτική** (*phantasia katalēptikē*) which is sometimes translated as 'cognitive impressions'.[32] Such impressions were taken by the Stoics to be self-evident or criterial for truth.

NOTES

1 It goes without saying that his constant presence in the Anglo-American appropriation of that mix of traditions that has gone by the name of 'Continental' philosophy has always been multi-faceted. Sometimes under the inspiration of remarks by, among others, Horkheimer, Foucault, or 'master' Heidegger himself, Sartre has been hailed or lampooned as—take your pick—heretical 'anthropologizer'

of Transcendental Phenomenology and defiler of the Husserlian purity, muddle-headed profaner of the temple of Freud and psychoanalytical simpleton, warmed-over Cartesian mangler of the gospel of Heidegger and puerile representative of nineteenth-century social and political phantasms, or, almost contrariwise, as harbinger of the postmodern deconstruction and death of 'the subject', and so on. As interesting and controversial as these interpretations may continue to be, we find certain recent trends more significant, because they were not foreseen, are based on a less ideologically slanted readings of Sartre's texts, and point, we think, to an element of the Sartrean legacy that is perhaps less subject to the ever-shifting winds of academic and cultural fashion, namely his substantive, if sometimes poorly understood, contributions to the phenomenological description of consciousness.

2 See Roderick Chisholm, 'On the observability of the self', *Philosophy and Phenomenological Research* 30 (1969), 7–21; Jay Rosenberg, 'Apperception and Sartre's pre-reflective cogito', *American Philosophical Quarterly* 18 (1981), 255–60; Panayot Butchvarov, *Skepticism in Ethics*, Bloomington, Indiana: University of Indiana Press, 1989, pp. 49–58; Daniel Dennett, *Elbow Room*, Cambridge, Massachusetts: The MIT Press, 1984, pp. 83, 89.

3 In Bryan Magee, *The Great Philosophers*, Oxford: Oxford University Press, 1988, pp. 276ff. Dreyfus mentions to Magee that he personally heard Heidegger refer to *Being and Nothingness* as *Dreck* ('muck' or 'filth'). One can gather from an unbiased reading of Merleau-Ponty's respectful and serious, if not uncritical, interaction with Sartrean ideas and themes in *The Phenomenology of Perception* and elsewhere (including in the review of *The Imagination* published in this volume) that he quite agreed with many theses of Sartrean origin. Of course, we forgive Dreyfus too, nor do we hate Heidegger or underestimate his profundity. Dreyfus has played an extremely important role in making the contributions of Phenomenological philosophy to the philosophy of mind well known and to making the mention of such philosophers in 'analytic' books and journals more 'respectable'. Arguably, the first real indication that the resurgence of interest in consciousness was going to be something 'big' was the 1974 publication of Thomas Nagel's 'What is it like to be a bat?' in the *Philosophical Review* 83, 435–50. We recall here Nagel's Sartrean allusion to the *pour soi* and the *en soi* (p. 437) in that classic article.

4 See Colin McGinn, *Mental Content*, Oxford: Blackwell, 1989, p. 22, n. 31 and *The Making of a Philosopher*, New York: HarperCollins, 2002,

pp. 39–44. One must read between the lines to see the Sartrean influence in Levine's 2001 book, *Purple Haze: The Puzzle of Consciousness*, Oxford: Oxford University Press; but Levine has since made his debt to Sartre explicit. See Joseph Levine, 'A "quasi-Sartrean" theory of subjective awareness' in S. Miguens, G. Preyer, and C.B. Morando (eds) *Pre-Reflective Consciousness: Sartre and Contemporary Philosophy of Mind*, London: Routledge, 2016, pp. 342–62.

5 Colin McGinn, *Mindsight: Image, Dream, Meaning*, Cambridge, Massachusetts: Harvard University Press, 2004. If McGinn had to rely on a translation of *L'Imaginaire* at all, he had to rely upon the rather abysmal version known under the title *The Psychology of the Imagination*. Jonathan Webber's translation of *L'Imaginaire* also came out in 2004 as *The Imaginary: A Phenomenological Psychology of the Imagination*, London: Routledge; all page references to *The Imaginary* are to this translation.

6 Lagache was Sartre's classmate at the Ecole Normale Supérieure and facilitated Sartre's legendary experiment with mescaline, an experiment, we should not forget, inspired by the very interest in images and the imaginary that produced the two books. Along with his rival Jacques Lacan, Lagache would become one of the two most important representatives and continuators of the Psychoanalytic tradition in France. It is of interest and an inadvertent symbol of this rivalry that Sartre claimed that sessions with Lacan helped him overcome the recalcitrant 'crab' hallucinations caused by the mescaline made available to him by Lagache. See John Gerassi, *Conversations with Sartre*, New Haven: Yale University Press, 2009, pp. 62–63. It should not be forgotten that Lacan also interacted, sometimes favourably, with Sartrean ideas. For the classic account of Sartre's 'cleansing of the doors of perception' see Simone de Beauvoir's *The Prime of Life*, New York: Paragon, 1991, pp. 168 ff. Because it is so little known and because his description in *The Imaginary* (pp. 156–57) is so threadbare, we reproduce here a passage from Merleau-Ponty's 1945 *The Phenomenology of Perception*, marked in a footnote as an 'unpublished self-observation of J. P. Sartre', that is a part of Sartre's original 'trip report':

> I perceive a world of puffinesses. ... it is as if one was suddenly changing the key of my perception and that one was making me perceive puffily, as one plays a piece in C or B flat. ... At this instant, all my perception transformed and, for a second, I perceived a rubber bulb. Is it to say that I saw nothing more? No, but I felt 'built' in such a way that I could not perceive otherwise. The belief that

> the world is such invaded me. ... Later, another change occurred. ... Everything appeared to me as doughy and scaly at once, like certain big snakes I have seen unfold their rings at the Berlin zoo. At this moment, the fear of being on a small island surrounded by snakes came to me.

(See the more recent translation of *The Phenomenology of Perception* by Donald A. Landes, London: Routledge, 2012, p. 356.) The ellipses are Merleau-Ponty's. We can thank Gautier Dassonneville for tracking down the manuscript of Sartre's 'trip report' in the Bibliothèque nationale de France and making some of it available in facsimile in 'Mescaline, between Psychopathology and Phenomenology: Sartre and experimentation in 1930s France' in E. Dyck and C. Elcock (eds) *Expanding Mindscapes: A Global History of Psychedelics*, Cambridge, MA: MIT Press, 2023, pp. 51–73. On the role that his mescaline experience might have played in the writing of *Nausea*, see Hazel Barnes, *An Existentialist Ethics*, New York: Alfred A. Knopf, 1967, pp. 231ff. and Thomas Riedlinger, 'Sartre's rite of passage', *The Journal of Transpersonal Psychology*, 14 (1982), 105–23. See also esp. ch. 7 of Mike Jay's *Mescaline: A Global History of the First Psychedelic*, New Haven, Connecticut: Yale University Press, 2019. It has, for many years, been, in some ways understandably, a matter of course to regard such experimentation as both morally and scientifically questionable, though this has now finally definitively changed. But it should be borne in mind that at the time it was not at all unusual for psychiatrists to administer doses of mescaline, which had been isolated from Peyote by Arthur Heffter around 1897, synthesized by Ernst Späth in 1919, and eventually made available for research purposes by Merck and other pharmaceutical companies. In 1927 there appeared two very substantial works reporting the results of some of this research, and much else of relevance, *Der Meskalinrausch* by Kurt Beringer (Berlin: Springer) and *Le Peyotl: La plante qui fait les yeux émerveillés* by Alexandre Rouhier (Paris: Gaston Doin). Both Beringer and Rouhier reported, in rich detail, the great range of physiological and psychological effects caused by mescaline, and both described its therapeutic and psychotomimetic potentials. In 1928 Heinrich Klüver's *Mescal* was published in London (better known in its 1966 reprinted form, along with an accompanying essay, *Mescal and Mechanisms of Hallucinations*, Chicago: University of Chicago Press). In 1934 Henri Claude and Henri Ey published their short report 'La mescaline, substance hallucinogène' in the periodical of the Société de Biologie of Paris (115, pp. 838–41) describing, among other things, its stunning effects on visual perception and noting its therapeutic potential for the treatment of depression. Thinking of Sartre's very negative experience and its lingering aftermath, it is of interest that Claude and Ey conclude that 'psychic troubles', and other psychedelic and psychotomimetic phenomena, are not brutely caused by mescaline but are, rather, a function of the interaction between the action of the substance and the 'set of ... affective and instinctive tendencies constituting the personality of the subject' (p. 841). Finally, though it was not published until 1973, we feel obliged to mention Henri Ey's massive and underappreciated *Traité des hallucinations* (Paris: Masson) which synthesizes decades of research, his own and that of others, into the variety and nature of hallucinations and their causes, including nearly 200 pages on the effects of hallucinogenic substances. It should also be noted that long before Aldous Huxley's famous experiment with mescaline recounted in *The Doors of Perception* (1954), other European intellectuals and writers, including Walter Benjamin (in 1934 in fact, see *Benjamin on Hashish* (Cambridge, Massachusetts: Harvard University Press, 2006) pp. 86–95) and Stanisław Ignacy Witkiewicz, had been conducting their own experiments (see Witkiewicz's *Narcotics*, trans. S.A. Gauger, Prague: Twisted Spoon Press, 2018). Given this multifaceted context, it is not at all surprising that Sartre experimented in this way (cf. Mike Jay's *Mescaline: A Global History of the First Psychedelic*, New Haven: Yale University Press, 2019).

7 The review originally appeared in 1941 as '*L'imaginaire*, de Jean-Paul Sartre' in the *Bulletin de la Faculté des lettres de Strasbourg*, no. 8, pp. 309–325. It is reprinted in Daniel Lagache, *Les hallucinations verbales et travaux cliniques: Oeuvres I (1932–1946)* (Paris: Presses Universitaires de France, 1977), pp. 339–61. This is the opening passage; our translation.

8 Simone de Beauvoir, *The Prime of Life*, New York: Paragon, 1991, pp. 168–71.

9 These days it is fashionable to think that the current efforts at bringing together the cognitive sciences, phenomenology, and the philosophy of mind represent something new. But in fact, Sartre, Merleau-Ponty, Gurwitsch, and Ey (to take some notable examples) and their counterparts in Germany (in the Phenomenological and Gestalt schools) and in Russia (in the work of Vygotsky and Luria) collectively made this very type of effort for the better part of the twentieth century. And we still have much to learn from them all. It is perhaps a sign of the ahistorical myopia, self-satisfaction, and naïve behaviouristic methodology, pseudo-scientific in spite of itself, that dominated the

Anglo-American approach for so long that it is only in relatively recent years that genuine efforts toward this sort of fruitful synthetic collaboration have been ongoing.

10 In contrast to Forrest Williams' translation of *The Imagination* (Ann Arbor, Michigan: The University of Michigan Press, 1962), we have preserved Sartre's own manner of organizing the book. Though we understand Williams' urge to divide the book into smaller and more readily digestible pieces, we think it is generally not the proper job of the translator to do that, especially when the author did provide some organizational structure.

11 If one is reminded of more recent debates about 'cognitive phenomenology', this is probably not an accident. Debates about the extent to which purely cognitive operations are introspectively accessible and have a distinctive phenomenological profile are nothing new. See the collection *Cognitive Phenomenology* edited by Tim Bayne and Michelle Montague, Oxford: Oxford University Press, 2011.

12 *The Imaginary*, pp. 148–59.

13 Lagache writes, 'if one considers the imaging consciousness as a noesis, its noematic correlative is the imaginary' (Daniel Lagache, *Les hallucinations verbales et travaux cliniques: Oeuvres I (1932–1946)*, Paris: Presses Universitaires de France, 1977, p. 340).

14 See Volume XXIII of the *Husserliana* series, *Phantasie, Bildbewusstsein, Erinnerung (1898–1925)*, not published until 1980, the year of Sartre's death. John Brough's English translation of the volume appeared in 2005 as *Phantasy, Image Consciousness, and Memory (1898–1925)*, Dordrecht: Springer. The extent to which the writings in this volume can be fruitfully compared or contrasted with Sartre's work on the image remains to be fully worked out. But see the classic 1970 book of Maria Saraiva, *L'Imagination selon Husserl* (The Hague: Nijhoff) and the more recent work of Beata Stawarska, 'Defining imagination: Sartre between Husserl and Janet', *Phenomenology and the Cognitive Sciences* 4 (2005), 133–53; Vincent de Coorebyter, 'De Husserl à Sartre. La structure intentionnelle de l'image dans *L'Imagination* et *L'Imaginaire*', *Methodos* 12 (2012); Sacha Carlson, 'Phantasia et imagination: perspectives phénoménologiques (Husserl, Sartre, Richir)'. *Eikasia: Revista de filsosofía* 11 (2015), 17–58; and Di Huang, 'Accounting for Imaginary Presence: Husserl and Sartre on the Hyle of Pure Imagination'. *Sartre Studies International* 27 (2021), 1–22; Alain Flajoliet, '*Analoga and Phantasmata:* On the Intuitiveness of Imagination in Husserl and Sartre'. *Research in Phenomenology* 51 (2021), 221–45.

15 Any such effort should begin with the texts in *The Debate between Sartre and Merleau-Ponty* (Jon Stewart (ed.), Evanston, Illinois:

Northwestern University Press, 1998) and with Caeymaex's and Cormann's 'Sartre and Merleau-Ponty', in *The Sartrean Mind*, M. Eshleman and C. Mui (eds), London: Routledge, 2020, pp. 475–86) and Annabelle Dufourcq's 2024 *Merleau-Ponty: An Ontology of the Imaginary*, trans. Bryan Smyth, Cham: Springer. Dufourcq's book is especially notable in the present context because it is organized around the *Problematik* of the imaginary and contains an important chapter (ch. 8) devoted to Sartre's work on the imagination.

16 See, for example, Sartre's remarks in the opening interview in *The Philosophy of Jean-Paul Sartre*, Paul Arthur Schilpp (ed.), La Salle, Illinois: Open Court, 1981, pp. 43–44: 'The entire ontology that emerges from Merleau-Ponty is distinct from mine. It is much more a continuum than mine. I am not much of a continuist .... Merleau-Ponty does not do ontology, but his reflections lead to an obscure ontology'.

17 On the early Sartre's relation to Marxism, see Sam Coombes, *The Early Sartre and Marxism*, Bern: Peter Lang, 2008.

18 Edmund Husserl, *On the Phenomenology of the Consciousness of Internal Time (1893–1917)*, trans. John Barnett Brough, Dordrecht: Kluwer, 1991 and *The Phenomenology of Internal Time-Consciousness*, trans. James S. Churchill, Bloomington, Indiana: Indiana University Press, 1964.

19 Edwin Bissell Holt, Walter Taylor Marvin, William Pepperell Montague, Ralph Barton Perry, Walter B. Pitkin, and Edward Gleason Spaulding, *The New Realism: Cooperative Studies in Philosophy*, New York: Macmillan, (1912). This book and other American Neo-Realist and adjacent efforts (notably by Roy Wood Sellars, Wilfrid Sellars' father) was, for example, discussed in a 1920 article entitled 'Le Néo-Réalisme américain et sa critique de l'Idéalisme' by R. Kremer in the *Revue Philosophique de Louvain* (85), 71–106.

20 Note that, in another sense, the Neo-Realists were ontological *pluralists*; so the uses of 'monism' in this context can be confusing. On neutral monism, see Leopold Stubenberg and Donovan Wishon, 'Neutral monism', in *The Stanford Encyclopedia of Philosophy* (Spring 2023 Edition), Edward N. Zalta and Uri Nodelman (eds), https://plato.stanford.edu/archives/spr2023/entries/neutral-monism/. On the relations of James and Bergson in this philosophical ballpark, see Jean Wahl, *Vers le Concret*, Paris: J. Vrin, 1932, which was known to Sartre in the early thirties. In the preface, Wahl briefly discusses Ralph Barton Perry. (For an English translation of the preface to the work, see Jean Wahl, *Transcendence and the Concrete: Selected Writings*, ed. A.D. Schrift and I.A. Moore, New York: Fordham University Press,

2017.) *Vers le Concret* is alluded to in a line in Chapter II of *The Imagination* where Sartre is criticizing Bergson and Bergsonism: 'Softening of the image, creation of the schema—is this progress towards the concrete? We do not believe so.'

21 See *The Transcendence of the Ego*, trans. Andrew Brown, London: Routledge, 2004, p. 2.

22 Gary Gutting, *French Philosophy in the Twentieth Century*, Cambridge: Cambridge University Press, 2001, pp. 9–25. Lalande, pp. 1019–24.

23 For the distinction see, for example, Henri Bergson's *Time and Free Will*, New York: Harper, 1960, pp. 90–91.

24 One can point out Sartre's disdainful attitude towards the expression 'contents of consciousness' in the 1939 article 'Intentionality: a fundamental idea of Husserl's phenomenology', trans. Joseph P. Fell, *Journal of the British Society for Phenomenology* 1 (1970), 4–5, in which he announces liberation from the 'alimentary', idealistic philosophy of Lalande and Brunschvicg and others thanks to the doctrine of intentionality brought to light by Husserl. Coorebyter argues persuasively that this article was most likely written in 1934; Vincent de Coorebyter, *Sartre face à la phénoménologie*, Brussels: Ousia, 2000, pp. 27–29.

25 See, e.g., Robert Sokolowski's classic book *The Formation of Husserl's Concept of Constitution*, The Hague: M. Nijhoff, 1964 and Bob Sandemeyer's more recent *Husserl's Constitutive Phenomenology: Its Problem and Promise*, London: Routledge, 2009.

26 See Sartre, *Sketch for a Theory of the Emotions*, trans. Philip Mairet, London: Routledge, 2002, pp. 49ff. And cf. Webber's remarks in his translator's notes to *The Imaginary*, p. xxvii.

27 Philip P. Hallie, *Maine de Biran: Reformer of Empiricism 1766–1824*, Cambridge, Massachusetts: Harvard University Press, 1959, p. 93.

28 See, e.g., Leibniz's 'On contingency', 'Primary truths', and *Monadology* §§31–35 and the entry for **identique (proposition)** in Lalande, p. 455.

29 See, e.g., a sophisticated defence of a version of Meinongianism in Panayot Butchvarov, *Being qua Being*, Bloomington: Indiana University Press, 1979 and *Skepticism about the External World*, Oxford: Oxford University Press, 1998. For a recent overview of Meinongianism, see Mary Elizabeth Reicher, *Meinongianism*, Cambridge: Cambridge University Press, 2024.

30 Leibniz, *New Essays on Human Understanding*, trans. Peter Remnant and Jonathan Bennett, Cambridge: Cambridge University Press, 1982, p. 110.

31 Benson Mates, *Stoic Logic*, Berkeley, California: University of California Press, 1961, pp. 11ff.

32 See, e.g., A.A. Long and D.N. Sedley, *The Hellenistic Philosophers: Volume I, Translations of the Principle Sources with Philosophical Commentary*, Cambridge: Cambridge University Press, 1987, p. 243.

INTRODUCTION

I look at this white page on my table. I perceive its shape, its colour, its position. These different qualities have common characteristics: first they give themselves to my gaze as existences that I can only bear witness to (*constater*) and whose being does not depend on my caprice in any way. They are for me; they are not me. But nor are they *others*, that is to say, they do not depend on any spontaneity, neither mine nor that of another consciousness. They are at once present and inert. This inertia of sensible content, which has often been described, is existence in itself. It is useless to discuss whether this sheet of paper can be reduced to an ensemble of representations or whether it is, and must be, *more* than that. What is certain is that the white that I bear witness to (*constater*) cannot be produced by my spontaneity. This inert form, which is set back from all conscious spontaneities and which one must observe and learn little by little, is what is called a *thing*. In no case could my consciousness be

DOI: 10.4324/9781003657408-1

a thing because its way of being in itself is precisely a *being for itself*. To exist is for it to have consciousness of its own existence. It appears as a pure spontaneity facing the world of things, which is pure inertia. We can then posit from the beginning two types of existence. Indeed, it is insofar as they are inert that things escape the domination of consciousness; it is their inertia that protects and preserves their autonomy.

But now I turn my head away. I do not see the sheet of paper anymore. Now I see the grey wallpaper. The sheet is no longer present. It is not *there* anymore. I know well though that it has not been annihilated; its inertia protects it from that. The sheet has simply ceased to be *for me*. Yet here it is once again. I did not turn my head back. My gaze is still directed towards the grey wallpaper; nothing has moved in the room. Nevertheless the sheet does appear to me again with its shape, its colour and its position; and I know very well, at the moment it appears, that it is precisely the sheet that I was seeing earlier. But is it the sheet *in person?* Yes and no. Certainly I affirm that it is *the same* sheet with *the same* qualities, but I am not unaware that the sheet has remained *over there*. I do know that I am not enjoying its presence. If I want to see it in fact, I have to turn back towards my desk and draw my gaze back to the blotter where the sheet is placed. The sheet that appears to me at this moment has an identity of essence with the sheet that I was looking at earlier. And by 'essence' I intend not only its structure but also its very individuality. However, this identity of essence is not accompanied by an identity of existence. It is indeed the same sheet, the one that is presently on my desk, but it exists differently. I do not *see* it, it does not *impose* itself as a limit to my spontaneity; nor is it an inert datum existing in itself. In a word, it does not exist *in fact*; it exists *as imaged (en image)*.

If I examine myself without prejudice, I will realize that I spontaneously make the discrimination between existence as thing and existence as image. I would not know how to count those apparitions we call images. But whether or not their evocations are voluntary, images give themselves, at the very moment they appear, as something other than presences. I am never mistaken about this. It would even greatly surprise someone who never studied psychology if, after explaining to him what the psychologist calls an image, one would ask him: Do you sometimes confuse the image of your brother with his real presence? The recognition of the image as such is an immediate given of the intimate sense (*sens intime*).

Now, it is one thing to immediately apprehend an image as an image, but it is something else to form thoughts about the nature of images in general. The only way to build a true theory of existence-as-imaged (*l'existence en image*) would be to rigorously keep oneself from asserting anything about such existence that does not directly find its source in a reflective experience. For existence-as-imaged is a mode of being quite difficult to grasp. Grasping it requires some straining of mind, but above all it requires us to get rid of our almost unbreakable habit of construing all modes of existence on the model of physical existence. Here more than anywhere else, this confusion among modes of being is tempting, since, after all, the sheet as imaged (*en image*) and the sheet in reality are but the same sheet on two different planes of existence. Thus, as soon as we turn our minds from the pure contemplation of the image as such, as soon as we think about the image without forming images, a slide occurs: from the affirmation of the identity of essence between the image and the object, one moves on to an affirmation of an identity of existence. Since the image is the object, one concludes that the image exists in the same way the object does. And in this fashion one fabricates what we will call the naïve metaphysics of the image. This metaphysics consists in making of the image a copy of the thing, which then itself exists as a thing. Here is the sheet of paper 'as imaged' ('*en image*'), imbued with the same qualities as the sheet 'in person'. It is inert, it does not exist anymore solely for consciousness; it exists in itself. It appears and disappears as it pleases, and not at the whim of consciousness. It does not cease to exist when it ceases to be perceived, but maintains, outside of consciousness, the existence of a thing. This metaphysics or, rather, this naïve ontology is everyone's. And this is why one notices this curious paradox: the same man, without psychological culture, who assured us earlier of being able to recognize immediately his images *as* images, will now add that he *sees* his images, that he *hears* them, etc. His first affirmation results from spontaneous experience and his second from a naïvely construed theory. And precisely, he does not realize that if he were to see his images, if he were to perceive them as things, he would not be able to distinguish them from objects anymore. And he ends by construing one single sheet of paper on two planes of existence as two rigorously similar sheets existing on the same plane. A beautiful illustration of this naïve thingism (*chosisme*) of images is provided by the Epicurean theory of 'simulacra'. Things keep emitting 'simulacra', 'idols', which are just sheaths. These sheaths have all the qualities of the object—content, shape, etc. And it is exactly the case that they are objects. Once emitted, they exist in themselves, just like the emitting object, and can wander in the air for some undetermined time. Perception will occur when a sensory apparatus encounters and absorbs one of these sheaths.

Pure *a priori* theory made a thing out of the image, but internal intuition (*l'intuition interne*) teaches us that image is not *a* thing. The data of intuition are thus going to be incorporated into theoretical constructions under a new form: the image is a thing, just as much as the thing it is an image of; but by the very fact that it is an image, it receives a sort of metaphysical inferiority in comparison with the thing it represents. In a word, the image is a lesser thing. The ontology of the image is now complete and systematic: the image is a lesser thing, which has its own existence, gives itself to consciousness as any other thing, and maintains *external* relationships with the thing it is an image of. One sees that it is only this vague and ill-defined inferiority (that can become only a sort of magical weakness, or that one will, on the contrary, describe as a lesser degree of distinction and clarity) and this external relationship that justify the appellation *image*. One can also foresee all the contradictions that will result from this.

It is nevertheless this naive ontology of the image that we will meet up with, as a more or less implicit postulate, in all the psychologists who have studied the question. All or almost all have made the confusion indicated above between identity of essence and identity of existence. All have built the theory of the image *a priori*. And when they came back to experience, it was too late. Instead of letting themselves be guided by experience, they forced it to respond yes or no to tendentious questions. To be sure, a superficial reading of the innumerable writings that have been dedicated to the problem of the image for the last sixty years seems to reveal an extraordinary diversity of points of view, but we would like to show that one can find a single theory underneath this diversity. This theory, which first resulted from the naïve ontology, was perfected under the influence of diverse preoccupations extraneous to the question and transmitted to contemporary psychologists by the great metaphysicians of the seventeenth and eighteenth centuries. Descartes, Leibniz and Hume have the same conception of the image. They only disagree when it comes to the determination of the relationships between image and thought. Positive psychology has retained the notion of the image inherited from these philosophers. But it did not know how to choose between the three solutions they had proposed to the *image-thought* problem, nor could it. We want to show that it had to be that way, necessarily, as soon as the postulate of an image-thing was adopted. But in order to stress this more clearly, we need to begin with Descartes and a brief history of the problem of the imagination.

I

THE GREAT METAPHYSICAL SYSTEMS

Faced with a Scholastic tradition in which species (*espèces*) were conceived of as half-material, half-mental (*demi-spirituelles*) entities, Descartes' main concern was to separate mechanism and thought with exactitude. The corporeal was to be entirely reduced to the mechanistic. The image is a corporeal thing; it is the product of the action of external bodies on our own body via the intermediaries of the senses and the nerves. Since matter and consciousness exclude one another, the image as it is depicted materially in some part of the brain could not be animated with consciousness. It is an object by the same right as external objects. It is exactly the limit of exteriority.

The imagination, or knowledge (*connaissance*) of the image, comes from the understanding; it is the understanding, applied to the material impression produced in the brain, that

DOI: 10.4324/9781003657408-2

provides us with a consciousness of the image. Incidentally, the image is not set in front of consciousness as a new object of knowledge, despite its corporeal nature; this would, in fact, throw back to infinity the possibility of a relation between consciousness and its objects. The image possesses this strange property of being able to motivate the actions of the soul. The motions of the brain, caused by external objects without resembling them, awaken ideas in the soul. The ideas do not come from the motions; they are innate in man. But it is on the occasion of the motions that the ideas appear in consciousness. The motions are like signs that provoke certain feelings in the soul. But Descartes does not develop this idea of the sign, to which he seems to give the sense of an arbitrary connection. And, above all, he does not explain how there is consciousness of this sign. He seems to admit a transitive action between the body and the soul that leads him either to introduce into the soul a certain materiality or to introduce into the material image a certain mentality (*spiritualité*). We do not comprehend how the understanding is applied to this very special corporeal reality that is the image or, conversely, how there can be an intervention of the imagination and of the body in thought, since, according to Descartes, even bodies are grasped by pure understanding.

The Cartesian theory does not allow one to distinguish sensations from memories or fictions, since, in all cases, there are identical cerebral movements, whether the animal spirits are set in motion by an excitation coming from the external world, the body, or even the soul. Only judgement and the understanding permit one to decide if images correspond to existent objects on the basis of their intellectual coherence.

Thus, Descartes limits himself to describing what happens in the body when the soul thinks and to showing what corporeal links of contiguity obtain between those corporeal realities that are the images and the mechanism of their production. But, for him, it is not a matter of distinguishing thoughts on the basis of these mechanisms that belong, as much as other bodies, to the world of dubitable things.

Spinoza asserts even more sharply than Descartes that the problem of the true image cannot be resolved at the level of the image but only by the understanding. The theory of the image is, as in Descartes, cut off from the theory of knowledge (*connaissance*) and is linked to the description of the body. The image is an affection of the human body; chance, contiguity, and habit are the sources of the connection between images and memory, which is the material resurrection of an affection of the body brought about by mechanical causes. The transcendentals and general ideas that constitute vague experience are the product of a confusion of images of an equally material nature. Imagination, or cognition via images, is profoundly different from the understanding; it can forge false ideas, and it only presents the truth in a truncated form.

Yet, even though the image is to be opposed to the clear idea, what it has in common with the latter is that it is an idea. It is a confused idea that presents itself as a degraded aspect of thought but in which are expressed the same connections as in the understanding. Imagination and understanding are not absolutely distinct, since a movement from the one to the other via the development of the essences embedded in the images is possible. They are like knowledge of the first kind and knowledge of the third kind, like human bondage and freedom, at once cut off from each other and continuously linked.

In Spinoza the image has a double aspect. It is profoundly distinct from the idea; it is human thought *qua* finite mode. And yet it is an idea and a fragment of the infinite world that is the collection of ideas. Separated from thought, as in Descartes, it also tends, as in Leibniz, to merge with it, since the world of mechanical connections described by Spinoza as the world of imagination is nevertheless not cut off from the intelligible world.

Every effort of Leibniz in regard to the image is to establish a continuity between these two modes of knowledge: image and thought. For him, the image is permeated by intellectuality.

He too at first describes the world of imagination as a pure mechanism in which nothing allows one to distinguish the images proper from sensations. Both express states of the body. Leibniz's associationism, furthermore, is no longer physiological. It is in the soul that images are maintained and connected to each other in an unconscious way. Only the truths of reason have necessary connections between them; only they are clear and distinct. There is thus a distinction here again between the world of images, or confused ideas, and the world of reason.

Their relation is conceived of in a standard way. First, according to Leibniz, the understanding is never pure because the body is always present to the soul, but, on the other hand, the image has only an accidental and subordinate role, the role of a simple auxiliary to thought, the role of a sign. Leibniz seeks to deepen this notion of a sign. According to him, the sign is an expression. That is to say, the same system of relations that is in the object is preserved in its image, and the transformation of the one into the other can be expressed by a rule valid for the totality as well as for each part.

The only difference between image and idea is thus that, in the one case, the expression of the object is confused, and in the other, it is clear. The confusion comes from this: every movement envelops in itself the infinity of the movements of the universe; and the brain receives an infinity of modifications to which only a confused thought can correspond, one enveloping the infinity of clear ideas that would correspond to each detail. Clear ideas are therefore contained in the confused ideas.

They are unconscious; they are perceived without being apperceived. Only their sum total is apperceived; this appears simple to us because of our ignorance of its components.

Therefore, between image and idea there is a difference that almost amounts to a pure mathematical difference: the image has the opacity of the infinite, the idea the clarity of a finite and analysable quantity. Both are expressive.

But if the image amounts to unconscious elements that are in themselves rational and to an infinity of expressive relations, and if it participates thereby in the dignity of thought, its subjective aspect is no longer explicable. How does the summation of unconscious perceptions, for instance, of yellow and blue, yield the conscious apperception of green? How, in diminishing the degree of consciousness of the elementary ideas, can their union (*consistance*) in the mind give rise to these abrupt combinations? This does not disturb Leibniz. He wants to find a meaning in the image which links it to thought and makes the image proper vanish. Moreover, he deceives himself with a mathematical analogy when he takes for granted that confusion is equivalent to infinity, opacity or irrationality. The mathematician's irrational is indeed only a certain rational that we do not know how to assimilate yet. But, in placing ourselves on the terrain of logic, we cannot ever find ourselves, at the end of a construction, confronted with an absolutely a-logical opacity in relation to which all thoughts would be worthless. Quality is not quantity, even when infinite, and Leibniz does not succeed in giving back to sensation its sensible, qualitative character that he stripped from it to begin with.

Moreover, the notion of expression that allows the attribution of an intellectual signification to sensory givens is obscure. It is a relation of order, says Leibniz, a correspondence. But there can be no natural representation of one 'kingdom' by another 'kingdom'. There must always be an arbitrary construction of the mind in order for it to be able to acknowledge later that it is in the presence of equivalent relations.

In trying to found the representational status of the image, Leibniz thus fails both to describe clearly the relation of the image to the object and to account for the originality of its existence as an immediate given of consciousness.

While Leibniz tends to regard the image as thought in order to resolve the Cartesian opposition between image and thought, Hume's empiricism strives on the contrary to make thought amount to a system of images. He borrows from Cartesianism his description of the mechanistic world of the imagination. And isolating this world from the physiological terrain it dipped into, that is, from below, as well as isolating it from the understanding, that is, from above, he makes of it the only terrain in which the human mind truly moves.

In the mind there are only impressions and copies of these impressions, which are ideas, and which are maintained in the mind by a kind of inertia. Ideas and impressions do not differ in their nature, so that perception is not in itself distinguished from the image. In order to recognize them, it will be necessary to have recourse to an objective criterion of coherence, of continuity, the sense of which is much more obscure than in Descartes. It is more obscure because one does not understand what the mind could rely upon in order to escape the impressions and rise above them by a judgement, if the mind is constituted solely by a mosaic of impressions.

Images are connected to each other by relations of contiguity and resemblance, which act like 'given forces'. They cluster according to attractions of a half-mechanical, half-magical nature. The resemblance of certain images allows us to attribute to them a common name, which leads us to believe in the existence of the corresponding general idea. However, only the set of images is real, existing 'potentially' in the name.

This whole theory supposes a notion that, however, remains unnamed: the notion of the unconscious. Ideas have no other existence than that of internal objects of thought, and yet they are not always conscious. They are only awakened by their connections with conscious ideas. They therefore persist in their being in the manner of material objects. They are always present in the mind, but they are not all perceived. Why? And how does the fact of their being pulled by a given force to a conscious idea confer upon them a conscious character? Hume does not raise the problem. The existence of consciousness vanishes completely behind a world of opaque objects that possess, from where one does not know, a sort of phosphorescence, which is, by the way, capriciously distributed and plays no active role.

Furthermore, to manage to reconstruct all of thought with the help of images, Associationism is obliged to deny the existence of an entire category of thought, namely, the type of thought whose object, as the Cartesians had well understood, is not given through any sensible impression.

*

* *

By the end of the first half of the eighteenth century, the problem of the image had been clearly formulated and three solutions had taken shape.

Will we say, with the Cartesians, that there is such a thing as pure thought that can always, at least in principle, be substituted for the image, like truth for error or the adequate for the inadequate? If so, then there is not a world of the image and a world of thought, but an incomplete mode of apprehension of the world, a mode that is truncated and purely pragmatic; and there is another mode of apprehension that is a total and disinterested vision. The image is the domain of appearance, but of an appearance to which our human condition gives a sort of substantiality. There is, therefore, between image and idea, at least on the psychological plane, a genuine hiatus. Images will not be distinguished from sensations. Or rather, the distinction that will be established between them will have mainly a practical value. The movement from the imaginative plane to the ideational plane occurs as a leap; there is here a primary discontinuity that necessarily implies a revolution or, as some have continued to say, a philosophical 'conversion'. This revolution is so radical that it raises the question of the very identity of the subject. That is to say, in psychological terms, that there would have to be a special synthetic form to unify, in *one consciousness*, the I that thinks of the wax with the I that imagines, and to unify concurrently, in the affirmation of the identity 'this is the *same* object', the imagined wax with the wax that is thought of. The image, by essence, will only be able to provide to thought a very suspect help. There are problems that are posed only to pure thought because their terms cannot be imagined at all. Other problems will permit the use of images on the condition that this use be rigorously regulated. In any case, the only function of these images is to prepare the mind to make the conversion. They are employed as schemas (*schèmes*), signs, symbols, but they never figure as real elements in the act of ideation proper. Left to themselves, they follow one another according to a purely mechanical type of connection. Psychology will be confined to the realm of sensations and images. The affirmation of the existence of pure thought removes the understanding itself from psychological descriptions; it can only be the object of an epistemological and logical inquiry into meanings.

But perhaps the independent existence of these meanings will appear to us as nonsense. Indeed, either we will have to take them as existing *a priori* in thought or as Platonic entities. In both cases they elude the inductive sciences. If we want to affirm the rights of a positive science of human nature, elevating itself from facts to laws, like physics or biology, and if we want to treat psychic facts as *things*, we will have to renounce this world of essences that gives itself to intuitive contemplation and in which generality is a given from the outset. We will have to affirm this axiom of method: one may attain no law without first going through facts. But by a legitimate application of this axiom to the theory of knowledge, we will have to resolve ourselves to recognizing the laws of thought as also issuing from facts, that is to say, from psychic sequences. Thus logic becomes a part of psychology. The Cartesian image becomes the individual fact from which induction will be possible. And the epistemological principle 'begin with facts in order to induce the laws' is going to become the metaphysical principle: *Nothing is in the intellect that was not first in sense (nihil est in intellectu quod non fuerit prius in sensu)*. Thus Descartes' image seems both like the individual object from which the scientist must start and like the primary element, which by combination produces thought, that is, the ensemble of logical meanings. We must speak here of the panpsychologism of Hume. The psychic facts are individuated things that are linked by external relations. Thus there must be a *genesis* of thought. Therefore, the Cartesian superstructures collapse; only image-things remain. But along with the superstructures, the synthetic power of the I and the very notion of representation also collapse. Associationism is above all an ontological doctrine that affirms the radical identity of the mode of being of psychic facts and the mode of being of things. After all, there are only things. These things enter into relation with each other and thus constitute a certain collection that we call consciousness. And images are nothing other than things insofar as they maintain a certain type of relation to other things. We see here the germ of American Neorealism. But all these methodological, ontological and psychological assertions follow analytically from the abandonment of Cartesian essences. Nothing happened to the image; it underwent no modification while the intelligible heaven was collapsing for the good reason that in Descartes it was already *a thing*. This is the advent of psychologism, which, under various forms, is nothing other than a positive anthropology, that is to say, a science that wants to treat man as a being of the world while neglecting the essential facts that man is also a being that *apprehends (se représenter)* the world and himself in the world. And this positive anthropology is already in embryo in the Cartesian theory of the image. It does not add anything to Cartesianism; it only subtracts from it. Descartes posits both the image and thought without the image; Hume keeps only the image without thought.

But perhaps one will want to keep everything inside a mental (*spirituelle*) continuity, affirm the homogeneity of fact and law, show that pure experience is already reason. In this case, we will remark that if from fact one can move on to law, this is because the fact was already like an expression of the law, a sign of the law. Or rather, the fact is the law itself. Nothing remains of the Cartesian distinction between necessary essence and empirical fact. But in the empirical, one would like to recover the necessary. Presumably the fact *appears* as contingent. Presumably no human intelligence could give the reason for the colour of this page or for its form. But it is only because this intelligence is by nature limited. We only induce where *by right* we could deduce. Leibniz's 'contingent truths' are *by right* necessary truths. The image thus remains for Leibniz a *fact* similar to other facts; the chair as imaged (*en image*) is nothing but the chair in reality. But just as the chair in reality is a confused knowledge of a truth that is reducible by right to an analytic proposition (*proposition identique*), so the image is just a confused thought. In a word, Leibniz's solution is indeed a panlogicism, but this panlogicism has only an existence of right (*une existence de droit*), which is superimposed upon an empiricism of fact. Psychologically, we will have to find, behind each image, the thought that it *by right* implies. But thought will never reveal itself to an intuition of fact. We will never have a concrete experience of pure thought as one finds it in the Cartesian system. Thought does not appear to itself; one separates it out by reflective analysis. This is why Leibniz can respond to Locke with the famous phrase: *except for the intellect itself* (*nisi ipse intellectus*). In sum, the empiricists' image, as such, is found here as a psychological fact, and it is only about its metaphysical nature that Leibniz is in disagreement with Locke.

A kingdom of thought radically distinct from the kingdom of the image, a world of pure images, or a world of fact-images behind which one must recover a thought that appears only indirectly as the sole possible reason for the organization and finality that one can recognize in the universe of images (a bit in the way that God, in the physico-theological argument, lets himself be inferred from the order of the world)—these are the three solutions proposed to us, the three great currents of Early Modern philosophy (*la philosophie classique*). In these three solutions, the image retains an identical structure. It remains a *thing*. Only its relations to thought change according to the point of view that one has taken on the relations of man to the world, of the universal to the particular, of existence-as-object to existence-as-representation, of the soul to the body. While following the continuous development of the theory of the image throughout the nineteenth century, perhaps we will observe that once one accepts the postulate that the image is only a thing, these three solutions are the only possible ones and that all are *equally* possible and *equally* defective.

II

THE PROBLEM OF THE IMAGE AND THE EFFORT OF PSYCHOLOGISTS TO FIND A POSITIVE METHOD

The problem of the image could have received a genuine renewal from Romanticism. Indeed, Romanticism, in philosophy as in politics and literature, manifests itself by a return to the spirit of synthesis, to the idea of faculties, to the notions of order and of hierarchy, and to a spiritualism (*spiritualisme*) that brings a vitalistic physiology along with it. And because of this fact, the way in which the image is thought of seems, for some time, very different from the three classical points of view we have enumerated. Binet writes:

DOI: 10.4324/9781003657408-3

> ... [M]any fine minds have been loath to admit that thought needs material signs in order to operate. It seemed to them that this would be to make a concession to materialism. In 1865, at the time when a big discussion about hallucination took place within the Société Medico-Psychologique, the philosopher Garnier and some eminent alienists such as Baillarger, Sandras and others still maintained that an unbridgeable abyss separated the conception of an absent or imaginary object—in other words, the image—and a real sensation produced by a present object, and that these two phenomena differed not only in degree but in nature ...[1]

The postulate that image and sensation have an identical nature, which was common to the theses of Descartes, Hume, and Leibniz, was thus put into doubt.[2] Unfortunately, this had rather to do with a general atmosphere than with a fixed doctrine, as one can see. The atmosphere changed quickly. Already in 1865 the thinkers cited by Binet could be considered conservatives: 'The idea of science', writes Giard, 'is intimately linked to those of determinism and of mechanism.'[3]

And probably this is a mistake, but it is this deterministic and mechanistic science that conquers the generation of 1850. Now, whoever says 'mechanism' says 'the spirit of analysis'. Mechanism seeks to resolve a system into its elements and implicitly accepts the postulate that these elements remain rigorously identical whether in a state of isolation or in combination. A further postulate follows naturally: The relations that the elements of a system maintain among themselves are exterior to those elements. It is this postulate that is ordinarily formulated under the name of the Principle of Inertia. Thus, for the intellectuals of the era we are considering, to take a scientific attitude towards any object whatsoever—be it a physical body, an organism, or a fact of consciousness—is to posit, prior to any investigation, that the object is a combination of inert invariants maintaining external relations to each other. By a curious detour, a simplistic interpretation of scientific progress led the philosophers back to the critical position of the eighteenth century and to a hostility of principle against the spirit of synthesis, even though the science of the scientists, science 'in progress', is in essence neither pure analysis nor pure synthesis but adapts its methods to the nature of its objects.

Ever since then, every effort towards developing a scientific psychology has necessarily had to be reduced to an attempt to render psychic complexity into mechanisms.

> The words *faculty*, *capacity*, *power*, which have played such a large role in psychology are, as one will see, only convenient names by means of which we put together in a distinct compartment all the facts of a distinct species;... they do not designate a mysterious and profound essence that persists and is hidden beneath the flux of facts ... By this, psychology becomes a science of facts, for our cognitions are facts; we can speak with precision and detail of a sensation, an idea, a memory, a prediction, as well as of a vibration, a physical movement. ... [V]ery small, well chosen facts that are important, significant, amply detailed and minutely recorded—here is what today constitutes the matter of all science ... our principal business is to know what are these elements, how they are born, in what ways and under which conditions they combine, and what are the constant effects of the combinations thus formed.
>
> Such is the method we tried to follow in this work. In the first part we have extracted the elements of knowledge; by reduction upon reduction we have arrived at the simplest, then, from there, at the physiological changes that are the condition of their genesis. In the second part, we first described the mechanism and the general effect of their assemblage, then, applying the discovered law, we examined the elements, the formation, the certitude and the scope of our principal types of knowledge....[4]

This is how Taine approaches the construction of a scientific psychology in the preface to his book *De l'Intelligence*, which appeared in 1871. One will note the resolute abandonment of the principles of psychological investigation put forward by Maine de Biran. The ideal here is to be able to consider a psychic fact as 'a physical movement'. And from this, we see coexisting in the same text the purely methodological and incontestable principle of making recourse to experience[5] ('very small, well chosen … facts', etc.) and a metaphysical theory, posited *a priori*, about the nature and ends of experience. Taine does not limit himself to prescribing a broad use of experience. He determines from unverified principles *what* this experience *must be*; he describes his results prior to consulting experience, and this description naturally implies a host of concealed assertions about the nature of the world and existence in general. One senses, from reading these first pages, that Taine's psychology, thanks to this originary contamination, will be deductive and that the innumerable facts we will be presented—which are, by the way, almost all false—will serve only to mask the purely logical sequence of the ideas.

Reading the book, unfortunately, only serves to confirm these expectations. One can maintain that nowhere will we find a concrete description or remark dictated by the observation of facts; everything is constructed. Taine first employs regressive analysis, and, thanks to this method, naively and without suspicion, makes a leap from the psychological plane to the physiological plane, which is itself nothing other than the terrain of pure mechanism. Then he goes on to synthesis. But by 'synthesis', we have to understand here a simple re-composition. We ascend from relatively simple groups to more complex groups and *presto* (*le tour est joué*): the physiological is introduced into consciousness.

> There is nothing real in the ego (*le moi*) except the queue of its events. These events, diverse in aspects, are the same in

> nature and all come down to sensation; sensation itself, considered from the outside and by the indirect means that we call external perception, is reducible to a group of molecular movements.[6]

And the image, an essential element of psychic life, will appear at its time in this reconstruction and will come to occupy a place in it determined in advance.

> Everything in the mind that goes beyond 'brute sensation' comes down to images, that is to say, to spontaneous repetitions of sensation.[7]

Thus the very nature of the image is deduced *a priori*. Not for a second do we consult the data of intimate experience (*l'expérience intime*). From the outset we know that the image is only a sensation being reborn, that is to say, it is, in the end, a 'group of molecular movements'. This is to posit the image as an inert invariant and by the same token to cancel out the imagination. The mind is a 'polypary of images'[8]—such is the ultimate finding of analytic psychology. But Taine did not see that this was also his initial postulate. The two large volumes of *De l'Intelligence* only fastidiously develop this simple sentence that we quoted above:

> ... [O]ur principal business is to know what are these elements, how they are born, in what ways and under which conditions they combine....

Once this principle had been posited, he only needed to explain how images combine in order to give birth to concepts, to judgement, and to reasoning. He naturally borrows his explanations from Associationism. But Hume, more skilled, had at least tried to construct a phantom of experience. He did not want to *deduce*. Thus, his laws of association are posited, at least in appearance, in the field of pure psychology. They are links between phenomena *as they appear* to the mind. Taine's initial confusion between experience and analysis leads him to construct a hybrid Associationism, which is expressed sometimes in physiological language, sometimes in psychological language, and other times in both languages at once. Thus, his purely theoretical empiricism is coupled with a metaphysical realism. From that comes this paradoxical contradiction: in order to construct a psychology on the model of physics, Taine adopts the Associationist conception, which, as Kant demonstrated, ends in a radical negation of all [rationally] legislative science (*toute science législatrice*). But at the very time that he unsuspectingly destroys the very ideas of necessity and science at the level of psychology, he maintains a system of necessary laws at the level of physiology and physics. And because he asserts that the physiological and the psychic are but the two faces of a single reality, it follows that the connection of images as facts of consciousness—the only thing that appears to us—is contingent, while the connection of molecular movements that constitute the images as physical realities is necessary. What has been taken as a kind of empiricism for a long time is, therefore, only a failed realist metaphysics.

But Taine's ideas seduced people by their scientific aspect and received confirmations from all quarters. Galton's investigations brought them new factual evidence.[9] At the same time, from 1869 to 1885, Bastian, Broca, Küssmaul, Exner, Wernicke, and Charcot founded the classical theory of aphasia, which tends towards nothing less than establishing the existence of differentiated centres of images. Déjerine still supported it in 1914. Other psychologists—like Binet in his first period[10]—attempted to conquer new domains for Associationism. The physical metaphor that makes the image into 'the survival of a perturbation (*ébranlement*) beyond the excitation that gave birth to it' and assimilates it to the pendular oscillations that still occur long after the pendulum has been moved away from its position of equilibrium by an extraneous force—these metaphors and many others of the same type knew a rare fortune. After J.S. Mill, Taine and Galton definitively fixed the nature of the image: it is a reborn sensation, a solid detached fragment of the external world. Whatever attitude psychologists come to take afterwards, they will always implicitly accept the idea that the image is a reviviscence. And the very same ones who will want to establish the existence of psychic syntheses will nonetheless maintain, as a vestige or as elements of support, the atoms that analytic psychology bequeathed them.

*

* *

Indeed, it is *from* Associationism and *against* it that a new generation of philosophers is going to define its position around 1880. Taine's or Mill's ideas of returning to inner experience are not rejected. But under the influence of diverse factors, they wish both to go beyond them and to preserve them at the same time in a broader synthesis. Among the principal reasons for this change one must cite the growing success of Kantianism, of which Lachelier made himself the champion in France.[11] From this point of view, the question that the philosophers pose to themselves could be formulated thus: How do we reconcile, on the terrain of psychology, the demands of a critique of knowledge with the data of experience? But what is significant is that Taine's descriptions are considered as the data of pure experience. It is only a matter of interpreting them. That there are image-atoms, no one doubts; it is a *fact*. That experience itself directly reveals nothing other than these images, many philosophers would have easily agreed. However, beside the question of fact, there is the question of principle. In principle, there must be something else, a thought that organizes and surpasses the images at each instant. It is a matter, therefore, of retrieving the principle behind the fact.

Reasons of a completely different kind militate in favour of this point of view: political and social ideas have come to change. From now on, critical individualism is distrusted because of its *moral* consequences. In politics it drives towards anarchy; it leads to materialism and atheism. For there is at this time a strong conservative reaction in France. The ideas of order and social hierarchy have retaken all their power. At the Assembly of Versailles they blacken the names of the '… thinkers of radicalism … [who] do not believe in God and in [whose] writings one finds concerning Man definitions that demean our species'.[12]

The Assembly denounces wholesale such radical 'detestable doctrines'. The conservative bourgeoisie, frightened by the Commune, turns back to Religion, as in the first part of the reign of Louis-Philippe. Hence the necessity for establishment intellectuals to combat the analytical tendency of the eighteenth century in every domain. One must posit, above the individual, synthetic realities: the family, the nation, the society. Above the individual image, one must re-establish the existence of concepts, of thoughts. Hence the subject proposed for the essay competition, on 30 April 1882, by the Academy of Moral and Political Sciences:

> Explain and discuss the philosophical doctrines that reduce the faculties of the human mind and the ego itself to the fact of association alone. Re-establish the laws, principles and beings that the doctrines in question tend to denature or suppress.

Thus official Science starts the race. But, again, it is not a matter of denying the existence of sensible images or the laws of association, from this point of view. Ferri, who was laureate of the essay competition, wrote:

> We are so convinced of the importance of association in the production of cognitions (*connaissances*) that the question for us is not to confirm (*constater*) it but to measure it.[13]

He even goes so far as to avow that the data of introspection deliver up to us only image-atoms. Experience is in favour of the Associationists. One has to adopt a critical stance to go beyond them:

> Pure thought is not an illusion because it captures itself in the reflective consciousness of intellectual processes and concepts. But *it does so by an effort of meditation and abstraction*. In reality, the brain never ceases to work for it, to provide it with visible, sonorous or tangible phantoms, the materials upon which it imprints its form....[14]

This text is striking. No other could better demonstrate the uncertainties of introspective knowledge. An author whose goal is to refute Associationism is so imbued with the theories that he wants to combat that he grants them the benefit of experience and grasps in himself only particular images. The activity of thought appears to him only following *an effort of abstraction*; he affirms it, in a way, *against* experience. Thirty years later, as we shall see, everyone will discover or believe himself to discover, at will, non-imagistic states in the slightest of intellectual processes.

And probably this timidity comes, in part, from the enormous success of the books of Taine. But there is something else. The reaction against Associationism is led first and foremost by conservative Catholicism. And for the latter, the theory of the image has a religious aspect that is not negligible. Man is a mix, as

Aristotle says, thought tightly united with a body; there is no thought not stained by the corporeal. The Cartesian idea of pure thought, that is, of an activity of the soul that would be exercised without the concurrence of the body, is a prideful heresy. It is because of this idea that Jacques Maritain could connect Descartes with the Protestants. Thus, one returns to Aristotle who wrote that we would not be able to exercise intellectual activity without the help of the imagination.[15] One returns to Leibniz who, even though a Protestant, had always been much closer to Catholic thought than Descartes. That is why they do not reject Associationism; they need only to integrate it. Associationism is the body; it is the weakness of Man. Thought is his dignity. But dignity never goes without weakness; thought never goes without images. It is in this sense that the Reverend Father Peillaube will write in 1910 in his book *Images*:

> Images are necessary to the formation of concepts. There is not a single concept that is innate. The goal of abstraction, in its originary function that is generative of the intelligible, is precisely to elevate us above the image and to allow us to cognize its object under a necessary and universal form. Our mind cannot directly conceive of an intelligible other than the abstract intelligible, and the abstract intelligible can only be produced from the image and with the image by intellectual activity. All the material that is susceptible to being exploited by intelligence is of a sensorial and imaginative origin.[16]

And here it is: the Leibnizian doctrine of the relation of the image to thought suddenly reappears. To tell the truth, here it does not have all the depth that Leibniz had given to it, but authors expressly invoked the name of Leibniz's doctrine. And it is indeed this doctrine that gives this particular nuance to *fin de siècle* philosophy. It is truly from Leibniz that the idea of thought everywhere present yet inaccessible to inner experience proceeds. This conception, which we were already finding in Ferri, Brochard is going to delineate further:

> ... *[B]ecause* the object can be changed, *I know* that the image is not equivalent to my concept. What the concept contains in addition is, following Hamilton's expression, a character of potential universality. Thought, constrained to take on a sensible form, appears for a moment as being such and such an object, such and such a particular example. It rests upon these in a way, but neither locks itself in them nor is absorbed by them. It goes beyond the images that express it and is capable of being incarnated later in other images that are more or less different.[17]

We thus arrive at a curious conception of thought. Thought has no real, concrete existence, accessible to immediate consciousness, since the datum of introspection is the image. It has no universality in act (*en acte*), because, if it were so, we should be able to grasp it directly. But it has a *potential* universality that one *derives* from the fact that a word can be accompanied by very different images. Over these particular images a kind of rule extends and guides their selection. But there is no 'consciousness of a rule' in the sense in which the Würzburg school will later understand this. The rule—which is the concept—is only ever given in a particular image and as the simple possibility of replacing it by another equivalent image. Thus, the aspect involving consciousness remains what Taine had described—images, words. But in place of the relation of pure habit that Taine established between the one and the other, Brochard and many of his contemporaries place a functional connection—this is thought. But if, thanks to this substitution, they can reintroduce all the Rationalism, it remains nonetheless that this strange thought floats, obscure to itself, between an existence *de jure* (*de droit*) and an existence *de facto* (*de fait*). Better: it exists as function but not as consciousness. It reveals itself only by its effects. It is not even the movement from one present image to another that defines it; it is the simple *possibility* of effecting this movement. And if this possibility is not currently present to consciousness, it must be because it is a pure logical possibility. At most it would manifest itself to reflection in the form of an insufficiency of the image as such.

Such is the timid attempt made by this re-emergent Rationalism to combat Associationism. It sees itself clasped between the alleged data of introspection ('there is never in consciousness anything but images and words') and the alleged discoveries of physiology (cerebral localizations). It thus abandons to Taine the terrain of facts and takes refuge on the plane of critique. Thus Leibniz once responded to Locke:

> Nothing is in the intellect that was not first in sense, except for the intellect itself. (*Nihil est in intellectu quod non prius fuerit in sensu nisi ipse intellectus.*)[18]

Thus Kant responded to Hume:

> It is possible that on the terrain of experience one cannot discover any relation between cause and effect other than empirical succession. But for an experience to be possible, *a priori* synthetic principles must constitute it.[19]

But this response, admissible as long as it is a matter of the constitution of experience, is no longer so when it is necessary to account for thought within this experience. The thought we are talking about is not a constituting one. It is the concrete activity of man, a phenomenon constituted in the midst of other phenomena. It is one thing to constitute my present perception (a bedroom, books, etc.) by categorial syntheses that *render* consciousness *possible*; it is another thing to form conscious thoughts about this perception *once it is constituted* (for instance, to think: 'the books are on the table', 'this is a door', etc.). In this second case, consciousness exists as facing the world. If, therefore, I form a thought about the world, it must appear to me as a real psychic phenomenon. There is no 'potentiality' ('*virtualité*') or 'possibility' that would hold here; consciousness is act and everything that exists in consciousness exists in act (*en acte*).

Be that as it may, it is not doubtful that this new atmosphere and these demands about the rights of synthesis in the face of mechanistic association strongly contributed to the education of Ribot, the founder of the psychology of synthesis. Certainly, it is not Kantianism that inspires Ribot, still less is he guided by religious preoccupations. His sole concern is to revise the Taineian notion of 'scientific psychology'. For him, presumably, science is analysis, but it is also synthesis. It is not sufficient to reduce everything to elements; there are syntheses in nature that must be studied as such. It thus seems at first glance that Ribot's point of departure is a reflection on the insufficiency of the method of the English psychologists and of Taine. But doesn't he borrow the very idea of psychic synthesis from the great current of thought that consecrates a renaissance of intellectualism at this period? It is rather curious to compare the text of Brochard that we just commented on with what Ribot wrote in 1914:

> Thought is a function that, in the course of evolution, was added to the primary and secondary forms of knowledge: sensations, memory, association. Consequent to what conditions could it have been born? One cannot, on this point, hazard hypotheses. Be that as it may, it made its appearance; it was fixed and developed. But as a function can only be activated under the influence of excitations that are appropriate to it, the existence of pure thought working without anything that provokes it is *a priori* implausible. Reduced to itself, it is an activity that

> dissociates, associates, perceives relations, and coordinates. One can even believe that this activity is, in its nature, unconscious, and that it only dons the conscious form through the data that it elaborates.... to conclude, the hypothesis of pure thought without images and without words is scarcely probable and, in any case, has not been proved.[20]

It could seem like one is reading the very text of Brochard but translated into a biological and pragmatist language. Ribot, like Brochard, retains the existence of sensations and images linked together by laws of association. These are the 'primary and secondary forms of knowledge'. Like Brochard, Ribot makes them into the immediate data of introspection. As for thought, Ribot, too, considers it as inaccessible to intuitive consciousness. But for Brochard, if thought does not reveal itself to intuition, it must be 'potential'; it is then a functional equivalence between very different images. As for Ribot, he expresses himself in resolutely thingist (*chosistes*) terms. Thought is a real but unconscious activity. 'It only dons the conscious form through the data that it elaborates.' And, satisfied with this obscure and contradictory notion of unconscious thought, this positivist psychologist concludes *a priori* that the existence of pure thought accessible to consciousness is implausible. One can see how profound Taine's influence is; it is profound to the point of leading an experimental psychologist to negate experimental results in the name of pure deductions.[21] For this entire generation, Associationism will remain a factual datum, and thought will only be a hypothesis necessary for explaining an 'organization', a systematization that is too difficult to account for by pure association. And Ribot's positivism, instead of being applied to the description of the image as such, will operate in the opposite direction by contriving this biological notion of an unconscious thought that 'appeared' in the course of human evolution.

We see what this idea of 'synthesis' signifies, and that wherein Ribot differs from Taine. It is a physiological idea. Man is a living organism within the world, and thought is an organ that has been developed by certain needs. Just as there is no digestion without food, there is no thought without images, that is to say, without material coming from the exterior. But just as the progress of physiology has made us envision digestion as a functional whole, the new psychology must, beginning from brute or elaborated materials that alone are conscious, reconstitute the synthetic unity of the organ that elaborates them. And even as synthetic psychology does not exclude determinism, the new psychology, considering the psychic activity of synthesis as a biological function, will be resolutely determinist. We thus find again here the Leibnizian theme of the inseparability of thought and image, but demeaned, fallen to the level of materialist thingism (*chosisme*): man is a living thing; the image is a thing; thought, as well, is a thing.

Nothing gives us a better sense of this degradation than Ribot's book *L'Imagination créatrice*. In this work, he attempts to analyse the mechanism of the creation of new images. But, naturally, he poses the problem in the very terms that Taine would have employed. He wonders how, beginning from the images furnished by memory, new ensembles or 'fictions' can be constituted. And, to be sure, he starts by affirming the rights of synthesis: 'Every imaginative creation demands a principle of unity.'[22] But this principle, which he calls, without much concern for coherence, a 'centre of attraction and a foothold' and that he conceives of as a 'fixed idea-emotion' ('*idée-émotion fixe*'), serves, in sum, only as a regulator for processes that are simply mechanical.[23]

Thus, first there will be dissociation; the image of the external object will undergo a work of dismemberment. The causes of the dissociation are 'internal and external'. The former or 'subjective' ones are: (1) selection with action in view; (2) affective causes 'that govern attention'; (3) intellectual reasons, 'designating under this name the law of mental inertia or law of least effort'.[24] The external causes are the 'variations of experience', which present a given object now imbued with or now deprived of a certain quality: 'what has been associated now with one thing, now with another tends to dissociate itself from both'.

This dissociation frees a certain number of imaged elements that are now going to be able to be associated in order to form new ensembles. We reach the second part of the problem: 'What are the forms of association that give rise to new combinations and under what influence do they form?'[25] We see that Ribot formulates the issue in terms of association. Associations can be oriented, directed from outside, but it would take a miracle to suspend their laws, just as it would to suspend the law of gravity. In sum, just as certain economists have proposed replacing the economic liberalism preached by the English empiricists by a directed economy, one can say that Ribot replaces the free Associationism of Taine and Mill with a *directed Associationism*.

There are three factors of creative association: an 'intellectual' factor, an 'affective' factor, and an 'unconscious' factor.

The intellectual factor is the 'faculty of thinking by analogy'. 'We mean by analogy an imperfect form of resemblance. The similar is a genus of which the analogue is a species.'

Regarding the affective or 'emotional' factor, Ribot scarcely explains himself in *L'Imagination créatrice*. But he returns to it in *La Logique des sentiments*. First there is what psychoanalysts have since named 'condensation'. 'States of consciousness combine because there is a common affective sense between them.'[26] One must also indicate transfer:

> When an intellectual state has been accompanied by a vivid sentiment, a similar or analogous state tends to elicit the same sentiment. ... When intellectual states have coexisted,

> the sentiment attached to the initial state, if it is vivid, tends to be transferred to the others.[27]

There can thus be condensation, then transfer, then condensation again, and, in this binary rhythm, imaged elements that primitively stand in no relation are compared and blended into new ensembles. As for the unconscious factor, it is not of a different nature from the preceding factors. It is intellectual or affective; only it is not directly accessible to consciousness.

To tell the truth, it was unavoidable that Ribot would have recourse to the unconscious, for none of the factors that he envisages appear to consciousness. We are never conscious of dissociation and never conscious of new combinations either. Images crop up suddenly and are given immediately for what they are. One must suppose then that all the work is done outside of consciousness. Neither the associations nor the synthetic factors appear to us; this entire generative mechanism (*mécanisme créateur*) is a pure hypothesis. Ribot is thus no more concerned with describing the facts than Taine. He begins with the explanation. Synthetic psychology, in its beginnings, thus remains theoretical, like analytic psychology. It just limits itself to complicating the abstract deductions while adding a factor into the combinations; it seeks to build up psychology on the model of biology, as analytic psychology tried to build it up on the model of physics. As for the image, it has remained for Ribot exactly what it was for Taine. It will not change for a long time.

*
* *

By the end of the century, however, there occurs what we are justified in calling a philosophical revolution. In his two books,

Essai sur les données immédiates de la conscience and *Matière et Mémoire*, appearing successively in 1889 and 1896, Bergson presents himself as being a determined opponent of Associationism. The classical conceptions of aphasia and cerebral localization do not withstand criticism. The image-memory is something other and more than a simple cerebral reviviscence. The brain could not have as a function the storing of images. Perception is a direct contact with the thing. And lastly, this notion of psychic synthesis, introduced by Ribot, is going to be radically transformed. Synthesis is not a simple factor of regulation; all consciousness is synthesis. This is the very mode of psychic existence; no longer are there any solid fragments in the flux of consciousness, nor any juxtaposition of states. But inner life presents itself as a multiplicity of interpenetration, it *endures* (*dure*). All of these celebrated affirmations seem called to bring about a renewal of the psychology of the image. Indeed, many believed it, and there is a whole literature on the Bergsonian problem of the image. Let us just refer to the article by Quercy, 'Sur une théorie bergsonienne de l'imagination',[28] and to the article by Chevalier and Bouyer, 'De l'image à l'hallucination'.[29] However, an attentive examination of Bergson's conception is going to show us that, in spite of the usage of a new terminology, he accepts the problem of the image in its classical formulation (*sous son aspect classique*) and that the solution that he gives to it brings with it absolutely nothing new.

Bergson is far from envisaging this problem as a pure psychologist. In his theory of the image we find again his entire metaphysics, and we must criticize first this metaphysical point of departure if we want to understand the role that he attributes to the image in the life of the mind.

Like the empiricists that he combats, like Hume, like the Neorealists, Bergson makes of the universe a world of images. Each reality has a 'kinship', an 'analogy', a certain relation to consciousness; and this is why all things that surround us are called images. But while Hume reserves the term image for the thing insofar as it is perceived, Bergson extends it to every sort of reality. It is not solely the object of a current cognition that is an image; it is every possible object of representation.

> An image can *be* without *being perceived*; it can be present without being represented.[30]

Representation adds nothing to the image; it does not communicate any new character to it or anything *more*. A representation already exists in fact, virtual and neutralized, before being a conscious representation; it is in the image. For it to exist in act (*en acte*), it has to be isolable from the images that have an effect on it, it has to '… detach itself from the surroundings like a painting, instead of remaining embedded in them like a thing'.[31]

Thus, there is no longer any point in distinguishing, with Descartes, between the thing and the image of the thing, in order to seek afterwards to understand how a relation is established between these two existences. Nor is there any point in reducing, with Berkeley, the reality of the thing to that of the conscious image; nor in reserving, with Hume, the possibility of an existence in itself of reality, but with the image alone being known. For Bergsonian realism, a thing is an image; matter is the ensemble of images:

> For images there is a simple difference in degree but not in kind between *being* and being consciously perceived.[32]

That is to say, the whole ensemble of reality is given first as partaking in consciousness or, better, as partaking *of consciousness*. Otherwise this reality could not ever *become* conscious, that is to say, borrow a character that would be foreign to its nature.

Bergson does not think that consciousness necessarily needs a correlate or, to speak like Husserl, that a consciousness is always consciousness of something. In Bergson, consciousness appears as a quality, a given character, almost a kind of substantial form of reality; it cannot be born where it is not, nor begin, nor cease to be. And, on the other hand, it can exist in a purely potential (*virtuel*) state, without being accompanied by any act nor even any manifestation of its presence. And Bergson will define this reality endowed with a secret quality as unconscious. But the unconscious that appears here is precisely of the same nature as consciousness. There is no non-conscious (*non-conscient*) for Bergson; there is only consciousness unaware of itself (*conscience qui s'ignore*). There is no opacity that is opposed to light and receives it, constituting thus an illuminated object. There is pure light, phosphorescence, without illuminated material, though this pure light, everywhere diffused, only becomes occurrent (*actuelle*) by being reflected on certain surfaces that serve at the same time as screens for the other luminous zones. There is a sort of inversion of the classical comparison: instead of consciousness being a light that goes from the subject to the thing, it is a luminosity that goes from the thing to the subject.

This centre of reflection and, at the same time, obscurity that actualizes potential (*virtuelle*) consciousness is the body. It is the body that, by isolating certain images, transforms them into occurrent (*actuelles*) representations. How does this movement happen?

There is no need to deduce consciousness, says Bergson, since, by positing the material world, one has given oneself a set of images. There is no need to generate consciousness from the thing if, in its very existence, the thing is already consciousness. But, in changing the terms of its formulation, Bergson has not, as he believes, eliminated the problem. It remains to be understood how one moves from the non-conscious image to the conscious image, how the potential (*virtuel*) can actualize itself.

Is it intelligible that it would suffice to separate one image from the rest of the images in order to give it this transparency, this existence for itself that makes it consciousness? Or, if one holds that it possessed it beforehand, is it admissible that this transparency neither existed for itself nor for any subject? Bergson regards as negligible this essential characteristic of the fact of consciousness, that is, to appear to itself precisely as conscious. And in having confused the world with consciousness, taken as a quasi-substantial quality, he also himself reduces psychological consciousness to being nothing but a sort of epiphenomenon, the occurrence of which one can describe but not explain.

In particular, how does this unconscious and impersonal consciousness become the conscious consciousness of an individual subject? And how, in making themselves 'present', do the potentially represented images suddenly envelop the existence of an 'I'? This is what Bergson does not explain. However, the whole theory of memory is founded on the existence of such a subject and on its possibility of appropriating certain images and of conserving them.

The body acts as an instrument of selection. Thanks to it, the image becomes perception. A perception is an image 'related to the possible action of a certain determined image', which is precisely the body. But how does this relation create the occurrence of a subject that will call this body 'my' body and the other images 'my representations'? Bergson says:

> Give me ... images in general and my body will necessarily end up drawing itself in the midst of them as a distinct thing, since they change constantly and it remains invariable.[33]

This explanation is amusing. Movement and immobility in all likelihood individuate matter, to speak like Descartes, or the 'images', as Bergson says. But they certainly leave to nature its materiality and to the image its character as image. The immobile does not appear as 'central'. A 'centre' does not appear as acting. And above all, the action itself, never being anything but an image, does not give birth to a subject that 'relates the actions to itself'.

But probably this is not exactly what Bergson means. In fact, one must suppose that there is, among the images, the presence of a mind (*esprit*) that defines itself as a memory. This mind makes comparisons between and syntheses of the images it collects, and it distinguishes its body from other surrounding images. Indeed:

> The images, once perceived, fixate and align themselves in memory.[34]

But this is to put us in the heart of insoluble difficulties.

And to begin with, if everything is consciousness, what can a consciousness be? Is it activity and unity, a reality distinct from all the others and capable of *gaining* (*prendre*) consciousness? But then it would be an abuse of words to call the passive realities that consciousness can apprehend 'consciousness', and one would be going back to a metaphysics that begins not from the world as conscious, but from consciousnesses facing a world. Is it individuated by its content, which is selected by the body to which consciousness is joined? But then we no longer understand how the very body, with the images in relation to it, distinguishes itself from the other bodies with the other images that surround them, since the image-body's relations of action with the other images are themselves images.

It is, however, this second solution that Bergson will stick to.

But here is another difficulty. How does the image transform itself into an image-memory? The image is, in sum, a *thing* isolated by the body; and its isolation confers a novel quality upon it, namely, the quality of being represented. But how can the image remain isolated and retain its representational character when the action of the body ceases? The table should again become a potentially (*virtuellement*) conscious table as soon as I cease to look at it, since it then recovers its relations with all the other images of the universe. How therefore can it remain at the same time a table in my memory? Or would it not then be that the representation does not define itself only by the isolation of the image, but that it appears as an existence radically distinct from *things*? The movement from the first to the second chapter of *Matière et Mémoire* is carried out by means of a pure sophism. The image-representation is first an image ideally isolated but really linked to all the others; then, as it becomes an image-memory, one sees its ideal isolation transform into a real isolation. It detaches itself from the world and is transformed in the mind. Bergson is fooled by the material comparison of the image with a painting. He resembles a man who, after having isolated a piece of landscape as a result of looking at it through a lens, would want to take with him not only the lens but also the piece of landscape carved out in it. The whole Bergsonian theory of memory is based on this sophism, which explains its realist character. For Bergson does not forget that this image-picture that memory takes with itself, precisely as one takes with oneself a painting taken down from a wall (memory 'gleans images along time [*le long du temps*] as they occur'[35]), is also an image-thing, embedded in other images and existing without being perceived, so that, playing on the dual meaning of the word 'image', he gives to the image-memory all the plenitude of the object. Better, it is the very object conceived as conforming to a new type of existence.

The formation of memory is thus contemporaneous with that of perception; it is, as it becomes representation, at the very moment it is perceived that the image-thing is transformed into memory:

> The formation of memory is never posterior to that of perception; it is contemporaneous with it. As perceptions are created, their memories take shape beside them at the same pace.[36]

The memory thus constituted

> ... is immediately perfect; time will not be able to add anything to its image without denaturing it; it will retain its place and its date for the sake of memory.[37]

The conception of the image that Bergson proposes here is far from being as different from the empiricist conception as he claims. For him, as for Hume, the image is an element of thought exactly conforming to perception, presenting the same discontinuity and the same individuality as the latter. In Hume, it appears as weakening of a perception, an echo that follows it in time. Bergson makes the image into a shadow of the perception, which doubles the perception. In both cases, it is an exact tracing of the thing, opaque and impenetrable like the thing, rigid, frozen, itself a thing.

> Images will indeed never be anything but things....[38]

And this is why we will see that the role of the image in the life of the mind is very close in Bergson to that which it plays in the eyes of the Empiricists. Here again, the image has first been defined as 'imprinting itself' in the mind as a content the memory of which is just the receptacle and not as a living moment of mental (*spirituelle*) activity.

Bergson, however, insists on pointing out that he has, contrary to the Empiricists, established a difference in nature—and not only in degree—between perception and memory. But this very distinction, more metaphysical than psychological by the way, is going to pose new problems. We have seen what it is. A perception is an image related to the possible action of the body, but it still remains nested among the other images. A memory is an isolated image detached from the others like a painting. Every reality possesses both of these characters at the same time. It disposes the body to action and deposits itself in the mind as an inactive memory.

> In its very gushing forth, the present splits itself at every instant into two symmetrical jets one of which falls back into the past while the other dashes forward towards the future.[39]

There is thus a profound difference between a memory, which is inactive, a pure idea, and a perception, which is an ideomotor activity. But—beyond the fact that this distinction will not allow us to discriminate an *actualized* memory (the image of this table that reappears) from a perception in concrete life—it is impossible to understand what this perpetual splitting of the present means, exactly as it was impossible before to know how a temporary isolation of a thing abruptly made it into a representation. This metaphor of the double gushing indicates an identical fundamental sophism.

What, indeed, is the present? 'My present is, by essence, sensory-motor.'[40] It is 'a section' that perception makes in a mass that is in the process of streaming down. This section is precisely 'the material world'. [41]It is also 'a thing absolutely determined and that demarcates my past.'[42]

The metaphysical insufficiency of such a definition of the present and the vicious circle that it implies (because this pragmatic present necessitates an ontological present to make it possible) jump right out at us. But it is off our topic to criticize this. Let us accept it as it is given. We have to note immediately that a present that is *pure action* could not by any splitting produce an inactive past, a past that is *pure idea* without any link to movements and sensations. Whether one considers the relation *action-memory* in the subject or the relation *image-thing—image-memory* in the object, one finds again the same hiatus between two kinds of existence that Bergson insists on positing as distinct (since he wants to separate mind from matter and memory from body) but that he nevertheless wants to bring back into unity. In order to justify these two contradictory operations, he relied on a syncretism of consciousness and matter. But, for having constantly confounded the noema and the noesis,[43] he was led to endow this syncretic reality he names *image* now with the significance of a noema, now with a noetic significance, depending on the needs of his construction. Unification? None. Rather, a perpetual ambiguity, a shifting from one domain to the other, perpetual and without good faith.

Thus, Bergson has attempted to explain what the Empiricists took as a datum: the existence of images that are born from perception. We just saw that he failed at it. But the position that he has taken obliges him to resolve a new problem: How can the image be reintroduced into the sensory-motor world of the body and perception? How does the past become present again?

The image-picture really remains in memory. Just like the image-things, it can be either currently conscious or potentially so, which comes down to a state of unconsciousness for it. The vast majority of our memories are unconscious. How do they return to consciousness?

There are, on this point, two irreconcilable theories in Bergson that are, however, never clearly distinguished. One has its root in psychology, in Bergsonian biologism; the other responds to metaphysical tendencies, to Bergsonian spiritualism (*spiritualisme*).

The first initially appears rather clear. The present is what is occurrent (*actuel*); the present is defined by the action of the body. Evoking a memory is making a past image present. But the evoked image is not a simple resurrection of the stored image, otherwise one would not understand how, of a face of which I possess a multiplicity of distinct memories corresponding to the multiplicity of perceptions, I evoke a single image, which can even fail to overlap exactly with any of the recorded memories. In order to reappear to consciousness, the image must insert itself into the body. A conscious psychological image is an incarnation, in the body and in its motor mechanisms, of pure memory; conscious psychological images were inactive, unperceived, and existing in the unconscious. For the mind, to live is always '... to insert itself into things by the intermediary of a mechanism'.[44] Memory is submitted to this condition. In the pure state it is '... clear, precise, but ... lifeless';[45] it resembles those souls of whom Plato speaks who must let themselves fall into a body in order to be capable of actualization. It is potential, impotent. To become present, it thus needs to insert itself into a corporeal attitude. Called from the depths of memory, it is developed into memory-images that are inserted into a motor schema (*schème moteur*), and it then becomes an acting reality, an image. In that sense, 'The image is a present state and can only participate in the past through the memory it came out of.'[46] And Bergson insists on the role of movement. He shows that every image, visual, auditory, etc., is always accompanied by an incipient sketch of movements, by the creation of motor schemas. If we kept to this theory, the image would appear as a present construction, as the consciousness of an attitude defined presently by movements of the body. Two consequences would result from this: First, nothing would distinguish image from perception, which is equally a present attitude; and the image, like perception, would be [a kind of] action and not knowledge. Second, the image would not be a memory but a new creation responding to the ever-new attitudes of the body.

But if consciousness is defined by Bergson in a vitalist manner as an occurrence (*actualité*) resulting from corporeal attitudes, it also represents for him the margin that separates an action from the agent (*l'être agissant*) and represents the power to escape from the present and from the body, memory. Hence the second orientation of his theory of images: a memory is not only conscious as present but also as past. It is thus that in his article on 'Le Souvenir du présent', Bergson, as we have seen, accepts that at the very same time that we perceive an object, we can have a memory of it, from which the phenomenon known by the name of paramnesia results. Of course, in that case the occurrence (*actualité*) of the memory is not defined by the body, since the representation that is born from the corporeal attitude before an object is called *perception*. A memory possesses here a *sui generis* consciousness that allows it to be *present* as memory, whereas a perception is *present* as perception.

In this case, the body does not appear positively useful for memory. It is just asked not to impede a memory from appearing. It is no longer about inserting a memory into the body but about, so to speak, suppressing the body, as this occurs in sleep where the tension of the nervous system diminishes. Dreams and the phenomena of hypermnesia show what richness of imagery can accompany this physiological annihilation.

But if, according to this second theory, consciousness is directly linked to the mind, the power that the body possesses of diverting consciousness from the mind, of making it grip onto action, becomes unthinkable. One does not see at all anymore what impedes the image-memories from being perpetually conscious.

This is why, as we indicated, Bergson kept both theories. It is the body that makes for the occurrence (*actualité*) of memory, that makes it move into clear consciousness. And it is nevertheless memory that makes of perception, which is a simple motor schema, a conscious representation. How does this junction work exactly?

Perception and present action create the motor schema. But what determines a memory to insert itself into it is a kind of force that properly belongs to this memory. However inactive such a memory may be, Bergson indeed confers on it tendencies and powers as magical as the powers of attraction that Hume conferred on images. In Bergson, images try to 'push themselves into full light'.[47] It requires an effort to 'inhibit their appearance'.[48] As soon as there is lessening of tension, 'the immobile memories, sensing that I have just put aside the obstacle and lifted the trap door that kept them in the underground of consciousness, start moving …'.[49] It is by a veritable tension that the body represses the appearance of the totality of memories, all of which would like to and, in principle, could exist. These metaphors are unfortunate, to say the very least. What thus becomes of the role of the screen and of the reflector that had been primitively allocated to the body? And what do we do with the famous definition 'the unconscious is the inacting (*l'inagissant*)'? Bergson seems to have forgotten it all right when he describes at length the 'dance' the memories give themselves up to.[50]

And anyway, from where does this appetite for an occurrent existence (*existence actuelle*) come to memories? The past, according to Bergson, is real at least as much as the present, which is only a limit. An unconscious representation exists as fully as a conscious representation. From where then does this ardour come to it for incarnating itself in a body whose nature is alien to it and that it has no need of in order to be? Why, instead of being inert or indifferent, are the memories '… in waiting … almost attentive'?[51] In a general way, to attribute an activity that is conceived on the model of mental activity to discontinuous elements, to contents of consciousness that one has first carefully separated from the whole of consciousness, is to be at risk of having recourse to physico-magical notions that are perfectly unthinkable.

As for the call that perception 'sends out' to memory, its nature is no clearer.[52] Perception is not a representation but a motor schema that endeavours to constitute the image that comes to grip onto perception. But, here again, why does perception, which is by nature activity and not speculation, endeavour to transform itself into representation? And above all, if perception is not representation, if memory is only the exact copy, the shadow of perception, *from where can the representation well up?* 'It is memory', says Bergson, 'that makes us see and hear. A perception would be incapable of evoking the memory that resembles it.'[53] And indeed, it would already have to have taken form; but the form comes only from the memory. A perception is an image in its relation to a certain attitude of the body. This attitude is at first very general and only answers to very exterior determinations of the object. It is through memory that it deepens, that it takes on a meaning. But where the initial forms and meanings can come from Bergson does not say anywhere. Incidentally, if, as he explains at length in *Matière et Mémoire*, '... to perceive is to remember',[54] taking perception this time not in the pure sense but in the sense of representation in the present, we have to admit one of two things: either the image, contrary to what he says elsewhere, does not carry in itself the mark of its origin in the past and gives itself as present, or else perception necessarily gives itself as an image coming from the past. Once again, we see that between an *image-memory*, which is a fragment of the past incarnated in a present motor schema, and a *perception*, which is a present motor schema where a past memory is incarnated, we would not be able to find a real difference. Despite his efforts, Bergson fails to distinguish them, and we find again, at the bottom of these specious theories, the simple affirmation of the Empiricists—image and perception do not differ in nature but solely in degree. Thus Bergson, after having carefully distinguished image and perception on the metaphysical plane, is obliged to confound them on the psychological plane.

It remains to determine what role this image-memory is going to play in the life of the mind. We have already seen that Bergson is led to conceive of it as the Associationists would, since, for them as for him, the image is a fixed element, a thing.

And surely, Bergson has fought the Associationist conception with force. But he did not understand that Associationism will always get the better of those who concede to it that the image is a thing, even if, in the face of this thing, they re-establish the mind. He did not see that the only means of being done with this invasive doctrine is to return to the image itself and to prove that it is radically different from an object. He thus softened the notion of consciousness; he attempted to restore to it fluidity, spontaneity and life. But try as he might, he let these inert images remain within pure duration (*la durée pure*), like cobblestones at the bottom of water. We must start all over again.

It is not that we do not find a sharp critique of Associationism in his books. He first tackles the ideas of resemblance and contiguity, conceived of as soft forces. The images, taken in themselves, do not possess, he says, the mysterious power of attracting each other. Their links come from the action in which they are embedded, from the body. All perception prolongs itself in motor reactions that utilize the motor mechanisms mounted by analogous perception, and these reactions drive other reactions that have been antecedently coordinated with them, and so forth. Such then is the source of links of resemblance and of contiguity, which therefore amount to mechanical links in the body, to body memory or memory-habit. Likewise, a general idea is not the result of a super-position of individual images. It is lived before it is thought. It is precisely an overall reaction to a total situation, and it is the similarity of the corresponding reactions to diverse situations that constitutes their generality. The mind thus does not start by forming images that reunite later to produce concepts and particular links. Perception furnishes us with syntheses that only afterwards are dissociated into images:

> Association is thus not the primitive fact; it is by a dissociation that we begin, and the tendency of every memory to aggregate

> with others is explained by a natural return of the mind to the undivided unity of perception.[55]

But how can this parcelling be carried out? The question is important, for Bergson conceives of the life of the mind as oscillating between two poles: that of synthetic perception, which defines the present, and that where the images are laid out exterior to each other. To understand, to invent, to remember, or, generally speaking, to think is always to move from one pole to the other through intermediary planes, less concentrated than the first, less dilated than the second. To live, for the mind, is not to connect separated elements but to contract or dilate a synthetic content always given in its totality. From where does the existence of these different planes of consciousness come, and, in particular, how does the plane of the past and of dream come out from the plane of action?

The relation of the image to perception appears in these descriptions as very different from what we have seen up to now. An image doubled a perception like its shadow. It was a perception itself falling into the past. It was the very image-thing just isolated from its surroundings in order to become an image-picture. Now, on the contrary, it seems that a perception synthetically contains a multitude of images to which the tension of the body gives an undivided unity but that are scattered as soon as the body relaxes.

As we have seen, this is because the role of the image in perception is not at all clear. One does not know whence, according to Bergson, primitive representations originate. In every complex perception there is embedded a multitude of images, shot up from the unconscious, that constitute, at the same time, the image-perception and the image-memory. In a sense, there is thus indeed in one perception a multiplicity of images. However, if one sees the image-perception as an undivided unity, the new image-memory that corresponds to it must also be taken as a unity. And inversely, if the latter is regarded as a compound, we must take the perception itself to be a compound. All the more so, the primitive images have exactly the same content and the same concentration as the primitive perceptions.

What, by the way, can the words 'parcelling', 'exteriority', and 'dissociation' mean in Bergson, who has otherwise shown so well that the life of the mind could not be translated into any spatial metaphor? If he is led to introduce them, it is, on the one hand, because he knows quite well that consciousness is a unity at each instant, but also, on the other hand, because his realist theory of memory obliges him to attribute to unconscious objects exactly the discontinuity and multiplicity of the objects of the material world. Since his metaphysics demands that this unconscious reality, this store of isolated images, always have an effective presence in the mind, consciousness can only become diversified via the diverse types of unities that it will give to this multiple reality. Hence the comparison with the different degrees of tension in a gas, in which the same amount of molecules can be contained in diverse volumes; hence the theory of diverse planes of consciousness. But the idea of synthesis, so dear to Bergson, is still conceived of by him in an extremely materialistic manner. No doubt, in place of the old *juxtaposition*, there is a *fusion* of elements. But the idea of elements is preserved. Bergson attempted to substitute a spiritualism (*spiritualisme*) for the geometric and spatial thought of Cartesianism and the Associationists, but he could only produce a physico-chemical fiction with connections that are often prelogical.

Besides, what meaning can this fusion have? Do we speak of a 'fusion' of molecules in the kinetic theory of gases? If the elements of a gas can occupy a variable volume, it is because we reduce the space that separates them. But we would not know how to make them interpenetrate. By what principle would these psychic molecules, Bergsonian images, merge into a synthesis of unification? Will we say that this type of synthesis is the peculiarity of consciousness? But one precludes oneself from affirming this *sui generis* power of the psychic once one has constructed a realist metaphysics of memory. Indeed, the image then remains a thing, a frozen element. By aggregating itself with other images, it can only produce a mosaic work. When the mind moves on a plane of consciousness, whatever it be, only mechanical links are produced, like those Associationism describes. There is even an entire region of psychic life that Bergson calls inferior or mechanical in which the links between images are by his own avowal purely associative; it is that of dream and of reverie.

What makes for the spontaneity of the mind is the possibility of moving from one plane to the other. The movement operates via what Bergson calls the dynamic schema (*schéma dynamique*). The schema (*schéma*) is a unity, a synthesis containing the rules of its development into images, containing '… the indication of what it must do in order to reconstitute the images.'[56] It '… contains, in a state of reciprocal implication, *what the image will develop in parts exterior to each other*'.[57]

One can let one's memory roam haphazardly. The images will follow one another on the same plane of consciousness; they will be homogeneous. But one can, on the contrary, '… transport oneself to a point at which the multiplicity of images seems to condense into a single, simple and undivided representation'.[58] In this case, recall will simply consist in going back down from the schema (*schéma*) onto the plane where the images are scattered.

To understand, to remember, to invent, these are always to form a schema (*schéma*) first, and then to go back down from the schema to the image, to fill up the schema with images, which can lead, by the way, to the modification of the schema throughout its realization. Thus would be explained the unity or organization of the mental activity, which is impossible to account for if, by contrast, one begins with separated elements; it is from the schema that the suppleness and the novelty come. And Bergson concludes:

> *Besides* the mechanism of association, there is that of mental effort.[59]

There we have it; this suffices to date his thought. Wouldn't we think we were reading a sentence from Ribot? No more than Ribot did Bergson see that one cannot make room for Associationism. If one accepts the conception of a frozen image and of mechanical links, if one introduces into consciousness an opacity, a resistance that is foreign to it, a world of 'things', one is precluded from understanding the nature of the conscious fact. How could consciousness master the foreign elements? Or in Bergsonian terms, how will the suppleness of the schema (*schéma*) be able to accommodate itself to the stiffness of the image? Here again we have to move into the magical. Between the schema and the image, Bergson says in very vague terms, there is 'attraction and repulsion'.[60] But we see well that he cannot account for the selection that the images effect between each other, their way of recognizing the schema in which they can embed themselves.

And above all, if images can only provide 'mosaics',[61] how can the schema modify them to the point at which they fuse into a new image of an irreducible quality? In short, how do we explain the creative imagination? For, after all, the schema acts only as a catalyst; it is not that different from the '... principle of unity, centre of attraction and foothold'[62] the existence of which Ribot posited. *Before* him, one only finds separated images, *after* him, images are classified in a new order of interdependence. But no 'soft force' directly ordering the images and emanating from them without intermediary could act in a more mysterious manner to yield the same results. Or else one has to admit that the schema has modified the internal structure of the images. But this would suppose a completely different theory of images, one in which they would appear as acts and not as contents, and in which, precisely, the schema would no longer play any role.

Bergson does not bring any satisfying solution to the problem of the image. He is limited to superimposing two planes of psychic life, to reclaiming the rights of the spirit of synthesis and of continuity. But he does not touch the psychology of the image; he does not enrich it with any new insight, and not for one instant did he *examine* his images. In spite of his frequent appeals to a concrete intuition, everything in him is dialectic and *a priori* deductions. It is Taine's image that has moved entirely, without scrutiny, and as an incontestable acquisition of science into Bergsonian metaphysics. And the world of thought that Bergson attempted to re-establish without much luck is irremediably cut off from the world of images and deprived of a multitude of resources.

Let us add that Bergson hesitated much on this point and that, in certain lectures, he attributed to the image a function incompatible with the nature that *Matière et Mémoire* and *L'Énergie Spirituelle* assigned to it. For example in *L'Intuition philosophique* he regards the image as '… intermediate between the simplicity of concrete intuition and the complexity of the abstractions that translate it';[63] and he shows the necessity of having recourse to this mediating term '… which is almost matter in that it still lets itself be seen, and almost mind in that it does not let itself be touched anymore'.[64] It is the concept that then appears as frozen, as spatial and fragmentary; the image is tighter, closer to intuition:

> It is into concepts that the system develops itself; it is into an image that it tightens itself, when pushed back towards the intuition from which it descends.[65]

Thus, every time Bergson talks about intuition, he tends, in defiance of discursive thought, to restore a great value to the image. But precisely by his theory of the dynamic schema, which enshrines the impossibility of moving from the reproductive imagination to the creative imagination, he cuts himself off from the means of relating this philosophical function of the image to its psychological nature.

We just noted Bergson's failure in his attempt to give a new solution to the problem of the image. But we do have to note that Bergson by himself is not the whole of 'Bergsonism'. He created, in fact, a certain atmosphere, a way of seeing, a tendency to search everywhere for mobility, the living; and, under this sort of methodological aspect, Bergsonism represents a great stream of pre-war thought. The principal characteristic of this state of mind seems to us a superficial optimism, without good faith, that believes it has resolved a problem when it has diluted its terms in an amorphous continuity. We can thus indeed suppose that the Bergsonians, taking up the problem of the image again *contra* Bergson, would confer on the image a suppleness and a mobility that the master had refused to it.

Thus it is that Spaier, in his first work,[66] which he relates explicitly to Bergsonian thought, attempts to show that images live: they are born and die, they have their 'dawns', their 'twilights'.[67] They grow and develop. The image in Associationism was in act (*en acte*), or it was not at all. The image according to the Bergsonians will be a passage from potentiality to act, like Aristotelian movement. It develops, goes towards actualization and complete individuation, that is to say, towards the existence of an individuated *thing*. The aspect that Associationism attributed to it is now only the ideal culmination of its development. But it can stop en route. Subjects point out a tendency of thought to economize its effort. It happens that the full comprehension of an idea precedes the full blooming of an image. Hence the image vanishes without having reached the end of its possibilities, without our even having been able to know exactly what the end of its actualization would be. The passage from one image to another was made in two steps for the Associationists. There was first a pure and simple annihilation of the first image, and then a creation *ex nihilo* of the second. And they followed each other without touching each other, as do two phenomena united by a relation of causality in the philosophy of Hume. Between two images that follow each other the Bergsonizing psychologists have re-established a transitive causality. One could even speak of the continuous transformation of *a single* image, where classic psychology would have seen a succession of discontinuous appearances. Hence the image rises from the mineral kingdom to the kingdom of living beings. Each of them develops according to its own law. They wanted to replace the mechanical causality of Hume and Taine, which supposes the inertia of the elements that it links, with a biological determinism. The image is a living form, a relatively autonomous life form in total psychic life. And they believe they have rendered the image homogeneous with thought by means of these metaphors.

At the same time, the notion of schema (*la notion de schème*) comes to know a rare fortune. Psychologists and linguists will routinely use this abbreviated image, intermediate between the pure sensible individual and pure thought. Indeed, one should not believe that the schema (*le schème*) owes its existence solely to Bergsonism. And men like Baldwin and Revault d'Allonnes underwent a good many other influences before establishing their psychology of the schematism. But the schema found in Bergsonism a favourable terrain for its development. It is, itself also, a potentiality. Thought as a power, image as a power—the schema maintains the role of 'medium', which it already had in Kant and that Bergson himself preserved. To tell the truth, it is even the only point on which its partisans agree with each other. It remains understood that the schema, like the 'daimon' of Platonic philosophy, has a mediating function. It establishes a continuity between two types of existences that are, at the limit, irreconcilable. It surmounts and resolves within itself the conflicts of image and thought. But, precisely because of this character of mixture, of conciliatory synthesis, the uncertainty concerning its nature is very great. Sometimes it is a principle of unity fully loaded with sensible matter; sometimes it is a very impoverished image, a skeleton. Sometimes it is an original image, a pure determination of geometrical space that purports to translate ideal relations into spatial relationships.

Softening of the image, creation of the schema (*schème*)—is this progress towards the concrete (*vers le concret*)? We do not believe so. We think on the contrary that these new theories are all the more dangerous as they present the appearance of a renewal of the question all the while being nothing but a perfecting, a making fashionable, of the antiquated Associationist error.

The image is *alive*, they say. But what do they mean by that? Is it simply a phase of the life of consciousness as a totality (*la conscience totale*) or is it rather only *a life in* consciousness? It suffices to peruse the abundant Bergsonian literature consecrated to the question to see that the image remains a *thing in consciousness*. First, it has not lost its sensible content and consequently its character of a reborn sensation. It has only been softened. The image à la Taine was always reborn similar to itself; it was a copy. The living image, as it reappears, draws its sense from the moment of psychic life in which it appears. The sensible content is always there but the form that it assumes undoes and redoes itself without ceasing. In this way, they thought they had done enough towards freeing the image from its past; and, in fact, they made it possible to better understand the creative function of the imagination, since every spontaneous, unforeseeable image is, in sum, a creation. But did they render more comprehensible the relation of form to matter in this psychic reality that we call an image? Where does this perpetual renewal of the image come from? Where does its perpetual adaptation to the present situation come from, if its sensible content remains the same? It is, one will say, from the fact that everything is activity in consciousness. Very well, but what does this mean, an *active* sensible content? Is it a sensible (*un sensible*) that has the property of spontaneously transforming itself? In such a case, it is no longer a sensible. So be it, one will say, it is no longer a sensible. It is enough for us that it retains its irreducible *quality* of red or of roughness or sharpness. But who does not see, precisely, that inertia, absolute passivity, is the condition *sine qua non* of this irreducible quality? Kant has well marked in the *Critique of Pure Reason* the radical difference that separates sensible intuition, which is necessarily passive, from an active intuition, which would produce its object. But, over and above this, the image of the Bergsonians is always posited in front of the thought that deciphers it. It is suppler and more mobile, most likely, but it remains impermeable. We must *wait for* it. If, for whatever reason, it disappears before being completely formed, we will never know what it should have been. It must be observed, deciphered. In a word, it teaches us something at every instant. What are we saying if not precisely that it is *a thing*? Certainly one has replaced the heavy stones of Taine with light living mists that transform themselves without ceasing. But these mists have not for all that stopped being things. If we had wanted to render the image homogeneous with thought, we should not have settled for simply rendering it diaphanous, moving, almost transparent. It is its very character of being a *thing* that one should have tackled. By not doing so, one is exposed to hearing oneself be told: certainly thought is fluid, diaphanous, moving; certainly we see, all right, that you apply the same terms to the image. But these identical terms do not have the same meaning in the one case and in the other. When you speak of the fluidity and of the diaphaneity of thought, in sum, you make use of metaphors that cannot be taken literally. When you endow the image with the same qualities, you *really* endow it with them, since you have made of the image a thing in front of thought. And it is under the cover of a pure and simple game of words that you can assert the homogeneity of thought and the image as you conceive of it. After this, it does nothing to say that the image is a living organism. You have not, for all that, eliminated its objectual nature; you have not freed it from the laws of association, no more than the fact of being alive frees an organism from the laws of attraction.

As for the schema (*schème*), it simply represents an attempt at reconciling two extreme terms. But the very fact that they use this notion shows all too well that they persist in affirming the existence of these extremes. Without image-things, there is no need for schemas. In Kant and in Bergson, the schema (*le schème*) has never been anything but a trick for re-joining the activity and unity of thought to the inert multiplicity of the sensible. The solution of the schematism therefore appears as a classic response to a *certain manner* of formulating the question. With another statement, the very meaning of the schema disappears. You have, so you say, presently in consciousness an abbreviated representation, too concrete to be of thought, too indeterminate to be assimilable to the individual things that surround us; and you call this representation a schema. But why wouldn't it be just simply an image? Do you not admit that you reserve the name of image for faithful and exhaustive copies of *things* by constituting for these abbreviated representations a separated class? But perhaps the images are never copies of objects. Perhaps they are only procedures *for rendering present to oneself* the objects in a certain way. In this case, what does the schema become? It is nothing but an image like the others, since what will define the image will be the way in which it aims at the object and not the richness of the details by means of which it renders the object present.

*

* *

At the beginning of the century, however, the problem of the image will undergo modifications very different in importance from this alleged Bergsonian 'upheaval'. We will indeed see reappearing the third attitude vis-à-vis the image-thing, the Cartesian attitude. Indeed, in rapid succession, Marbe publishes his *Experimental Psychological Investigations of Judgement* (1901),[68] Binet brings out his *Étude expérimentale de l'Intelligence* (1903)[69] and definitively abandons his position of 1896; in 1905 Ach writes his article 'On voluntary activity and thought'[70] and Messer his *Experimental Psychological Investigations of Thought;*[71] and from 1907 to 1908 Bühler writes his *Facts and Problems for a Psychology of Thought Processes.*[72] At the same time, Marie publishes his *Révision de la question de l'aphasie* in 1906 and later contributes an article, 'Sur la fonction du langage', to the *Revue philosophique.*[73]

These works, which are of a very different nature and inspiration, will nevertheless result in the rebirth of the Cartesian conception of the *image–thought* relation. We remember the quandary in which Brochard, Ferri, and all the Rationalists of the 1880s found themselves. They believed themselves to be caught between the factual data of physiology and those of introspection. Despite these two great scientific laws—there are cerebral localizations, and consciousness never observes within itself phenomena other than imaged representations—despite these inductions, which seemed supported by an imposing quantity and variety of observations, these philosophers wished to attempt to re-establish the existence of synthetic thought, thought that makes use of concepts, grasps relations and whose manoeuvres are set by logical laws. Hence the recourse to Leibniz and the pure and simple affirmation of the rights of thought. But the physiological theory of localizations will suddenly lose its credit with the physicians. It had been built, in sum, upon dubious material; recourse to experience had been made according to the methods advocated by J.S. Mill and was worth only as much as these methods themselves. Marie takes up again the question of aphasia, which is at the origin of the scientific theory of localizations, and shows that, in place of innumerable disturbances each corresponding to a lesion of a particular centre, there is only one single type of aphasia, which simply corresponds to a general lowering of the psychic level and thus to a synthetic incapacity. Aphasia is a disturbance of intelligence. From there, physiology will slowly orient itself towards a synthetic conception of the brain. It is an organ in which one can certainly distinguish different regions each of which have different functions, but it cannot be resolved into a mosaic of cellular groups.

At the same time, the work of the Würzburg School will transform the very conception of the data of intuition. Subjects have grasped within themselves non-imaged states; thought has revealed itself to them without intermediary. They have observed the existence of pure knowledge, of 'consciousness of rules', of 'tensions of consciousness', etc. As for that which concerns images properly so called, the data of the intimate sense (*sens intime*) come to confirm the theories of the Bergsonians: the image is supple, mobile; the objects that appear as imaged (*en image*) are not subjected to the same individuation as those of perception.

Such then is the great novelty of the theories of Würzburg: thought appears to itself without an intermediary; to think and to know that one thinks are but one. Earlier we were able to compare to the physico-theological argument the effort of Leibniz and his successors to prove the existence of thought beyond images from the very order of images. But here, there is no more need for a proof: as God offers himself to the contemplation of the mystic, so thought lets itself be grasped by a privileged experience. And the value of this privileged experience is guaranteed by the Cartesian '*cogito*'.

It does not enter into our plans to present the work of the Würzburg School. One can find on the question a wealth of monographs in French, English, and German. Concerning the value and import of experimental introspection, everything has been said. We would just like to point out that the German psychologists did not come to experience without preconceived ideas.

To tell the truth, their works do not have an exclusively psychological goal. One could even say that they aim at rigorously limiting the domain of psychology. They were conceived under the influence of Husserl's *Logische Untersuchungen* of which the first volume is filled with an exhaustive critique of psychologism in all its forms. To this psychologism, which aims at reconstituting the life of thought by means of 'contents of consciousness', Husserl opposes a novel conception: there exists a transcendent sphere of meanings, which are 'representeds' (*«représentés»*) and not 'representations' and which cannot themselves be constituted by contents in any way. To this world of meanings there evidently corresponds a type of special psychic state: the states of consciousness that *represent* to themselves these meanings and that can be empty intentions or intuitions that are more or less clear and more or less full. In any case, meaning and consciousness of meaning escape psychology. The study of meaning as such will go to logic. The study of the consciousness of meaning will belong, after a special 'conversion' or 'reduction', to a new discipline, Phenomenology. Here we find again what we had pointed out in Descartes: essences and the intuition of essences, acts of judgement, and deductions entirely escape psychology conceived of as a genetic and explanatory study that goes from fact to law. On the contrary, it is essences that render psychology possible.

Now, one of the concerns of the psychologists of Würzburg has precisely been to verify, on the terrain of experimental introspection, the anti-psychologism of Husserl. If Husserl was telling the truth, there should be special states in the stream of consciousness that are precisely consciousnesses of meaning. And if these states existed, their essential characteristic would be to limit psychology, to constitute its boundaries. They would indeed let themselves be described and classified and, by this fact, would still belong to the psychologists. But it would be necessary, by the very fact of their existence, to give up explaining them or showing their genesis from prior contents. Indeed, they represent the way the logical gives itself to human consciousness.

When the psychologists of Würzburg discovered pure thoughts they thus thought they had proved the existence of the purely logical, and this *a priori* conception of thought dictated to them their attitude vis-à-vis the image. The latter remains the purely psychic facing the purely logical, the inert content facing thought. Between the world of images and the world of thought there is a gulf, precisely the gulf that one found in Descartes. And Bühler will make his own the famous passage of the *Meditations* in which Descartes shows that only the understanding can think a piece of wax in its true nature. Indeed, he will write:

> I affirm that in principle, every object can be fully and exactly thought without the aid of images.[74]

It follows that the image, in the opinion of these psychologists, could only be a quandary for thought. It represents the inopportune reappearance of the thing amidst the consciousnesses of meaning. This is why Watt can write:

> Every image presents itself as an impediment (*Hemmung*) for ideational processes.[75]

The image is a survival, an organ on the way to regression. And since we can always render an object present to ourselves in its pure essence, it is always a waste of time and a degradation to make use of images. Thus, for Watt and Bühler the image retains the nullifying (*dirimant*) character of a *thing*. They have not studied it for itself; they have not taken advantage of the rich harvest of facts that their experiments had brought to them. Their theory of the image thus retains a purely negative character, and, as a result, the image remains in them what it was in Taine—a reviviscence of the thing.

*

* *

Whether the Würzburg psychologists understood Husserl well and whether there wasn't an entirely novel psychology to construct from the *Logische Untersuchungen* is what we will attempt to determine later. For now it will suffice for us to show how this conception of pure thought—which despite Ribot, Titchener, etc., becomes a given of psychology—still remains uncertain and confused. Indeed, around the same period, Binet makes experiments on his nieces and discovers thought without images.[76] But he does not have recourse to experience freely and without prejudices. He started from Associationism and only later came under the influence of the psychology of synthesis. It follows that he kept, almost unwittingly, the old conception of the Taineian image. What he wants is to establish the existence of thought *in opposition to* the image. And immediately the image appears to him like a 'meagre engraving', like a sou coin, whereas thought is like a thousand francs. Now without a doubt it enters into synthetic combinations, but it is as a discrete element.

But above all he does not expect experience to reveal either the existence or the nature of thought to him; he already has his conception, or rather he hesitates between two opposed conceptions.

Thought often appears to him as a *fact* accessible to introspection—for instance, when he comments on the celebrated formula of one of his subjects: 'Thought seems like a feeling to me, like any other one.'[77] But, in this case, under the influence of the biological pragmatism of the time, he makes of it the coming to awareness of a bodily attitude. We are thus dealing with a fallen Cartesianism, fallen onto the plane of naturalism, just as Ribot represented the fall of Leibnizianism. Thus at this time do we find not only the great metaphysical systems (which reappeared in Brochard and Bühler, for example) but, further, their projections onto the terrain of a naturalism that believes itself to be all the more 'positive' as it is the cruder.

But from this conception Binet slips insensibly into another one. Meditating, in the manner of Brochard, on the inadequacy of the image and of signification, he concludes that thought *cannot* be something other than the image. In this case, without leaving the naturalist plane, he transports himself onto the terrain of principle. He writes then this famous sentence, in full contradiction with his previous descriptions:

> Thought is an unconscious act of the mind that, to become conscious, requires images and words.[78]

Thus thought remains a reality, since the notion of principle is weighted down and hypostatized into that of the unconscious, but it is no longer accessible to itself. If I think the sentence 'I will leave tomorrow for the country', it may be that it will only be accompanied in my mind by the vague image of a square of grass. In this case, says Binet, the image is insufficient to render all the meaning contained in the words. We must therefore posit its necessary complement outside of consciousness in the unconscious.

But there is here a grave confusion. *By right* (*en droit*) this phrase, 'I will leave tomorrow for the country', encompasses the infinite. First, indeed, there must be a 'tomorrow', that is to say, a solar system, physical and chemical constants. It is also necessary that I still live, that no grave event comes to upturn my family or the society in which I live. All these conditions are, surely, implicitly required by this simple sentence. Moreover, as Binet well said, the meaning of the word 'country' is inexhaustible. We should add: and the meaning of the word *I* and that of the words 'to leave' and 'tomorrow'. Finally, one recoils, frightened before the depth of this innocent little sentence. This is the occasion to recall Valéry's remark that there is no speech that we can understand, if one goes to the bottom.

But Valéry adds, 'whoever hastens has understood',[79] which means that *in fact* we never go to the bottom. The inexhaustible meaning of the cited sentence does exist, but it is virtual and social. It exists for the grammarian, for the logician, for the sociologist, but the psychologist does not have to be preoccupied by it because he will never encounter its equivalent, neither in consciousness nor in a problematic unconscious invented for the sake of the cause. Surely cases in which thought tends to make explicit the entire comprehension of a sentence can be found. But if, as in the case that occupies us here, we scarcely find a meagre image, wouldn't it be worth more to ask oneself if there was not also a meagre thought in our mind? Better still: we have only had consciousness of the image. After all, wouldn't this image be the very form under which thought has appeared to consciousness? This square of green grass, it's not just any square. I recognize it; it's a piece of the large meadow that is located at the bottom of my garden. It is there that I am accustomed to go and sit. On the other hand, it is not an anonymous square of this meadow. It is exactly the place where I choose to lie down. Precisely, one will say, how do you know it, if not by thought? But this question contains a hidden postulate: that the image is different from thought; that it is thought's support. In this case it would stand in the same relation to the latter as the sign to the signification. But what proves this? Isn't it possible *a priori* that the image, instead of being an inert support to thought, is thought itself under a certain form? Perhaps the image is nothing less than a sign. Perhaps this square of grass, far from being an anonymous engraving, constitutes a precise thought. At the threshold of a study of the relations of the image to thought, it would have been necessary to get rid of the Associationist prejudice that makes of the image an inert mass, and to get rid of a false conception of thought that, by the confusion of the real and the virtual, makes the infinite enter into the slightest of our ideas. Binet did not go up to that point. That he remained an Associationist at the bottom of his soul, the following text, which dates to a time shortly before his death, shows well:

> ... [Psychology] studies a certain number of laws that we call mental in order to oppose them to the laws of external nature, from which they differ, but which, strictly speaking, do not deserve this name of mental since they are ... laws of images and since the images are material elements. Despite the fact that this appears absolutely paradoxical, psychology is a science of matter, the science of a portion of matter that has the property of preadaptation.[80]

*

*   *

Thus indeed in 1914 we find again without change the three great attitudes that we described in the first chapter. Associationism still survives, with a few lingering partisans of cerebral localization. It is above all latent in a multitude of authors who, despite their efforts, were not able to get rid of it. The Cartesian doctrine of a pure thought that can substitute itself for the image on the very terrain of the imagination knows, with Bühler, a renewal of favour. Finally, a very large number of psychologists hold, with the R.F. Peillaube, the conciliatory thesis of Leibniz. Experimenters like Binet and the psychologists of Würzburg affirm having observed the existence of thoughts without images. Other psychologists, no less concerned with the facts, like Titchener and Ribot, deny the existence and even the possibility of such thoughts. We are no more advanced than at the time when Leibniz published his *Nouveaux Essais* in response to Locke.

This is because the point of departure has not changed. First, the old conception of the image has been retained. Surely it has been made suppler. Surely experiments like those of Spaier[81] have revealed a sort of life where one only saw frozen elements thirty years earlier. Images have dawns and dusks. The image transforms itself under the gaze of consciousness. Surely, the investigations of Philippe[82] have shown a progressive schematization of the image in the unconscious. They now admit the existence of generic images; the work of Messer has revealed a multitude of indeterminate representations in consciousness, and Berkeleyan particularism (*individualisme*) is completely abandoned. The old notion of a *schema* (*schème*) comes back into fashion with Bergson, Revault d'Allones, Betz, etc. But the principle is not abandoned; the image is an independent psychic content that can serve as a support for thought but that also has its own laws. And if a biological dynamism has replaced the traditional mechanist conception, it nonetheless remains that the essence of the image is passivity.

In the second place, the problem of the image is still approached with the same preoccupations. It is still a matter of taking a position vis-à-vis the metaphysical question of the soul and the body or the methodological question of analysis and synthesis. To be sure, the problem of the soul (*l'âme*) and the body is not always formulated or, at least, is not formulated in the same terms, but it has no less retained all its importance. The imagination has remained with sensibility the domain of corporeal passivity. When Brochard, Ferri, and Peillaube struggle against Taine's Associationism and seek to limit it without suppressing it, it is because they want to re-establish over and above the laws of the body the dignity and the rights of thought. The centre of the question has not been moved. It is still a matter of understanding how matter can receive a form, how sensible passivity can be *enacted* (*agie*) by the spontaneity of the mind. At the same time, psychology still searches for its method, and the solutions it gives to the great problems of the imagination appear more like *demonstrations of method* than like positive results. In place of going straight to the thing and of shaping the method around the object, one first defines the method (Taine's analysis, Ribot's synthesis, Watt's experimental introspection, Brochard's reflexive critique, etc.) and one *then applies* it to the object, without suspecting that by giving oneself the method one has at the same time forged the object.

If one accepts these premises, there are and there can only be three solutions. *Either* one posits *a priori* the value of analysis: in this case, one affirms at the same time a materialism of method, since one will, as Comte has profoundly shown, attempt to explain the superior by the inferior; and this materialism of method will be easily convertible into a metaphysical materialism.

Or one affirms the necessity of simultaneously utilizing analysis and synthesis: and by that one re-establishes the syntheses of thought facing the image. In this case, depending on the metaphysical attitude adopted, thought will represent the mind (*esprit*) facing the body or the biological organ facing an element. But image and thought will be given as inseparable and the former as the material support of the latter.

Or one will simultaneously stick up for the metaphysical rights of pure thought and for the methodological rights of unanalysable syntheses. But, as the image has been maintained as an inert element, one will limit the domain of pure syntheses and one will see two types of psychic existence coexist: the inert content with its associative laws and the pure spontaneity of the mind. In this case there will be between imaginative thought and thought without images not only a difference in nature but, as we showed about Descartes, a *difference in subject*. The difficulty here will be to show how these two subjects will be able to merge in the unity of an ego (*un moi*).

Must we choose between these three conceptions? We have done the historical exposé of the difficulties raised by each of them. We are now going to attempt to show that all three must necessarily fail because all three accept the initial postulate of the rebirth of inert sensible contents.

NOTES

1 Alfred Binet, *La psychologie du raisonnement; Recherches expérimentales par l'hypnotisme*, 2nd edn, Paris: Alcan, 1896, p. 16. [*The Psychology of Reasoning, Based on Experimental Researches in Hypnotism*, Chicago: Open Court, 1899, pp. 10–11.]

2 One might read with interest an essay by the Belgian Ahrens toward a new theory of the image in his *Cours de Psychologie* delivered in Paris in 1836, published by Brockhaus and Avenarius. [Heinrich Ahrens, *Cours de psychologie, fait à Paris sous les auspices du gouvernement*, vol. 1, Paris: J.-A. Merklein, 1836; vol. 2, Paris: Brockhaus and Avenarius, 1838.]

3 [Alfred Giard, *Controverses transformistes*, Paris: Masson, 1904, p. 8.]

4 Hippolyte Taine, *De l'Intelligence*, 6th edn, vol. 1, Paris: Hachette, 1892, pp. 1–2. [*On Intelligence*, London: L. Reeve, 1871, pp. ix–x.]

5 Even though experience is here conceived of in much too narrow a manner.
6 Hippolyte Taine, *De l'Intelligence*, vol. 1, p. 7.
7 [Taine, ibid. p. 18.]
8 [Taine, ibid. p. 124; *On Intelligence*, p. 71.]
9 Francis Galton, 'Statistics of mental imagery', *Mind*, 5 (1880), 301–18 and *Inquiries into Human Faculty and its Development*, London: Macmillan, 1885.
10 Alfred Binet, *La psychologie du raisonnement; Recherches expérimentales par l'hypnotisme*, 2nd edn, Paris: Alcan, 1896.
11 Cf. Jules Lachelier, 'Psychologie et métaphysique', *Revue philosophique de la France et de l'étranger*, 19 (1885), 481–516.
12 *Rapport Batbie*, 26 November 1872. [Quoted in Ernest Lavisse and Philippe Sagnac, *Histoire de France contemporaine depuis la révolution jusqu'à la paix de 1919*, Paris: Hachette, 1920–1922, vol. 7, p. 349.]
13 [Louis Ferri, *La psychologie de l'association depuis Hobbesjusqu'à nos jours (histoire et critique)*, Paris: Germer Baillère, 1883, p. 232.]
14 [Ibid. p. 320 (emphasis added).]
15 Cf. Aristotle, *De anima*, III, 8, 432a, 8: ὅταν τε θεωρῇ, ἀνάγκη ἅμα φαντάσματι θεωρεῖν ['... when one contemplates a thing, one is forced to contemplate it in conjunction with an internal image....' *Aristotle's De Anima*, William Alexander Hammond, trans., New York: Macmillan, 1902, p. 127].
16 [Émile Peillaube, *Les Images: Essai sur la mémoire et l'imagination*, Paris: Marcel Rivière, 1910, pp. 470–71.]
17 Victor Brochard, *De l'erreur*, Paris: Berger Levrault, 1879, p. 151. My emphasis.
18 [Leibniz, *Nouveaux Essais*, II.i; 1982, p. 110; see Notes on the Translation.]
19 [Kant, *Critique of Pure Reason*, cf. B5, B123–24, A112, etc. We believe but are not certain that this is a paraphrase.]
20 Théodule Ribot, *La Vie inconsciente et les mouvements*, Paris: Alcan, 1914, pp. 113–115. In these pages, Ribot attempts to refute the conclusions of the Würzburg psychologists about the existence of thought without images.
21 Ribot will indeed contest the value of the experiments of the Würzburg psychologists.
22 [Cf. Théodule Ribot, *Essai sur l'Imagination créatrice*, Paris: Alcan, 1900, p. 9; *Essay on the Creative Imagination*, Chicago: Open Court, 1906, p. 12.]
23 [Cf. ibid., p. 66ff.; 79ff.]

24 [Cf. *Essai sur l'Imagination créatrice*, pp. 17ff. [*Essay on the Creative Imagination*, pp. 20ff.]
25 Ibid., pp. 19–20. [Ibid., p. 23.]
26 Théodule Ribot, *La Logique des sentiments*, 4th edn, Paris: Alcan, 1912, p. 22. [We have reason to believe that Sartre actually had in mind here Ribot's *La Psychologie des sentiments*, Paris: Alcan, 1896, pp. 21–22; *The Psychology of the Emotions*, London: Walter Scott, 1897, p. 21.]
27 [*La Logique des sentiments*, 1912, p. 4.]
28 *Annales médico-psychologique*, 1925. [P. Quercy, 'Remarques sur une théorie bergsonienne de l'hallucination', *Annales médicopsychologiques*, no. 2 (1925), 242–59. Sartre mistakenly has 'l'imagination' instead of 'l'hallucination' in his reference to this article by Quercy.]
29 *Journal de psychologie*, 15 April 1926. [J. Chevalier and H. Bouyer, 'De l'image à l'hallucination', *Journal de Psychologie normal et pathologique*, 23 (1926), 439–55.] See also an essay in the Bergsonian interpretation of hallucination in Lhermitte, *Le Sommeil*. [Jacques Jean Lhermitte, *Le Sommeil*, Paris: Colin, 1931.]
30 Henri Bergson, *Matière et Mémoire*, 26th edn, Paris: Alcan, 1929, p. 22. [*Matter and Memory*, New York: Zone Books, 1988, p. 35.]
31 [*Matière et Mémoire*, p. 24; *Matter and Memory*, p. 36.]
32 [*Matière et Mémoire*, p. 25; *Matter and Memory*, p. 37.]
33 [*Matière et Mémoire*, p. 36; *Matter and Memory*, p. 47.]
34 [*Matière et Mémoire*, p. 78; *Matter and Memory*, p. 81.]
35 [*Matière et Mémoire*, p. 73; *Matter and Memory*, p. 77.]
36 'Le Souvenir du present et la fausse Reconnaissance' in Henri Bergson, *L'Énergie spirituelle*, 6th edn, Paris: Alcan, 1920, p. 138. [*Mind-Energy: Lectures and Essays*, London: Macmillan, 1920, p. 157.]
37 [*Matière et Mémoire*, p. 80; *Matter and Memory*, p. 83.]
38 [*Matière et Mémoire*, p. 133; *Matter and Memory*, p. 125.]
39 'Le Souvenir du present et la fausse Reconnaissance' in *L'Énergie spirituelle*, p. 140. [*Mind-Energy*, p. 160.]
40 [*Matière et Mémoire*, p. 149; *Matter and Memory*, p. 138.]
41 [*Matière et Mémoire*, pp. 162, 165; *Matter and Memory*, pp. 149, 151.]
42 [*Matière et Mémoire*, p. 149; *Matter and Memory*, p. 138.]
43 See further on, in our chapter on Husserl, the meaning of this distinction, which must impose itself on all who consider the relation of consciousness to the world.
44 [*L'Énergie spirituelle*, pp. 60–61; *Mind-Energy*, 1920, p. 71.]
45 [*L'Énergie spirituelle*, p. 103; *Mind-Energy*, p. 118.]
46 [*Matière et Mémoire*, p. 152; *Matter and Memory*, p. 140.]
47 [*Matière et Mémoire*, p. 82; *Matter and Memory*, p. 85.]

48 [Ibid.]
49 [*L'Énergie spirituelle*, p. 102; *Mind-Energy*, p. 117.]
50 [Ibid.]
51 [*L'Énergie spirituelle*, p. 106; *Mind-Energy*, p. 151.]
52 [*L'Énergie spirituelle*, p. 184; *Mind-Energy*, p. 210.]
53 [*L'Énergie spirituelle*, p. 181; *Mind-Energy*, p. 207.]
54 [Cf. *Matière et Mémoire*, p. 59; *Matter and Memory*, p. 66.]
55 [*Matière et Mémoire*, p. 180; *Matter and Memory*, p. 165.]
56 [*L'Énergie spirituelle*, p. 172; *Mind-Energy*, 1920, p. 196.]
57 'L'Effort intellectuel', in *L'Énergie spirituelle*, p. 174. My emphasis. [*Mind-Energy*, p. 199.]
58 [*L'Énergie spirituelle*, pp. 170–71; *Mind-Energy*, p. 194.]
59 [*L'Énergie spirituelle*, p. 201; *Mind-Energy*, p. 229; Sartre's emphasis.]
60 [Ibid.]
61 [*L'Énergie spirituelle*, p. 200; *Mind-Energy*, 1920, p. 228.]
62 [Ribot, *Essai sur l'Imagination créatrice*, p. 67; *Essay on the Creative Imagination*, p. 80.]
63 [Henri Bergson, *L'intuition philosophique: Communication faite, au Congrès philosophique de Bologne le x avril M. CM. XI*, Paris: Helleu & Sergent, 1927, reprinted in Henri Bergson, *La Pensée et le mouvant: essais et conferences*, Paris: Alcan, 1934; 63rd edn, Paris: Presses Universitaires de France, 1966, p. 119 (our page references are to the 63rd edn); *The Creative Mind: An Introduction to Metaphysics*, New York: Citadel Press, 1992, p. 109.]
64 [*La Pensée et le mouvant*, p. 130; *The Creative Mind*, p. 118.]
65 [*La Pensée et le mouvant*, pp. 131–32; *The Creative Mind*, p. 119.]
66 Albert Spaier, 'L'image mentale d'après les experiences d'introspection', *Revue Philosophique de la France et de l'étranger*, 77 (1914), 283–304.
67 [Spaier, 'L'image mentale', pp. 290–93.]
68 [Karl Marbe, *Experimentell-psychologische Untersuchungen über das Urteil: eine Einleitung in die Logik*, Leipzig: Engelmann, 1901.]
69 [Alfred Binet, *Étude expérimentale de l'Intelligence*, Paris: Schleicher, 1903.]
70 [Narziß Ach, *Über die Willenstätigkeit und das Denken. Eine experimentelle Untersuchung mit einem Anhange: Über das Hippsche Chronoskop*, Göttingen: Vandenhoeck & Ruprecht, 1905.]
71 [August Messer, 'Experimentell-psychologische Untersuchungen über das Denken', *Archiv für die gesamte Psychologie*, 8 (1906), 1–224.]
72 [Karl Bühler, 'Tatsachen und Probleme zu einer Psychologie der Denkvorgänge: I. Über Gedanken', *Archiv für die gesamte Psychologie*, 9 (1907), 297–365; 'Tatsachen und Probleme zu einer Psychologie der Denkvorgänge: II. Über Gedankenzusammenhänge, III. Über

Gedankenerinnerungen', *Archiv für die gesamte Psychologie*, 12 (1908), 1–92.]

73 [Pierre Marie, 'Révision de la question de l'aphasie: La troisième circonvolution frontale gauche ne joue aucun rôle spécial dans la fonction du langage', *Semaine Médicale*, 26 (1906), 241–47; 'Révision de la question de l'aphasie: Que faut-il penser des aphasies sous-corticales (Aphasies pures)?', *Semaine Médicale*, 26 (1906), 493–500; 'Révision de la question de l'aphasie: L'aphasie de 1861 à 1866: essai de critique historique sur la genèse de la doctrine de Broca', *Semaine Médicale*, 26 (1906), 565–71. These can be found in English translation in *Pierre Marie's Papers on Speech Disorders*, New York: Hafner, 1971. Pierre Marie, 'Sur la fonction du langage: Rectifications à propos de l'article de M. Grasset', *Revue de Philosophie*, 9 (1907), 207–29. Sartre's '*Revue philosophique*' is a mistake here.]

74 Bühler, *Tatsachen und Probleme*..., etc. *Über Gedanken*, 321. *Arch. f. ges. Psych.*, 1907, t. IX. [Sartre's reference. See note 72 for full reference.]

75 [The German word *Hemmung* is in Sartre's text. We have been unable to locate a sentence from Watt's publications in German that matches this exactly but it seems likely that Sartre had the following work in mind: Henry Watt, 'Experimentelle Beiträge zu einer Theorie des Denkens', *Archiv für die gesamte Psychologie*, 4 (1905), 289–436; for Watt's own English summary of this work see his 'Experimental contribution to a theory of thinking', *Journal of Anatomy and Physiology*, 40 (1906), 257–66.]

76 *Étude expérimentale de l'Intelligence*, 1903. The choice of the subjects (too young) and that of the tests (much too easy) have often been criticized. Cf. Ribot, *La Vie inconsciente et les mouvements*.

77 [Binet, *Étude expérimentale de l'Intelligence*, p. 107.]

78 [Binet, *Étude expérimentale de l'Intelligence*, p. 108.]

79 [Paul Valéry, *Monsieur Teste*, 'Lettre d'un ami' in Paul Valéry, *Oeuvres* vol. 2, Paris: Gallimard, 1960, p. 53.]

80 Binet, *L'Ame et le corps*, Paris, 1908. Binet died in 1911. [Alfred Binet, *L'Ame et le corps*, Paris: Flammarion, 1905, p. 181; *The Mind and the Brain*, London: Kegan Paul, 1907, p. 175.]

81 Albert Spaier, 'L'image mentale d'après les experiences d'introspection', *Revue Philosophique de la France et de l'étranger*, 77 (1914), 283–304.

82 Philippe, *L'Image*. [Jean Philippe, *L'Image mentale (evolution et dissolution)*, Paris: Alcan, 1903.]

III

THE CONTRADICTIONS OF THE CLASSICAL CONCEPTION

M. Spaier, in his work on *La Pensée concrète*, appearing in 1927, points out that experimental investigations on the nature of the mental image have become increasingly rare after the work of the Würzburg School.[1] This is because most psychologists consider the question settled. Here as almost everywhere they have arrived at an eclecticism. The article that M. Meyerson has just published in the *Nouveau Traité* of Dumas is very indicative of this tendency to reconcile, to attenuate, to weaken.[2] In the stream of consciousness one still considers the image as a substantive state, but one grants to it a certain mobility. It lives, it transforms itself, there are dawns and dusks of the image; that is to say, one tries to make this old psychic 'atom' benefit from

DOI: 10.4324/9781003657408-4

the suppleness that the idea of continuity has conferred on the entirety of psychic life.

> We have to make traditional psychology understand that its images with sharp edges only constitute a very minimal part of a concrete and living consciousness. To say that consciousness only contains these sorts of images comes down to saying that a river only contains buckets of water or such and such other volumes poured and moulded in their containers, pots, litre bottles, or barrels. If you insist, let's put all these buckets and these containers into the river: there remains next to them the free water into which they plunge and that continues to flow between them.[3]

They maintain an autonomous structure in front of thought that they call the image, but they acknowledge that thought profoundly penetrates the image, for, they say, every image *must be understood*.

> Our consciousness of the image implies our consciousness (more or less explicit) of its meaning, and the images that psychology deals with are not pure signs deprived of meaning. In other terms, the image is understood and ... in ordinary thought our attention is not always nor most of the time directed at images; it is directed in the first place towards their meaning.[4]

Likewise, M. Spaier writes:

> ... Most of the time our attention does not fall onto the object of sensible intuition (onto the image or onto the perception) but onto the meaning.[5]

No one envisions denying the sensory structure of the image, but they insist on the fact that it is already *elaborated* by thought.

This elaboration, in its turn, is conceived of under the old guise of 'fragmentation' and 'recomposition', that is to say, in sum, of a combination of material elements. They maintain a mode of linkage proper to images, and it quite resembles association because it remains mechanical. But a smaller and smaller part is reserved for this mode, and they enjoy themselves when they can write, 'It is thus a new domain that escapes from association',[6] as if the function of the psychologist was to capture new territories or polders from association.

Thus, they have recovered everything, replaced everything. The plane of the image and that of thought have been kept, but they have sought to make the idea of continuity prevail. The sharp delimitations have been suppressed; the idea of the unity of consciousness has been insisted upon. And this permits, by sleight of hand, the melting of thought into the image and of the image into thought in the name of the predominance of the whole over the elements that compose it. Satisfied, they then come to write pages like those that follow, in which the will to reconcile and vindicate everyone affirms itself in a quite amusing way.

> The image therefore serves as a sign. ... It has a signification, a relation to something other than itself; it is a substitute. It has an intellectual content; it is the indication of a logical reality. It is never completely isolated. It is part of a system of image-signs; it is understood thanks to this system. It is not entirely fluid. It has enough stability, precision, form and homogeneity of form for being amenable to comparison with other images and other signs. It is a complex: the signifier and the signified, the 'sensible' and the 'intelligible' merge themselves into it forming an indissoluble whole. One can catch sight of sides, faces, layers of signification or details of sensible aspects, but when one thus isolates a part, one must, in order to understand it, remember the totality. ...[7] It can be

> more or less active. This can be a simple illustration that sort of drags itself behind thought and does not serve its progress. And it can also be an activity, a positive activity that orients and guides or a negative activity that retains or arrests. It is a guardrail that prevents thought from falling out of its path, but it is also sometimes a barrier across the path. It is when it is supple, plastic, and mobile that it can be of some slightly efficacious help to thought; when, on the contrary, it is too precise, too concrete or too stable, when it endures (*dure*), it stops thought or makes it deviate.[8]

The attitude of M.I. Meyerson is that of many good authors. However, the solution that they are satisfied with does not stand up to a serious examination. Following the words of Pascal, they have 'covered' the difficulties; they have not 'removed' them. In a general way, one must be in defiance of the modern tendency to substitute for Associationist atomism a sort of amorphous continuum in which the oppositions and the contrasts dilute themselves and vanish. Thought, synthetic apperception of relations, and the Associationists' images are quite certainly incompatible. But now it is once again the Associationists' images that our 'synthetic' psychology wants to give to thought as a support. However, a veil of haze has been thrown over the mechanical linkages; this is what is called duration (*la durée*). Thought endures (*dure*), one says, and images endure (*durent*); this is the basis of a possible rapprochement. But what does it matter if they do not endure in the same way? Contemporary eclecticism has wanted to keep, under the auspices of a Bergsonian penumbra, the Rationalist nominalism of Descartes and the 'experimental data' of Würzburg, Associationism, as the lowest-level mode of sequencing, and the Leibnizian thesis of a continuity between the different modes of knowledge, notably between image and idea. The existence of brute givens that would constitute the very matter of the image is indeed accepted. But it is claimed that these givens, in order to be a part of consciousness, have to be *rethought*. One thus dialectically constitutes a sort of Neoplatonic process from the almost brute image, 'stable, precise, concrete', to the almost pure thought that still contains, regardless, a sensible, almost imponderable materiality. But under these vague and general descriptions the incompatibility persists; the image indeed remains profoundly material. For instance, when M. Meyerson explains to us that the image must be understood for what it represents and not for how it appears, he introduces in this very way a distinction between the proper nature of the image and the way in which thought apprehends it; and, by this fact, he assimilates the image to a material symbol—as a flag is, for instance—which is always *in itself* something other (wood, fabric, etc.) than what we want to see in it. In a general manner, by the way, as soon as one makes of the image a sign that must be understood, one posits the image outside of thought by this very act. The sign, indeed, remains, in spite of everything, an external and material support for the signifying intention. Thus the metaphysical conception of the image-trace reappears with the theory, purely functional in appearance, of the *image-sign*. Likewise, when M. Spaier grants to judgement alone the possibility of distinguishing the image from a perception, he effects quite naturally an assimilation of the object as it appears as imaged (*en image*) to the material object of perception. Indeed, extrinsic characteristics alone would permit one to differentiate them. This image that thought *deciphers, penetrates, dissociates, and recomposes* may well have acquired for a few years a suppleness that it did not have until then. It remains, profoundly, the material image of Early Modern philosophy (*la philosophie classique*); and when they tell us that the image is nothing if one does not think it, we confess to not understanding clearly, since they recognize, at the same time, that it is yet something other than what one thinks about it. In place of dissolving these theses in the presence of a vague continuism, it would have been better to consider them squarely and to attempt to extract their common postulate and the essential contradictions to which they lead. We have shown in the previous chapter that the common postulate of these different theories was that of the fundamental identity of image and perception. We are going to attempt now to show that this metaphysical postulate, no matter which conclusions one derives from it, must necessarily lead to contradictions.

1. THE PROBLEM OF THE 'CHARACTERISTICS OF THE TRUE IMAGE'

The first move of our philosophers has been to identify image and perception; the second must be to distinguish them. The fact that brute intuition delivers to us is that there are images, and there are perceptions; and we know very well how to tell the one from the other. Next, after the *metaphysical* identification, we must of all necessity take into account this *psychological* datum: *in fact*, we spontaneously make a radical distinction between those psychic states. Let us note immediately that there were two ways to pose this new question. One could have asked oneself how the psychic structure called 'image' gave itself to reflection *as image* and the structure called 'perception' as perception. One would have then limited the problem to its strictly psychological aspect and would not have made the *objects* of perception and of the image intervene. Perhaps this way of proceeding would have led sooner or later to this observation: in spite of metaphysics, there is between image and perception a difference of nature. But most authors have envisioned the question quite differently. They did not ask themselves if the psychic formations are not immediately given to consciousness *for what they are*; they placed themselves at the metaphysico-logical point of view of truth. They tacitly transformed the discrimination that every consciousness spontaneously makes between image and perception into a distinction between the true and the false. Thus Taine was able to say 'that perception was a true hallucination'.[9] Still truth and falsehood are not conceived of here as intrinsic criteria in the manner of Spinoza. It is a matter of a relation to the object. We are before a world of images. Those that have an external correspondence are called true or 'perceptions'. The others are called 'mental images'. We see the trick of prestidigitation: the givens of the intimate sense (*sens intime*) are transformed into external relations between a content of consciousness and the world, and the immediate distinction between the contents is replaced by a classification of these contents with respect to something other than themselves. In this way, the metaphysical theory of the image intends to meet up with the data of psychology. But it does not truly meet up with them; it only harmonizes with a logical *equivalent*.

Moreover, the most difficult thing is not done; it remains to find the 'characteristics of the true image',[10] it being well understood that the true image does not exhibit any difference of nature from the false image. There are only three possible solutions.

The first is that of Hume: image and perception are identical in nature but differ in intensity. Perceptions are 'strong impressions', images are 'weak impressions'. We have to grant to him the merit of presenting the distinction between image and perception as immediate; it happens by itself, without the need of making recourse to an interpretation of signs or a comparison. It operates mechanically in some way; by themselves, strong impressions throw weak impressions into an inferior level of existence. Unfortunately, this hypothesis does not withstand examination. The stability, richness, and precision of perceptions could not distinguish them from images. First, because these qualities are quite exaggerated.

'Constantly,' observes M. Spaier on this subject,

> our eyes, our ears, our mouth experience very confused impressions, very indistinct, to which we scarcely pay attention, either because they are from too distant an origin or because even from a very close source they are without direct relation to our conduct.[11]

Are we going to make them into images for that? Moreover, there is the question of thresholds. For a sensation to cross the threshold of consciousness, it must have a minimum intensity. If the images are of a same nature, they will have to have at least this intensity. But then won't we confuse them with sensations of the same intensity? And why doesn't the image of the noise of a cannon blast appear like a weak but real cracking? How is it that we *never* took our images for perceptions? But, someone will say, sometimes it happens to us. I can, for example, take a tree trunk for a man.[12]

Surely, but there is not in this case a confusion between an image and a perception; there is a false interpretation of a real perception. There is no example—and we will come back to this—in which an image of a man having suddenly appeared in our consciousness is taken for a real man really perceived. If we made use only of intensity in order to distinguish image from perception, error would be frequent. At some times intermediary worlds would even constitute themselves, at dusk for instance, composed of real sensations and of images halfway between dream and wakefulness. 'To believe', writes M. Spaier,

> that well-founded certitude is a matter of the strength or vivacity of the impressions is simply to restore the φαντασία καταληπτική [cognitive impressions] of the Stoics.[13]

In a word, if image and perception are not differentiated in *quality* first, it is vain to seek then to distinguish them by quantity.

This is what Taine understood well. '[The image],' he writes,

> is sensation itself but consecutive (*consécutive*) and resuscitating and, *no matter what point of view one considers it from*, one sees it coincide with sensation.[14]

Next it will be necessary to make an intrinsic distinction between an *isolated* image and an *isolated* sensation. In a word, there is no longer an immediate recognition of the image as image. On the contrary, the image gives itself to the intimate sense (*sens intime*) first as sensation.

> There are two moments in the presence of the image: one affirmative and the other negative, the second restraining in part what was posited in the first. If the image is very precise and very intense, these two moments are distinct: at the first moment it seems external, situated at such and such a distance from us when it's a matter of a sound or a visible object, situated in our palate, our nose, our limbs when it's a matter of a sensation of odour, of flavour, of pain, or of local pleasure.[15]

Thus, the image *by nature* affirms itself as sensation; it spontaneously drives our belief in the existence of its object. We see what follows, which is the direct result of the metaphysical attitude that we have signalled: it is that the image as such loses its character as an immediate datum. In order to become aware that the object here is given to me presently *as imaged* (*en image*) there must be an operation. We thus arrive at the second solution to the problem of the 'characteristics of the true image'.

According to Taine, who proposes the solution, a mechanical discrimination between sensations and images is in operation.

> The ordinary image is thus not a simple but a double fact. It is a spontaneous and consecutive (*consécutive*) sensation that, by the conflict of another non-spontaneous and primitive sensation, undergoes a diminishment, a restriction, and a correction. It includes two moments: the first in which it seems situated and exterior, the second in which this exteriority and this situation are taken away from it. It is the work of a struggle; its tendency to appear exterior is fought and defeated by the contradictory and stronger tendency that the shaken nerve has evoked at the same instant.[16]

Thus, the consciousness of an image is not immediate, and the struggle between the consecutive sensation (*sensation consécutive*) and the primitive sensation is only an episode in the Darwinian struggle for life.[17] The strongest wins. Taine takes care to add that the victory can belong to the 'consecutive and spontaneous' sensation. In such a case there is hallucination. In order for the image to be recognized as an image, that is to say, for it to 'produce its normal effect', it is necessary that there exist an *antagonistic* sensation. In the absence of this sensation—or if it happens that the image is stronger—we have in front of us an object that *in fact* does not exist.

To tell the truth, this thesis is quite obscure. First, is it of a physiological or a psychological order? Where does the discrimination get made? Taine seems to hesitate and not to want to choose. Sometimes one could be led to believe that sensations and images oppose each other as conscious events:

> ... The memory returning, the images and the ideas reappear, envelop the image with their procession, enter into conflict

> with it, impose their ascendancy on it, pull it from its solitary life, bring it back to its social life, and plunge it back into its habitual dependence.[18]

At other times we read the description of a genuine cortical mechanism of inhibition:

> When a hallucinator, eyes open, sees an absent figure three feet away and there is in front of him a simple wall covered with grey paper with green stripes, the figure covers a piece of it that it renders invisible; the sensations that the piece should provoke are thus null; however, the retina and probably the optic centres are shaken in the ordinary way by the grey and green rays; in other words, the preponderant image annihilates the portion of sensation that would contradict it.[19]

It seems here to be a matter of cortical inhibition, all right, and, besides, we do not understand why the sensations of green and grey are *inhibited* instead of being simply thrown back to the rank of images. To tell the truth, Taine does not decide because, as we have seen above, he never had a clear idea of the distinction between the physiological and the psychological.

Moreover, how must we understand this 'rectification', this 'correction'? The spontaneous and consecutive (*consécutive*) sensation, we are told, is first *situated* and *exterior*. And Taine cites a multitude of examples. It is the bookseller Nicolai who glimpses a figure of death '*at a distance of ten feet*'. It is an English painter who 'takes' his models 'in his mind' and 'puts them on a chair'. It is a friend of Darwin who, having one day 'looked quite attentively, head inclined, at a little engraving of the Virgin and infant Jesus … was surprised [in standing up] to glimpse a figure of a woman with an infant in her arms *at the extremity of the apartment*'.[20]

Then, under the influence of the antagonistic sensation, the spontaneous sensation loses its situation and its exteriority. That seems difficult to admit. Exteriority is indeed an intrinsic quality of the first as well as of the second representation; it is not a relation. How then, in contact with a contradictory impression, could the first sensation lose its exteriority? Certainly it is difficult to conceive, for example, of a man and a table occupying the same place. But if the man is 'ten feet from me', it is not the presence of the table at the same place that will make him cease to be ten feet away. Perhaps, by the way, Taine, whose vocabulary is, like his mind, very imprecise, confuses exteriority and objectivity. But the difficulty remains the same: I ask, what mechanical antagonism will be able to make an image, which first affirms itself as an object, move into the subjective?

One sees what Taine was missing. His Associationism forbade him from having recourse to a discriminatory judgement. But all his explanations aim at constructing an Associationist equivalent of this judgement with mechanical operations.

He does not succeed in this. First his concept of 'contradictory sensation'[21] underhandedly borrows from judgement one of its qualities. Indeed, only two judgements can contradict each other. I cannot say at the same time of the same object: *it is white* and *it is not white*. But two sensations cannot contradict each other; they *combine*. If I project the image of a square of white fabric 'ten feet away', and at this same distance and instant, there happens to be a square of black fabric, there won't be two antagonistic objects to mutually hold each other in check. I will simply see a square of grey fabric. To suppose in this way that sensations and images mutually exclude each other, we must have, under the name of image, already meant a judgement.

Another remark will make us understand this better still. I am in my bedroom, seated at my table. I hear the light noises that the maid makes in the next room. At the same time I distinctly remember, with its rhythm, its timbre, its intonation, a sentence that I heard pronounced the day before yesterday. How can the light creakings that come from the next room 'reduce' the 'consecutive sensation' of the sentence, while they do not succeed in covering the faint sounds of voices that rise from the street? Wouldn't one say that the creakings distinguish between what needs to be reduced and what must be allowed to pass? Wouldn't these sensations of creakings already involve some *judgement*? Or, if one must grant the theory of Taine the benefit of a rigorous logic, I must have here an auditory hallucination. But, in this case, it is not a hundred nor a thousand, but an incessant series of hallucinations that I am going to have. For the silence of my bedroom and that of the country, which *are not* sensations, could not act as reducers. Will it suffice to be suffering from deafness to become a raving lunatic?

There is, by the way, in Taine, beside the thesis of a purely mechanical and probably physiological reduction—that, in spite of itself, makes an appeal to judgement—the sketch of another theory of the reduction that does put judgement to work explicitly. Indeed, does he not write this?

> ... Beyond the weights constituted by sensations, there are others that are lighter, which nevertheless *suffice ordinarily and in the state of health to take off from the image its exteriority*; these are memories. These memories are themselves images but coordinated and affected with a recoil that situates them on the line of time. ... General judgements acquired by experience are attached to them, and altogether they form a group of elements linked to each other in equilibrium with respect to each other such that the whole is of a very great consistency and lends its force to each of its elements.[22]

It is true that two pages later, probably dreading the consequences of this explanation that risks dragging the mechanical theory of reducers to ruin, he adds:

> When an image acquiring an extraordinary intensity annuls the particular sensation that is its special reducer, the order of memories may well subsist, and the judgements may well be produced; but we have a hallucination. To tell the truth, we know ourselves to be hallucinators, but the image appears no less external. Our other sensations and our other images still form an equilibrated group, but this reducer is insufficient because it is not special.[23]

In a word, Taine's theory of reducers is an attempt to translate into mechanistic terms a suppler and more profound thesis that would entrust the spontaneity of judgement with the task of discriminating between image and sensation. It is this last conception—the only one that counts and that one will find already implied in the two others—that we are going to discuss now. We have already encountered it in Descartes, and we saw then its insufficiencies within the Cartesian system. It is a matter now of explaining in a completely general fashion why we could not be satisfied with it.

We begin again with the assertion that sensation and image are identical in nature. We assert one more time that an *isolated* image does not distinguish itself from an *isolated* perception. But this time the discrimination will be the product of a judicative act of the mind. It is judgement that will constitute two worlds, that of the imaginary and that of the real; and it is again judgement that will decide, once these two worlds are constituted, if such psychic contents must be placed in the one or in the other. It remains to be known *over which characteristics* one will judge. It can only be over external relations, that is to say, on the one hand, over the mode of appearance, succession and sequencing, and, on the other hand, over the compatibility or incompatibility of the envisaged content with the universes that we have constituted. What would not be compatible with the coherence and order of the real world, which a long apprenticeship has allowed us to recognize and to build, we would cast to the side of pure subjectivity. M. Spaier who defends this thesis writes:

> It is in judging the agreement or disagreement of a sensible datum either with the system of my current external universe or with that of my imagination (which long, incessant trials have taught me to distinguish from the former), it is in making judgements of comparison, adequacy, inadequacy, belonging, etc., that I class an impression among the real perceptions or among the images.[24]

Here two remarks impose themselves: first, the criterion of truth has evolved. It is no longer a matter of a relation of conformity to the external object. We are in a world of representations. The criterion has become the agreement of representations with each other. We are thus freed of naive realism. But the index of the true remains external to the representation itself. It is by comparison that one establishes whether or not one must incorporate it into the 'reality' group.

At the same time, the problem of the 'characteristics of the true image' changes profoundly in meaning. There are no longer 'image' data or 'object' data. But it is a matter of building an objective system from neutral data. The real world is not; it has to be made. It undergoes incessant retouching; it becomes supple; it is enriched. Such and such a group taken as objective for a long time is finally rejected; on the contrary, another such group, for a long time isolated, will be all of a sudden incorporated into the system. The problem of the discrimination of images is but one with that of the construction of the objective. Among the sensible data, the image is what cannot proceed to the objective. The image is subjectivity. We have never been farther from the psychological. Rather than the nature of the image as such being revealed to us by an immediate intuition, we must finally make use of a system of infinite references in order to affirm of a content that it is an image or a perception. Naturally, in practice one will content oneself with a few well-made comparisons, but a rather grave consequence will result from this: the discriminative judgement will only ever be *probable*. It is thus that Maldidier, in the article cited above, speaks of the '*probable* characteristics of the true image'.[25] Indeed, this is because the certitude could only come from a comparative examination pushed to the infinite; and moreover, the system of references modifies itself constantly. For instance, if some positivist atheist gets converted, accepts the dogmas and believes in miracles, he will no longer have the same system of references as before. We thus arrive at this paradoxical conclusion: far from the deep nature of the image being revealed to us by an immediate and certain knowledge, we will *never* be *sure* that such and such psychic contents having appeared on such and such a day and at such and such an hour were really truly an image. Introspection is entirely deprived of its rights to the benefit of judgement, and consciousness, facing its own data, adopts the hypothetico-experimental attitude that it normally takes vis-à-vis the external world.

The artificial character of this conception jumps right out at us. Nobody will accept that recourse to a system of infinite references is needed to establish the discrimination between an image and a perception. Let everyone consult their internal experience (*expérience interne*). I am sitting, I am writing, I see the objects that surround me; I form for an instant the image of my friend Pierre. All the theories in the world will not prevent it from being the case that at the very moment at which the image appeared I *knew* that it was an image. The example that

Spaier cites to support his thesis[26] is not convincing. It is a light crackle that he hears one day before going out:

> Would that be rain beginning to fall? I listen; I repeat the operation. It reveals to me the persistence of the noise. There is a first observation, a first *clue*. Will that content me? Not the least bit in the world. *Because* the ear can ring. I go to the window; not a drop of water on the tiles. But rain can fall straight. I *therefore* open the window and I lean outside ... etc.[27]

Who has ever made so much effort to distinguish an image from a perception? If the image of a creaking had crossed my mind, I would have recognized it right away as an image, without needing to look at the windowpanes or open the window. To tell the truth one may well admit that the scene related by Spaier has not been completely contrived for the sake of the cause. But a grave error has slipped into this reasoning. It is not in order to distinguish the image of a creaking from a perception that this series of experiences (which goes on for two more pages) has been produced. It's in order to distinguish a false from a true perception. And, naturally, when one does not admit any difference between image and perception other than that which separates the false from the true, it is fatal that one calls every false perception an image. But this is exactly what is inadmissible for a psychologist. To perceive a man in place of a tree is not to form an image of a man, it is quite simply to *misperceive* a tree. We remain on the terrain of perception and, up to a certain point, we perceive correctly. There is indeed an object—ten feet away—in the half-light. It is indeed a thin body, slender, about a metre and eighty centimetres tall, etc. But we were mistaken in our manner of apprehending the *sense* of this object. Likewise, if I prick up my ear in order to know if I really heard a creaking, at bottom this means that I try to discern if *it really was a creaking* that I heard. I could have taken an organic noise, the sound of my breath, for example,[28] for the crackling of the rain.

But, by the way, in accepting the discussion on the very terrain where M. Spaier placed himself, how can we admit that judgement in classing a representation among the images, could, by the same stroke, suppress its exteriority? Taine, who had glimpsed discrimination by judgement, had not fooled himself about it. We have seen that he wrote:

> … [T]he order of memories may well subsist, and the judgements may well be produced; but we have a hallucination. To tell the truth, we know ourselves to be hallucinators, but the image appears no less external. …[29]

This is indeed what seems to have to occur on the hypothesis of M. Spaier. If I see a man seated in front of me, my judgement may well convince me that I'm dealing with a vision, with a phantom. I won't cease seeing the man seated in front of me because of that. Or must one believe that judgement cuts and builds exteriority and interiority in parallel within a group of neutral psychic contents? This would be to go against good sense and the current data concerning the problem of perception.

But even if we admitted that this procedure of discrimination could sometimes succeed, it would be ineffective in the majority of cases. First—and very often—it would make one take perceptions for images. Indeed, this is because at each instant there arises around us a multitude of strange little incidents, objects that move by themselves (in appearance), that creak or groan, appear or disappear, etc. All these fantastic events are explained upon reflection in the simplest way in the world, but at first pass, they should surprise us. We should be, at least for an instant, tempted to rank them among the images. I was sure to have put my hat in the armoire, but here I find it on the chair. Will I doubt myself or 'not believe my eyes about it'? Not for an instant. I could exhaust myself in finding explanations. But what I would take for granted from one end of my reflections to the other, without even bothering to go touch the hat, is that the hat that I see is indeed *my real* hat. I believe my friend Pierre to be in America. There I catch sight of him at the corner of the street. Will I tell myself 'it's an image'? Not at all. My first reaction is to seek to find out how it is possible that he has already come back. Has he been recalled? Was somebody ill at his place? Etc. I even recall having encountered one day an old classmate from the lycée whom I believed dead. In fact, a contamination between two memories had occurred, but I would have sworn that I had received an announcement of his death. This conviction did not prevent my first thought from being, 'I was mistaken then. He is not the one who is dead, it must be so-and-so, etc.', as soon as I caught sight of him. What do we want to come of this? The following: far from the possibility that rational motives could make us put our perception in doubt, it is our perceptions that rule and direct our judgements and our reasonings. It is to them that we constantly adapt our systems of reference. I can be persuaded that X is dead or that he is travelling afar. If I see him, I revise my judgements. Perception is a primary source of knowledge; it delivers to us the objects themselves; it is one of the cardinal types of intuition, what the Germans call an 'originary giving intuition' (*originär gebende Anschauung*), and we feel it so well that our disposition of mind in its regard is the inverse of that which M. Spaier describes. Far from criticizing it, we only seek to justify it by all means once it has appeared. Certain people, if they believe they have seen Pierre while it is *impossible* that Pierre be in France (they have seen him embark for New York three days ago), will even defend the rights of their (false) perception against the rights of reasoning by the most sophisticated and improbable arguments.

Moreover, and inversely, this procedure of discrimination would be very insufficient most of the time for detecting the images as images. Indeed, for it to succeed, it would be necessary that our imaginations most often be fantastic, unreasonable, lyrical, and so different from everyday perceptions that judgement would be able to set them aside from the real world with some probability.

In place of that, what, in outline, is the imaginary world where I live? Well, I await my friend Pierre, who can come at one instant or another, and I represent his face to myself. I went yesterday evening to Jean's, and I recall his suit. Then I think about the detachable collars that are in my armoire, then about my inkwell, etc., etc. None of these familiar images are contradicted by anything real. The door of the antechamber is open onto the half-light. Nothing keeps me from projecting the image of Pierre onto this black background. And if this were the case, since he has the key to the apartment, I would have no reason to put into doubt the reality of this image. But, one will say, what if he doesn't approach? If he doesn't respond when you call to him, if he completely disappears? Surely, I will take him then for a hallucination. But who, I ask, will dare to assert in good faith that he had made recourse to these means for classing an appearance among the images or the perceptions? In fact, most of the time, the course of our images adjusts itself to that of our perceptions, and what we imagine precedes only by a little what will happen next or follows by a little what just happened. In these conditions, perception should at each instant be a conquest over dream; one would have to continually risk denying, based on sheer presumptions, the reality of such and such a figure, and risk affirming, without decisive reasons, the real existence of such and such another. The sensible universe, so painstakingly constructed, would be perpetually invaded by completely plausible visions that one would nonetheless have to set aside, as well as one could, without ever being absolutely sure of having the right to do so. We see that the world thus described—a world where one has never finished correcting the appearances, a world where all perception is conquest and judgement—does not correspond in any way to the world that surrounds us. As a matter of fact, objects are relatively stable, relatively clear. To be sure, one often has to wait before being sure about the nature of an object, and surely this waiting can be given as the very essence of the perceptual attitude. But the appearances that thus dissipate are not images; they are only incomplete aspects of things. No image, ever, comes to entangle itself with real things. And this is quite fortunate, for, as we just saw, if it were thus, we would not have any means of putting them aside, and the world of wakefulness would not distinguish itself so sharply from that of dream.

Thus when one has first asserted the fundamental identity of perceptions and images, one is constrained to have recourse to judgements of probability in order to distinguish them later. But these judgements of probability would not be able to find a solid basis. In fact, it would be necessary that the order of perceptions and that of images sharply differentiate themselves and render possible a discriminative judgement. This comes down to saying that if the differentiation is not first *given* in some way, no power of the understanding can suffice to establish it. And this could have been predicted from the beginning. Indeed, if one begins by affirming the essential identity of two objects, this affirmation removes, by its very nature, the possibility of distinguishing them later. Thus the metaphysical theory of the image definitively fails in its attempt to recover the spontaneous consciousness of the image, and the first step of a concrete psychology must be to get rid of all metaphysical postulates. On the contrary, it has to begin from this irrefutable factual datum: it is impossible for me to form an image without knowing at the same time that I form it; and the immediate knowledge that I have of the image as such will be able to become the basis for existence judgements (of the type: I have an image of X—this is an image, etc.). But it is itself *antepredicative evidence*.

One would surely find more than one psychologist today to grant us this principle. But there are only a few who clearly see what this endorsement commits them to. It is thus that M. I. Meyerson can write in the article we cited above:

> The image is not a weakened perception or sensation; it is not a pale reflection of the past. The image is on the path of abstraction and generalization; it is on the path of thought. ... The image is thus a perception rethought and, however unsophisticated it may still appear, rationalized; it is already a rationalization of the sensible given.[30]

It is all very well to affirm that the image is not a perception. But it is not enough to affirm it. One must still support this affirmation on the basis of a coherent description of the psychic fact, 'image'. If one is reduced to implicitly confusing image and perception, it is quite in vain to cry so strongly that they are distinct from each other. Now, it suffices to read with some attention the text that we just cited to see that the description that M. Meyerson gives of the image would be suitable, word for word, for perception. The image, one says, is a 'rationalization of the sensible given'. But is it otherwise with perception? Is there any perception that is not an act of thought? Is there a perception that is a pure sensible given, deprived of an intentional synthesis? The image is 'on the path of abstraction and generalization'? What do we mean? That there is no absolutely particular image? First, this is not entirely exact; it is an erroneous interpretation of a real fact that we will try to explain elsewhere. But, even if this were so, wouldn't that be rigorously the same for perception? I perceive an 'inkwell', a 'table', 'a Louis XVI armchair'. To arrive at the individual, at the sensible matter, at *this particular tint* of the fabric that covers the armchair, one has to make an effort, invert the direction of attention. Or more, as M. Spaier says, someone smiles at me and I perceive *benevolence*. Someone waves a flag, and I perceive the nation, the emblem of the party or of the class. Am I not more than halfway to abstraction and generalization? If I compare the perception of *a* house (I saw a flag at the window of *a* house) to the image-memory of *the* house in which I spent my childhood, which of these two acts of consciousness is on the general side and which on the particular side? The image is a perception rethought, says M. Meyerson. But when then will the perception be 'rethought'? Must one imagine the darkness to be propitious for an unconscious where a whole little work of polishing can be carried out unnoticed? Or will we rather say that the transformation happens at the moment in which the image appears to consciousness? But in this case why would we now rethink this reborn perception? Why didn't we *think* it when it appeared to us for the first time? We see it. M. Meyerson, similar in this respect to many contemporary psychologists, has rightly made the distinction that stands out, but he did not know why he was making it.

The text that we just cited makes us understand clearly what this affirmation commits us to: 'There is a difference of nature between perception and image.'[31] M. Meyerson has, in some way, distinguished in the image the matter and the form. Matter is the sensible given. It is also the matter of perception. But it has received another form. That is to say that it is penetrated by reason. But the failure of his attempt at differentiation shows us that the form could not suffice to distinguish image from perception. Surely we will see later that the *intention* of an image is not that of a perception. But we must still posit that the image and the perception do not have the same matter. One finds again here the famous Aristotelian problem: is it form or matter that individuates? We will respond, as it concerns the image: the one and the other. If, as one rightly thinks, the matter of perception is the sensible given, then it is necessary that the matter of the image not be sensible. If, for some reason, the psychic structure, 'image' has a reborn sensation for a basis—even rationalized and recomposed—it becomes radically impossible, however one proceeds, to establish some distinction between the image and the real, between the universe of wakefulness and the world of dream.

2. THE PROBLEM OF THE RELATIONS OF THE IMAGE WITH THOUGHT

The image is thus almost universally considered as having a sensible content, that is to say, as having an impressional matter that is identical to that of perception. This matter requires from the mind a receptive part; it is an irrational, a *given*. In admitting, with M. Spaier, that 'becoming conscious is to *bear witness to (constater)*',[32] there is something that just is and that lends itself to being witnessed (*se laisse constater*) at the basis of the image. This is also, one will say, a fact about perception. Surely. But, precisely, the perceived object opposes itself to and imposes itself on thought. We have to adjust the course of our ideas to it; we have to *wait for* it, make hypotheses about its nature, observe it. Is this attitude possible? Does it keep the same meaning when it is an image, that is to say, something that presents itself as an aid for thought? The image is used for deciphering, for understanding, for explaining; but must one decipher it, understand it, explain it first? And how can one? By means of another image? To tell the truth, these difficulties, which jump right out at us, could not be evaded. Indeed, the image, which was first assimilated to perception, is also from thought. We *form* images; we *construct* schemas (*schèmes*). And what necessarily complicates the question is that most authors, after having made an external object of the image, make an idea of it on top of that. Thus, M. Spaier, after showing that one had to make recourse to judgement and even to reasoning to distinguish the image from perception, is not afraid to write:

> There aren't *images* on the one hand and *ideas* on the other; there are only concepts more or less concrete.[33]

It is true that after having attempted to shed light on the way the image is elaborated and schematized by thought, he insists, in parallel, on the amount of construction that we find in external perception. Every image is signification, but insofar as every perception is judgement.

> ... There are brute sensations no more than there are pure images and nothing opposes itself from this side to the identification of consciousness, as well as of its most sensible contents, with thought.[34]

But, first, the fact that sensible contents are rationalized by thought evidently does not mean that these contents are *identical* with thought, quite the contrary. And then, under these definitive affirmations, one divines a wavering of ideas. The image, for Spaier, does not have the same *function* as perception. It demonstrates a mobility, a transparency, a docility thanks to which one can assimilate it to judicative and discursive thought. But if it is *thus* that an image is a thought, then a perception is not a thought. It is indeed its sensible content that makes for the exteriority and the objectivity of perception. How then to admit that the sensible content *here* opposes itself to consciousness and obliges one to observe, be patient, make conjectures, and that *elsewhere* it participates in the fluidity, mobility, and transparency of the subjective? In a word, if the image has a sensible content, it will perhaps be possible to think *on* it, but one could not then think *with* it.

This participation of the image in the sensible one can understand in two ways: like Descartes or like Hume.

Descartes, for his theory of the imagination, places himself, we have seen, on the psycho-physiological plane. There is a soul *and* there is a body. The image is an idea that the soul forms on the occasion of an affection of the body. If we rid this conception of Cartesian vocabulary, this still remains: the psycho-sensory centres can be excited by an internal stimulus or by an external stimulus. One calls the state of consciousness that corresponds to the first sort of excitation an image and that which corresponds to the second a perception. The foundation of this thesis is the affirmation that the nerve cells or groups of nerve cells have the capacity to get back, under diverse influences, into the state in which an external stimulus had put them—whether one calls this possibility a cerebral *trace* or an *engram*. But, if this is so, the order of appearance of images in consciousness will be the result of the trajectory of 'animal spirits', that is to say, will depend on the associative circuits and the trajectory of the nervous influx. In a word, it is a physiological determinism that will regulate the successions of images in consciousness. Some representation or other will surge into consciousness on the occasion of the 'awakening' of such and such an associative group. But then, how will we be able to propose the image as an effective aid to thought?

Descartes, who anticipated the objection, imagined a sort of physiological contingency that would permit the soul to direct the animal spirits at will. We have seen above that this strange theory is not admissible. The hypothesis of an integral physiological determinism remains. In this case, the order in which the images appear will be regulated, as Claparède has rightly seen, by a real and material contiguity, that of cerebral 'traces' in space.[35] But then the succession of images will be regulated by mechanical and objective laws. The image becomes a part of the external universe. Surely, it is above all else a psychic act (*un acte psychique*). But this act corresponds rigorously to a physiological modification. Otherwise put, we must *wait for* our images as we *wait for* objects; hope for the image of Pierre as I hope for my friend Pierre in person. What does thought become then? Well, it is, precisely, facing the images as it faces perception; it is *what is not* image, what is not perception. But it cannot call on the images for help, no more than it can call on an external object. If one accepts these premises, it becomes necessary to accept as well James' observations (which, by the way, Claparède cites in his work): one cannot admit that the thought of a resemblance will make an image that resembles a perception surge up on the occasion of that perception.[36] But, rather, the mechanical contiguity makes the image surge up at the same time as the perception or as the image considered, and it is then only that thought can notice the resemblance. In a word, thought cannot serve as a directing theme around which the images organize themselves, like tools or approximations. Thought is rigorously reduced to a single function: to grasp relations between two types of objects, object-things and object-images. As Alain says, in a scarcely different sense: 'One does not think as one wants.'[37]

That's all quite fine, but what then do the logical laws become? Surely one can attempt to bring them down to associative connections too. In this case, under one form or another, we find again Taine's Associationism. But if we must maintain the existence of an autonomous thought, here we are constrained to reduce it to immediate judgement alone, affirming in the instant such and such a relation between two perceptions, two images, or one image and one perception, which appeared outside of it and as in spite of it. Who will recognize in this broken, bouncing thought, stopped short in its developments by ever-new appearances, and without logical relations between them, the faculty of reasoning, of conceiving, of building machines, of conducting thought experiments, etc.?

There is only one way to get out of this quandary. It is to accept the integral parallelism of the modes of extension and those of thought. In this case, corporeal affections will correspond as well to logical thoughts, and nothing would be able to hinder these new affections from leading, by a purely physiological mechanism, to the 'awakening' of the traces that would correspond to images. Thus we could admit a thought that chooses images and modifies, to a certain extent, the order of their appearance. At least there would no longer be any impossibility *from the point of view of mechanism*. But it escapes no one that this integral parallelism is only acceptable in a Spinozistic metaphysics. If indeed we had to understand this corporeal mechanism as directing and *explaining* the succession of psychic facts, the spontaneity of consciousness would vanish; the logical laws would reduce to being only symbols of physiological laws, and we would fall into epiphenomenalism. We therefore must understand this parallelism quite otherwise, that is to say, as Spinoza repeats tirelessly, that a thought will have to be explained by a thought and a movement by another movement. So that, in psychology at least, this parallelism, in wanting to explain everything, does not explain anything at all anymore.

It comes down to saying that one must study the domain of consciousness in terms of consciousness and the domain of the physiological in physiological terms. In a word, for having wanted to find a mechanical system that would account for the organizational power of thought, we are sent back to consciousness and constrained to formulate the question in strictly psychological terms. We cannot hold on to Cartesian dualism, we must abandon all explanations in terms of traces, nervous contiguity, etc. One can admit, if one wants, that a corporeal affection corresponds to each image, to each thought; but *precisely for that*, the body explains nothing, and one must envisage the relation of thought to the image such as it appears to consciousness.

Here we are led by necessity to consider the participation of the image in the sensible from the second point of view, that is to say, in the manner of Hume. Hume, at the beginning, does not know anything about the body anymore. He starts—or believes he starts—from the immediate data of experience: there are strong impressions and weak impressions. The second are images and differ from the first only in intensity. Have we surmounted by this conversion the difficulties that we had encountered at first? We don't believe so. We would like to show that they don't depend on the point of view chosen but on the conception of the image as a sensible content.

The first characteristic of Hume's 'impressions' is indeed their opacity. And it is this very opacity that constitutes their quality of being sensible. There is nothing truer, by the way, when it comes to perceptions. There is indeed, finally, in the yellow colour of an ashtray, in the roughness of this piece of wood, something irreducible, incomprehensible, *given*. This given represents not only the share of opacity but also the share of receptivity in perception. And anyway opacity and receptivity are but two faces of a single reality. But Hume does not limit himself to describing the sensible contents of perception. He wants to build the world of consciousness out of these contents alone; that is to say, he doubles the order of perception by an order of images that are these very sensible contents at a lesser degree of intensity. Thus, Associationism's images represent centres of opacity and receptivity. The yellow colour of this ashtray, when it is reborn as a weakened impression, keeps its character as a *given*; it remains an irreducible, an irrational. Above all else, and precisely because it is pure passivity, it remains an inert element. What must we understand by that? That it could not find in itself, in the intimacy of its being, the reason for its appearance. It couldn't be reborn or disappear of itself. It has to be evoked or pushed back by something other than itself. But this 'something else' cannot be a systematizing spontaneity. This is in fact because a spontaneity could not enclose passive parts. It is entirely activity, and, by consequence, translucent to itself—or indeed it does not exist. In reality, the positing of sensible contents transports us into a world of pure exteriority, that is to say, into a world where inert contents are determined in their modes of appearance by other equally inert contents, a world where all changes, all impulses come from the exterior and remain profoundly exterior to the content that they animate. This is why the great laws of Associationism each had to contain something like an implicit affirmation of the principle of inertia. They don't fall short of this. What is the law of resemblance if not the positing of external relations between psychic contents? It is indeed an accident for Pierre to resemble Jean. What, above all, is the law of contiguity if not the pure and simple translation of the principle of inertia into psychological terms? According to this latter law, indeed, the sole principle of connection between two contents is encounter, contact. Thus, every content of consciousness is in some way exterior to itself. A shock makes it appear; a shock pushes it back outside of consciousness. We now see what consciousness is for

Associationism. It is just the world of things. Indeed, there exists only a world of exteriority; it is the exterior world. Between this red bowl and the perception of this bowl there is no difference. This bowl is an inert body that remains immobile as long as no force comes to communicate movement to it and that persists infinitely in its movement if nothing comes to impede it. The perception of this bowl is an inert content that could not appear without being pushed to the centre of consciousness by some other content, and, once it has appeared, it will remain present indefinitely if nothing repels it. It is with reason that M. Laporte was able to compare Hume to the Neorealists.[38] For him, as for them, there exist only objects maintaining external relations between each other. Consciousness is nothing but a collection of these objects envisaged from the standpoint of a certain type of relations (the laws of association). But then, one will say, what difference is there between the law of contiguity as Descartes understands it and the same law as Associationism presents it? We will answer: none. The Cartesian law of contiguity concerns cerebral traces. Contiguity is understood in the spatial sense and rests expressly upon the principle of inertia. The Associationist law of contiguity derives as well from the principle of inertia, and although not strictly understood in the spatial sense, it also implies exteriority and contact. But in Descartes, the associative connections are established between the marks left by the objects, whereas in Hume, they form ties between the objects themselves.

But Hume is perfectly logical. His system must be accepted or rejected en bloc. Having posited that the elements of consciousness have passive natures, he applied the principle of inertia to the psychic domain and reduced consciousness to a collection of inert contents linked by external relations. It would seem then that a psychology that claims to be 'synthetic' and that affirms the existence of a spontaneity at the heart of consciousness should expressly renounce all the theses of Hume. Naturally, one should indeed accept the existence of sensible contents in perception. But one will recognize, from this very fact, that the order of their succession is rigorously independent of consciousness. And, in fact, I am not free to see a hat on this coat rack, or a piano at the location of this armchair. The appearance of these sensible contents would thus remain regulated by a certain type of association. This is what Husserl expresses by saying that the principle of the connection of sensible contents is *passive genesis by association*, of which the essential form is temporal flow.[39] Psychological consciousness[40] could not direct this succession; but, all consciousness being act (*étant acte*), it 'bears witness to' it (*elle la «constate»*), as Spaier says.[41] With this witnessing (*constatation*), the structures of which must be made the object of a special description, the perception of the external world appears.

However, when returning to images, one would expect the psychology of synthesis to expressly reject their sensible origin and their assimilation to 'weak impressions'. Indeed, from two things one: either they remain inert contents, and in this case one must limit the role of spontaneity to the apprehension (*l'aperception*) of relations between images that evoke each other by the laws of association; or one affirms that consciousness is organization, systematization, that the flow of psychic facts is regulated by directing themes, and in this case the image can no longer be assimilated to a content of receptive opacity. Thus, we have gained nothing in moving to the plane of pure psychology. On the contrary, the necessity of choosing appears more pressing; at present, one can no longer take refuge in psycho-physiological loopholes.

Now, the psychologists of synthesis *have not chosen*. Certainly, they assert that every state of consciousness is synthesis, that the whole gives to the parts their meaning and value, that thought directs and chooses its images. But they keep the sensible basis of these images, and nothing more is needed to skew radically their psychology.

If one posits sensible contents, one must indeed link them together, one way or another, by laws of association, since they are the only ones that are suitable to inertia. And, by this fact, there are very few psychologists to deny absolutely the laws of association. It seems that they *belong* so much to the sensible given that they are preserved on an inferior plane, the plane of dream, of distraction, of 'low power'. But, at the same time, they admit a constant harmony between the images currently present in consciousness and the current directing themes of thought. How is that possible?

It is, they say, because thought *chooses* its images. But how can this choice operate? Is there a suspension of the laws of association, or does thought use them to its benefit? Thus, the problem that Cartesian physiology posed reappears in its entirety on the plane of pure psychology. Earlier we asked, how can thought direct the animal spirits or use cerebral contiguity to its benefit? At present we pose the same question in scarcely different terms: How can thought direct associations or use psychological contiguity to its benefit? It is well understood that thought does not create its images. How indeed could this spontaneity create something inert? How could this transparency produce something opaque? It is thus necessary that it *go seek them*. Here, naturally, a reservoir of inert contents is conceived for the sake of the cause—it is the unconscious. We have indeed seen how much Hume was hindered by the absence of this notion. He does not go as far as inventing it, but it is implied by all his psychology. The modern authors make great use of it. But isn't it clear that this unconscious in which inert contents exist like things, that is to say, without being conscious of *themselves* nor *for others*, in which opaque data have only relations of contact or resemblance between them, isn't it clear that this unconscious is a spatial milieu that can be rigorously assimilated to the brain?

Thus, only the words have changed. And if one comes to say then that thought is *seeking* the images, the consequence is unavoidable. One transforms thought into a material force. The confusion arises thanks to an analogy: in the external world, there are, likewise, inert objects. But I can take them, change their place, take them out of a drawer or put them back in. It seems then that one could conceive of an *activity* that exerts itself on passive givens. But it is easy to detect the error. In fact, if I can lift this book or this cup, it is insofar as I am an organism, that is to say, a body subject to the same laws of inertia. The mere fact that I can oppose my thumb to my four other fingers in a gesture of prehension already supposes all of mechanics. Activity here is but an appearance. It is thus impossible to give to thought a power of evocation over inert contents without materializing it by that very stroke. Transforming this positive power of evocation into a negative power of *selection* resolves the difficulty only in appearance. *Setting aside* supposes indeed a material power of prehension, an action by contact, just like *evoking*. But, one will say, you are fooled by an image; when one says that thought evokes, sets aside, that consciousness selects, one speaks figuratively. Surely, but we demand to know what is *behind* these images. If words are metaphors, let someone make us understand the reality that hides itself beneath the words. But it is evident that there is *nothing* under the words, behind the images, because nothing can be there. We call an existence spontaneous that determines itself to exist by itself. In other terms, to exist spontaneously is to exist for itself and by itself. One reality alone thus merits the name spontaneous, and that is consciousness. Indeed, for it, to exist and to have consciousness of existing are but one. In other terms, the great ontological law of consciousness is the following: *The sole manner of existing for a consciousness is in having consciousness that it exists*. It evidently follows that consciousness can determine itself to exist but cannot act upon something other than itself. One can form a consciousness on the occasion of a sensible content but one cannot act on this sensible content by consciousness, that is to say, pull it out of nothingness (*néant*)—or out of the unconscious—or send it back there. If then the image is a consciousness, it is pure spontaneity, that is to say, consciousness of itself, transparency for itself, and it exists solely to the extent that it knows itself. It is therefore not a sensible content. It is absolutely in vain to represent it as 'rationalized', as 'penetrated with thought'. It is all the one or all the other. Either it is entirely thought—and then one will be able to think with an image; or it is sensible content, and in this case one will be able to think *on the occasion* of an image. But in this second case, the image becomes independent of consciousness. It *appears* to consciousness according to the laws that are proper to it but it *is not* consciousness. And so this image that one must await, decipher, observe, it is quite simply *a thing*. Thus, all inert and opaque content places itself, by the very necessity of its type of existence, among the objects, that is to say, in the external world. It is an ontological law that there be only two types of existence: existence as a thing of the world, and existence as consciousness.

What will show clearly that the image, which has become 'sensible content', is ejected out of thought, is that contemporary psychologists will implicitly accept a radical distinction between an image and the thought of that image. Hoernlé, we have seen, distinguishes the image and its meaning, that is to say, in sum, the *thing* 'image' and that which the image is *for thought*.[42] Likewise Spaier:

> Our attention does not bring itself onto the object of sensible intuition (onto the image or onto the perception) but onto the meaning.[43]

Here then is the image posited as an independent object; it is apprehended by thought in one way or another, but it exists *in itself* in a way different from what it is for consciousness. Spaier gives an example that retains an indisputable value for perception: I *see* a smile (the corners of the lips lift, the nostrils dilate, the eyebrows rise, etc.) and I *perceive benevolence*. But what must one understand by that? It is that there exists a certain *thing* outside of me, that is, a face. This face has its own existence, it is what it is, it has an infinite multitude of aspects; moreover, it contains an infinity of details that I cannot see (pores, cells). The knowledge of this face demands an infinite approximation. It is therefore infinitely richer than it appears to me. Hence the necessity of awaiting, observing, and being mistaken. But, since the assimilation of the image to perception is explicitly made in the text we cited above, we have the right to apply word-for-word the description we have just made to the *image* of a face that smiles. The face that is reborn as imaged (*en image*) must also have its pores, its cells, its multiplicity of aspects. Then, since this is what defines the transcendence of the thing, it is also itself *a thing*. We simply apprehend this thing as a meaning. If then we want to get ourselves out of inextricable difficulties and posit the image as a fact of consciousness, we will have to renounce distinguishing what it is from what it appears to be or, if one prefers, to posit that the mode of *being* of the image is exactly its 'appearing'.

We can conclude. Every theory of imagination must satisfy two requirements. It must account for the spontaneous discrimination that the mind makes between its images and its perceptions, and it must explain the role that the image plays in the operation of thought. Whatever form it has taken, the classical conception of the image could not fulfil these two essential tasks. To give to the image a sensible content, is to make a *thing* of it, obeying the laws of things and not those of consciousness. In this way, one removes from the mind every possibility of distinguishing the image from other *things* of the world. It becomes impossible at the same time to conceive in some way of the relation of this thing to thought. In fact, if one subtracts the image from consciousness, one removes from the latter all its freedom. If one makes it enter consciousness, the entire universe enters with it and consciousness is solidified all at once like an oversaturated solution.

How understandable then is the offensive against the image that we have seen take shape before the war! It hinders thought, as Binet and several other psychologists of Würzburg had already said. Others have gone further. If the image can only exist on the bases of a sensory reviviscence, we are constrained, they said, to accept Associationism, atomistic psychology, the juxtaposition of the contents of thought. The image is a being of reason that could only be adequate during the era of cerebral localization. With the hypotheses of Broca and Wernicke, it must disappear. There is no place for it in a psychology of synthesis. Moutier, a disciple of Marie, writes in 1908:

> The great error in the question of images has been to believe in them as in realities. We have lost sight of their completely hypothetical existence, completely conventional, and, little by little, we have ended up detaching them from the word and the idea. We ended up allowing into the brain images without words, without ideas, without any attributes—pure images. We have opposed images of words to the words properly speaking, ideas have been freed up from words and images, and we have ended up discovering in the interior language three manners of being: by words, by images of words, and by pure ideas. It is with images as it is with the *thinking substance*: They are 'metaphysical realities' not corresponding to any experience. ...[44]

This conception, which represents, in sum, the spirit of synthesis in its purest form, refuses to consider isolated elements in psychic life. But it remains rather obscure. First, we are on the uncertain terrain of physiological psychology; they speak to us about images and ideas 'in the brain'. And we do not know what that means. Does it have to do with a physiological hypothesis presenting the brain as an organ that functions like the heart or the liver in the unity of a biological synthesis? Does it have to do with a psychological theory concerning the indivisibility of psychic states? Does it have to do with the two at the same time? And then to what extent do they negate the reality of the image? Must we understand that the image is a 'metaphysical reality', an 'abstract', the way the individual is for certain sociologists? In this case, one would have to understand simply that it has no *functional* reality, that it is never independent. But then we would re-encounter M. Spaier's point of view. Or must we believe in a radical negation of the image as a structure of consciousness? Or is it still Broca's image-trace that Moutier intends to repulse? To tell the truth, Moutier is not a psychologist. What he defends against the analytic tendencies of a Broca or a Taine is the unity of the living being. And, surely, there is some progress here, but it is only a progress of method. Moutier does not care about the direct testimony of consciousness anymore more than Taine. He *deduces* his negation of the image from general and abstract principles. Taine had chosen the image as a single principle of explanation because he was trying to build a scientific psychology on the model of physics. And, at the same time, because emerging biology had introduced the idea of organic synthesis, and because, sharper than Ribot, he realizes that the idea of synthesis is incompatible with that of psychic atoms, Moutier, without examining the concrete data further, dismisses the image as being among 'metaphysical entities'. In both cases, the procedure is the same.[45]

*
* *

It is his theory of knowledge and judgement that leads Alain to take an attitude of radical negation towards the image.

> That we keep in memory copies of things and that we can in some way page through them is a simple, convenient idea but a little too puerile.[46]

The image does not exist, it could not exist; what we call by this name is always a false perception.

> In every fact of imagination, one will find three types of causes: the external world, the state of the body, and movements.[47]

But every false perception is just a false judgement, since to perceive is to judge. A crowd in Metz believed it had seen an army in the windows of a house. It *believed* it had seen it, but it did not see it. There were lines, colours, reflections there, but no army. But nor was there a 'representation' of an army in their minds. There was no *projection* of an image on the window. One has not merged a memory with the data of perception. Fear and haste led to judging too fast, to wrongly interpreting.

> When one imagines a voice in the strikings of a clock, one still only hears a striking of a clock; and the least bit of attention assures us of this. But in this case and probably in all, the false judgement is rescued by the voice itself, and the voice creates a new object that substitutes itself for the other. Here we forge the imagined thing; being forged, it is *ipso facto* real and is perceived without a doubt.[48]

> … A strong emotion is felt and perceived, inseparable from bodily motions, and at the same time … a belief, plausible but anticipated and finally without an object, is produced; the ensemble has the character of a passionate suspense, imaginary in a sense but very real through the tumult of the body. … Thus disorder in the body, error in the mind, the one feeding the other, that's the real (*le réel*) 'of the imagination'.[49]

What we have explained in the previous pages enables us, we believe, to understand the position of Alain, Cartesian Rationalist. Alain, like Descartes, accepts the initial postulate of the fundamental identity of images and perceptions. However, a more profound and scrupulous thinker than the psychologists of which we attempted a critique, he is struck right away by the contradictions that result from it. It is absurd to claim that there exist images entirely similar to perceptions and then to think that one will be able to distinguish them from each other. Yet, by accepting the idea that the products of the imagination are distinguished from the objects of perception *as error is from truth*, isn't it possible to muddle through by reversing the position? To distinguish image and perception by the external criteria of truth and falsity is necessarily to affirm that *every false perception is an image*. It is thus, we have seen, that M. Spaier proceeds. But, in this case, there remains this famous re-emerging 'sensible content' that one could not explain. Why not instead say, starting from the same principles, that *every image is a false perception*? In this case the 're-emerging sensation' has no longer a *raison d'être*; there are no sensible data other than those currently provided by my perception. But, depending on whether I judge them true or false, I constitute these data as real objects or as phantoms. These phantoms are precisely the images. But, of course, there are several sorts of imagination. One, turned towards the outside, consists in false judgements about the exterior objects. The other, turned towards the inside, '... turns itself away from things and closes its eyes, especially attentive to the movements of life and to the weak impressions that result from them'.[50]

The real object that the judgement will distort by too great a haste or by passion is the cœnaesthetic given—or a thousand more fugitive perceptions: complementary images and entoptic spots. There are thus never any independent representations with their own content and an autonomous life; an image is just a skewed perception.

As a result, we no longer need to pose the question of the 'mode of sequencing' of the images. There is no association of ideas, nor selection operated by thought, since there are no longer any rèvived sensible contents. One judges based on the present sensible contents, and these follow each other as the laws of the world require.

> Our dreams come to us from the world, not from the Gods.[51]

Thought is a spontaneous judgement—true or false—about the current data of the external world and of the body. Here we find again this conception, which we pointed out above and which restricts thought to judgement. But while earlier this judicative thought was hampered and bounced along by the double succession of 'sensible' images and perceptions, Alain frees it from the order of images. It is alone facing the world and regulates itself on the basis of it:

> One does not think as one wants. What makes one believe that one thinks as one wants is that the ideas coming to the mind of a man are almost always those that are suited for the circumstances. If I wander on the harbour, the course of my ideas does not differ much from the series of things that I see, water cranes,

> coal heaps, boats, wagons, and barrels. If sometimes I follow some reverie, this does not last more than the shadow of a swallow. Soon some vivid impression puts me back in the middle of present things; and as I look after my preservation, in the middle of these masses going up and down, rolling, creaking, and banging together, my attention finds itself by this token disciplined; and I fix in my mind true relations between real things.
>
> But where do these flights of reverie that cut across my perceptions from time to time come from? If I searched well, I would almost always find some real object that I have seen only for an instant, a bird in the air, a tree afar or the face of a man, turned towards me an instant and pouring at my feet, in a flash, a rich freight of hopes, fears and angers. Our thoughts are copied from the present things and our power to dream does not go as far as they say.
>
> I recall that I was conferring about these things with a friend. We were walking, adventuring in the middle of the woods. He was asking me if we were not able to pull treasures out of ourselves, as out of a casket, without the help of a present thing. At that time, there came to my mind the word 'Byrrh', which indeed had no relation to the trees and the birds. I said it to him. We discoursed about it. We were approaching a sort of shack, half devoured by branches. As I applied my gaze to it, I saw a piece of cardboard nailed on the window ... on which one could read the word 'Byrrh'.[52]

Alain's theory is expressly conceived to avoid the contradictions that we have enumerated in the course of the present chapter. And one has to acknowledge that it reaches its goal, but it does so by abandoning the very notion of an image. One could not find a better conclusion to our critical exposé. If one assimilates the mental image to perception, the image destroys itself; and one is led like Alain to produce a theory of the imagination without images.

Is it possible for us to content ourselves with this? We do not believe so. This theory, conceived of *a priori* like the others, does not fit with the facts. For not having referred to the testimony of consciousness, Alain, by suppressing the image, grants to the *imagination* at once too much and not enough.

Too much: for him the imagination is necessarily a belief in a false object. I'm taking a walk in the evening on a dark road. I'm afraid. My fear hastens my judgement and I take a tree trunk for a man. That's the imagination according to Alain. Since it is judgement, it envelops by nature an affirmation of existence, and the distinction introduced by this philosopher between the imagination turned inward and that turned outward could not change anything about it. Hence the imaginary object begins by being posited as a real object. The imagination presents itself as a succession of little instantaneous dreams followed by abrupt awakenings. And this *affirmative* character of imaginative thought is perhaps sharper in Alain than in psychologists who admit a re-emerging sensible content at the basis of images. Indeed, in them, judgement—if it exists as an autonomous spontaneity—can posit itself *facing* the image. We can exercise the Stoic ἐποχή [*epochē*], abstain. The image will not disappear for all that, since it is first a sensible content. It will remain like an irreal, and precisely then it will take on its essential character, which is precisely non-existence. For Alain, on the contrary, the constitutive element of the imaginative act is judgement. One must thus choose. Either we are in the imaginative act, and then we *perceive falsely*. Or we awaken, we are out of the imaginative act, we straighten up our judgement, and then there is no more fiction; there is the real, the true judgement. Very well, dream and awakening. But reverie, is precisely not dreaming. The man who lets himself go into it tells himself stories *he does not believe* in and that are, however, something other than simple abstract judgements. There is here a type of affirmation, a type of intermediary existence between the false assertions of dream and the certitudes of waking life; and this type of existence is, of course, that of imaginary creations. To make these out to be judicative acts is granting them too much.[53]

But it is also not granting them enough. One must still go back to the data of consciousness. There exists an 'image' *fact*, and this fact is an irreducible structure of consciousness. When I evoke the image of my friend Pierre, I do not make a false judgement about the state of my body, but my friend Pierre *appears* to me. Indeed he does not appear to me as an *object*, as currently present, as 'there'. But he appears to me as *imaged (en image)*. Perhaps, in order to formulate the judgement 'I have an image of Pierre', it is appropriate that I go into reflection, that is, that I direct my attention no longer onto the object of the image, but onto the image itself, as a psychic reality. But this movement to reflection does not alter at all the positional quality of the image. It is not an awakening, a straightening up; I do not suddenly *discover* that I have formed an image. Quite the contrary, at the very moment that I bear the affirmation 'I have an image of Pierre', I realize *that I always knew that it was an image*. Only, I knew it in a different fashion. In a word, this knowledge was but one with the act by which I constituted Pierre as imaged (*en image*).

The image is a psychic reality for certain. The image could in no way be reduced to a sensible content, nor constitute itself on the basis of a sensible content. Such are, at least so we hope, the observations that impose themselves at the end of this critical exposé. If we wish to go further, we must return to experience, and describe the image in its full concretion, such as it appears to reflection. But how can we avoid the mistakes that we pointed out? Neither the experimental method of Würzburg, nor pure and simple introspection could satisfy us. We have seen that they cannot set aside metaphysical prejudices. Isn't there here a radical impossibility?

But perhaps the error does not slip into the reflective act itself. Perhaps it appears at the level of induction, when, starting from facts, one establishes laws. If it were so, would it be possible to constitute a psychology that, while remaining a psychology of *experience*, would not be an inductive science? Is there a type of privileged experience that puts us immediately in contact with the law? A great contemporary philosopher has believed so, and he is the one we will presently ask to guide our first steps in this difficult science.

NOTES

1 [Albert Spaier, *La Pensée concrete: Essai sur le symbolisme intellectuel*, Paris: Alcan, 1927.]

2 [Ignace Meyerson, 'Les Images' in *Le Nouveau Traité de Psychologie*, vol. 2, bk. 4, Paris: Alcan, 1932, 541–606.]

3 James, *Précis de psychologie*, p. 214, cited by Ignace Meyerson, 'Les Images' in *Le Nouveau Traité de Psychologie*, vol. 2, bk. 4, Paris: Alcan, 1932, p. 559. [William James, *Précis de psychologie*, E. Baudin and G. Bertier, trans., Paris: Marcel Rivière, 1909, p. 214; *Psychology: The Briefer Course*, New York: Henry Holt, 1892; Notre Dame, Indiana: University of Notre Dame Press, 1985, p. 32 of the Notre Dame edition. We leave our translation because it reflects the rather free French translation Sartre cites. Here is the original: 'What must be admitted is that the definite images of traditional psychology form but the smallest part of our minds as they actually live. The traditional psychology talks like one who should say a river consists of nothing but pailsful, spoonsful, quartpotsful, barrelsful, and other moulded forms of water. Even were the pails and the pots all actually standing in the stream, still between them the free water would continue to flow.']

4 R. F. Alfred Hoernlé, 'Image, idea and meaning', *Mind*, 16 (1907), 75–76. Cited by Meyerson. [See Ignace Meyerson, 'Les Images' in *Le Nouveau Traité de Psychologie*, vol. 2, bk. 4, Paris: Alcan, 1932, 541–606,

pp. 575–76. Presumably this is Meyerson's translation. The original reads: 'Our consciousness of the idea involves our consciousness (more or less explicitly) of its meaning, and the ideas with which Psychology deals are not mere signs without signification. In other words, ideas are understood, and, as I have already mentioned, in ordinary thinking our attention is not directed always or even mainly to the ideas, but primarily to their meanings.' Hoernlé uses 'idea' where the text (in Meyerson and Sartre) has 'image'. But Hoernlé treats ideas as the genus and images and meanings as species; the former are psychological ideas, the latter are logical ideas. See Hoernlé, p. 71. Meyerson in effect justifies this modification in a footnote (4) on p. 575.]

5 Albert Spaier, *La Pensée concrete: Essai sur le symbolisme intellectuel*, Paris: Alcan, 1927, p. 201.

6 Meyerson, ibid., p. 578.

7 Meyerson, ibid., p. 582.

8 Meyerson, ibid., p. 588.

9 [Hippolyte Taine, *De l'Intelligence*, 6th edn, vol. 2, Paris: Hachette, 1892, p. 10. *On Intelligence*, London: L. Reeve, 1871, pp. 222.]

10 Cf. for example Jules Maldidier, 'Les Caractéristiques probables de l'image vraie', *Revue de Métaphysique et de morale*, 16 (1908), 281–320.

11 Spaier, *La Pensée concrete,* pp. 120–121.

12 The example that Albert Spaier discusses on p. 121 [of *La Pensée concrete: Essai sur le symbolisme intellectuel*, Paris: Alcan, 1927] is exactly of this type.

13 Spaier, *La Pensée concrete,* p. 120.

14 Taine, *De l'Intelligence*, vol. 1, p. 125. [*On Intelligence*, p. 72. Sartre's emphasis and bracket.]

15 Taine, *De l'Intelligence*, vol. 1, pp. 88–89. [*On Intelligence*, p. 44.]

16 Taine, ibid., vol. 1, p. 99. [*On Intelligence*, p. 52.]

17 [The phrase, 'struggle for life', is in English in the original.]

18 Taine, ibid., vol. 1, p. 99. [*On Intelligence*, p. 52.]

19 Taine, ibid., vol. 1, pp. 100–101. [*On Intelligence*, p. 53.]

20 [Taine, ibid., vol. 1, pp. 90, 92–93, 105–108; *On Intelligence*, pp. 45–47, 56–59. Sartre's emphases and brackets.]

21 Taine, ibid., vol. 1, p. 101. 'It is the *special reducer*, to wit, the contradictory sensation.' [*On Intelligence*, p. 53.]

22 Taine, ibid., vol. 1, p. 115. [*On Intelligence*, pp. 63–64.]

23 Taine, ibid., vol. 1, p. 117. [*On Intelligence*, p. 66.]

24 Spaier, *La Pensée concrete,* p. 120.

25 [Maldidier, 'Les Caractéristiques probables de l'image vraie', *Revue de Métaphysique et de morale*, 16 (1908), 281–320.]

26 It is not certain that Spaier would have accepted without reservation the thesis that we explained on the preceding page. But we have above all wanted to indicate a direction and describe an attitude generally adopted today.
27 Spaier, *La Pensée concrete*, p. 121. His emphasis.
28 See on this topic the interesting observation of Lagache on the role of respiratory rhythm in auditory hallucinations in *Les Hallucinations verbales et la parole*, Paris: Alcan, 1934.
29 [Taine, *De L'Intelligence*, vol. 1, p. 117; *On Intelligence*, p. 66.]
30 Meyerson in *Nouveau Traité de Psychologie*, vol. 2, p. 594.
31 [Meyerson, 'Les Images' pp. 594–595.]
32 [Spaier, *La Pensée concrete*, p. 169. Emphasis Spaier's.]
33 [Spaier, *La Pensée concrete*, p. 159. Emphasis Spaier's.]
34 [Albert Spaier, *La Pensée concrete*, p. 172.]
35 Édouard Claparède, *L'Association des idées*, Paris: Octave Doin, 1903. [e.g., pp. 55ff., 100.]
36 [See, e.g., Édouard Claparède, *L'Association des idées*, Paris: Octave Doin, 1903, p. 18; cf. William James, *Principles of Psychology*, vol. 1, New York: Henry Holt, 1890, p. 551.]
37 [Alain (Émile Chartier), *Les Propos d'Alain*, vol. 1, Paris: Nouvelle Revue Française, 1920, p. 33.]
38 [Jean Laporte, 'Le scepticisme de Hume', *Revue philosophique de la France et de l'étranger*, 115 (1933), 61–127.]
39 Cf. the description of this passive genesis in *Méditations cartésiennes*. [Edmund Husserl, *Méditations cartésiennes*, Paris: A. Colin, 1931/ Paris: Vrin, 2001, pp. 131ff. (page references are to the Vrin edition); *Cartesian Meditations*, Dordrecht: Kluwer, 1991, pp. 77ff.]
40 To be distinguished, according to Husserl, from absolute or phenomenological consciousness.
41 [Spaier, *La Pensée concrete*, p. 169.]
42 [Hoernlé, 'Image, idea and meaning', pp. 75–76.]
43 [Spaier, *La Pensée concrete*, p. 201.]
44 François Moutier, *L'Aphasie de Broca*, Paris: G. Steinheil, 1908, Part 3, Chapter VII, 'Des images verbales', p. 237.
45 It is also for reasons of a methodological order and, at bottom, metaphysical, that the *behaviourists* deny the existence of images: 'I would completely reject images', says Watson, 'and show that all thought naturally comes down to sensori-motor processes having their seat in the larynx.' Cf. *Behavior*, vol. 1 and 'Image and affection in behavior', *Journal of Philosophy*, July 1913. [This quotation seems to be Sartre's summary of Watson's view. See John B. Watson, *Behavior:*

An Introduction to Comparative Psychology, 1st edn, New York: Henry Holt, 1914, Chapter 1; 'Image and affection in behavior', *Journal of Philosophy, Psychology, and Scientific Methods*, 10(16) (1913), 421–428.]

46 Alain, *Système des Beaux-Arts*, Paris: Gallimard, 1920, p. 22.

47 Alain, *Quatre-vingt-un chapitres sur l'esprit et les passions*, Paris: Camille Bloch, 1921, p. 41.

48 Alain, *Système des Beaux-Arts*, Paris: Gallimard, 1920, p. 16.

49 [Ibid., pp. 17–18.]

50 [Alain, *Quatre-vingt-un chapitres sur l'esprit et les passions*, p. 42.]

51 [Alain (Émile Chartier), *Les Propos d'Alain*, vol. 1, p. 33.]

52 Alain (Émile Chartier), *Les Propos d'Alain*, vol. 1, pp. 33–34. One may read similar considerations in Dr Pierre Vachet's work, *La Pensée qui guérit*. [Pierre Vachet, *La Pensée qui guérit*, Paris: B. Grasset, 1926.]

53 One will object perhaps that there exist judgements of probability or possibility. But this is not a solution. Saying 'what I see here is perhaps a man' and imagining the body of a man in the course of a reverie is accomplishing two obviously very different operations. Alain's thesis implies, by the way, a conception of the perceptual act that is not acceptable, as we have shown above.

IV

HUSSERL

The great event of pre-war philosophy is certainly the publication of the first volume of the *Jahrbuch für Philosophie und phänomenologische Forschung*,[1] which contained the main work of Husserl, *Ideen zu einer reinen Phänomenologie und phänomenologischen Philosophie*.[2] As much as philosophy, this book was destined to shatter psychology. Certainly, phenomenology, a science of pure transcendental consciousness, is a discipline radically different from the psychological sciences, which study the consciousness of the human being, indissolubly linked to a body and before a world. For Husserl, psychology, like physics or astronomy, remains a 'science belonging to the natural attitude',[3] that is to say, a science that implies a spontaneous realism. On the contrary, phenomenology starts 'when we put the general positing of existence that belongs to the essence of the natural attitude out of play'.[4]

But the essential structures of transcendental consciousness do not disappear when this consciousness imprisons itself in

DOI: 10.4324/9781003657408-5

the world. Thus the main acquisitions of phenomenology will remain valid for the psychologist *mutatis mutandis*. Moreover, the very method of phenomenology can serve as a model for psychologists. Surely, the essential approach of this method remains the 'reduction', the 'ἐποχή' [*epochē*], that is to say, the parenthesizing of the natural attitude. And it is well understood that the psychologist does not carry out this ἐποχή [*epochē*] and that he stays on the terrain of the natural attitude. But it remains that the phenomenologist, once the reduction is made, has a means of research that will be able to serve the psychologist. Phenomenology is a description of the structures of transcendental consciousness founded on the intuition of the essence of these structures. Naturally, this description operates on the plane of reflection. But one must not confuse reflection with introspection. Introspection is a special mode of reflection that seeks to grasp and fix the empirical facts. In order to convert its results into scientific laws, one *then* needs an inductive passage to the general. But there is another type of reflection that phenomenology employs. Phenomenology seeks to grasp essences. That is to say, it starts by placing itself from the outset on the terrain of the universal. Of course, it works well with examples. But it matters little that the individual fact that serves as a support for the essence is real or imaginary. Even if the 'exemplary' datum is a pure fiction, from the very fact that it could be imagined, it must indeed have realized in itself the essence sought, because the essence is the very condition of its possibility:

> It is thus permitted, if one likes paradoxes and on the condition of understanding adequately the ambiguous meaning of this sentence, to say in all truth that Fiction is the vital element of Phenomenology as of every eidetic Science[5] and the source from which the knowledge of eternal truths is drawn.[6]

What is valuable for the phenomenologist is valuable for the psychologist as well. We of course do not want to deny the essential role that experimentation and induction must play in all their forms in the constitution of psychology. But before experimenting, isn't it appropriate to know as exactly as possible *on what* one is going to experiment? About this, experiment will never yield anything but obscure and contradictory information.

> The great era (of Physics) begins in modern times when, suddenly and broadly, one starts using, for the physical method, Geometry, which, ever since Antiquity (principally among the Platonists), had been pushed quite far as a *pure eidetics*. One realizes then that it is the essence of the material thing to be a *res extensa, and that, as a result, geometry is the ontological discipline that relates to an essential moment of the thing:* spatial structure. But one also realizes that the universal essence of the thing embraces many other structures. This is what the fact that the scientific development immediately follows a new direction shows well: We want to constitute a series of new disciplines that we will coordinate with geometry and that are meant to fulfil the same function: *to rationalize empirical data.*[7]

What Husserl writes about Physics, one can repeat about Psychology. The latter will make the greatest progress when it will start clarifying the essential structures that constitute the object of its research and renounce cluttering itself up with ambiguous and contradictory experiments. We just saw, for instance, that the classical theory of the image contains a whole implicit metaphysics, and that they moved on to experimentation without getting rid of this metaphysics, carrying in experiments a crowd of prejudices that sometimes go back to Aristotle. But isn't it possible to ask oneself first, *before* any recourse to experiments (be it experimental introspection or any other procedure): *What is an image?* Does this very important element of psychic life have an essential structure accessible to intuition that one could fix with words and concepts? Are there assertions that are incompatible with the essential structure of the image? Etc., etc. In a word, Psychology is an empiricism that is still searching for its eidetic principles. Husserl, who has often been quite wrongfully reproached for a hostility of principle toward this discipline, proposes, on the contrary, to render it a service. He does not deny that there is an experimental psychology, but he thinks that to deal with the most pressing matters, the psychologist must construct (*constituer*) *before* all else an eidetic psychology. Naturally, such a psychology will not borrow its methods from mathematical sciences, which are *deductive*, but from phenomenological sciences, which are *descriptive*. It will be a 'phenomenological psychology'. It will bring about on the intra-mundane plane investigations and fixations of essences as phenomenology does on the transcendental plane. And indeed, one must still speak of experience here, since every intuitive viewing of an essence remains an experience. But it is an experience that precedes all experimentation.

A study of the image must therefore be presented as an attempt at realizing phenomenological psychology on a particular point. One must seek to construct (*constituer*) an eidetics of the image, that is to say, to fix and describe the essence of this psychological structure such as it appears to reflective intuition. Then, when we will have determined the set of conditions that a psychic state must necessarily realize in order to be an image, then only must we move from the certain to the probable and ask of experience what it can teach us about the images such as they present themselves in a contemporary human consciousness.

But, as for what concerns the problem of the image, Husserl does not content himself with furnishing us a method. There are in the *Ideen* the bases of an entirely new theory of images. To tell the truth, Husserl only touches on the question in passing, and besides, as we will see, we do not agree with him on all points. On the other hand, his remarks demand to be deepened and completed. But the indications that he gives are of the greatest importance.

The fragmentary character of Husserl's observations makes the exposition of them particularly difficult. One must not expect to find in the paragraphs that follow a systematic construction but only a set of fruitful suggestions.

The very conception of *intentionality* is destined to renew the notion of the image. One knows that, for Husserl, every state of consciousness or rather—as the Germans say and as we will say with them—every *consciousness* is consciousness of something.

> All the 'Erlebnisse' that have this essential property in common are also called 'intentional Erlebnisse': to the extent that they are consciousness of something one says that they 'relate intentionally' to this something.[8]

Intentionality—this is the essential structure of all consciousness. There naturally follows a radical distinction between consciousness and *that of which there is consciousness*. The object of consciousness whatever it is (save in the case of reflective consciousness) is in principle outside of consciousness; it is transcendent. This distinction, to which Husserl returns without tiring, has as a goal the fighting of the errors of a certain immanentism that wants to constitute the world from contents of consciousness (for example, the idealism of Berkeley). Without a doubt there are contents of consciousness but these contents are not the object of consciousness. Through them intentionality aims at the object that, itself, is the correlate of consciousness but is not *of consciousness*. Psychologism, starting from the ambiguous formula 'the world is our representation' makes the tree that I perceive vanish into myriad sensations of coloured, tactile, thermal, etc. impressions that are 'representations', in such a way that, finally, the tree appears as a sum of subjective contents and is itself a subjective phenomenon. On the contrary, Husserl begins by putting the tree *outside of us*.

> As an absolutely universal rule a *thing* cannot be given in any possible perception, that is to say in any possible consciousness in general, as a real immanent (*immanent réel*).[9]

Certainly, he does not deny the existence of visual or tactile data that make up part of consciousness as subjective immanent elements. But they are not the *object*. Consciousness is not directed at them; through them, it aims at the external thing. This visual impression that presently makes up part of my consciousness is not *the red*. The red is a quality of the object, a transcendent quality. This subjective impression, which is, probably, 'analogous' to the red of the thing, is only a 'quasi-red'. That is to say, it is the subjective matter, the '*hylē*' to which is applied the intention that transcends itself and seeks to catch the red outside of itself.

> One always has to keep present the idea that the impressional data that have for a function to 'profile' the colour, the surface, the form[10] (that is to say that have for a function to 'represent') are, as a matter of principle, radically distinct from the colour, the surface or the form, in short, from all the qualities of the thing.[11]

We see the immediate consequences for the image: the image is also an image of something. We are thus dealing with an intentional relation of a certain consciousness to a certain object. In a word, the image ceases to be a psychic *content*; it is not in consciousness as a constituting element. But, in the consciousness of a thing *as imaged* (*en image*), Husserl will distinguish, as in a perception, an imaging intention and a '*hylē*' that the intention comes to 'animate'.[12] The *hylē*, naturally, remains subjective but, by the same token, the object of the image, detached from the pure 'content', is camped outside of consciousness as something radically different.

> [Couldn't one object to us that ...] a centaur who plays the flute, a fiction that we freely form, is, precisely because of that, a free assemblage of representations in us?—We will respond: Sure ... the free fiction is effected spontaneously and what we generate spontaneously is, of course, a product of the mind. But, as for what concerns the centaur who plays the flute, it is a representation to the extent to which one calls a representation that which is represented and not in the sense in which representation would be a name for a psychic state. The centaur itself is, naturally, nothing psychic, it exists neither in the soul, nor in consciousness, nor anywhere; it does not exist at all, it is entirely an invention. To be more exact: the state of consciousness of invention is invention *of* this centaur. To this extent surely we can say that 'Centaur-aimed-at', 'centaur-invented' belongs to the 'Erlebnis' itself. *But let us not confuse this 'Erlebnis' of invention with that which, through it, has been invented as such.*[13]

This text is capital. The non-existence of the centaur or of the chimera thus does not give us the right to reduce them to mere psychic formations. Surely, there are here, at the occasion of these inexistents (*inexistants*), real psychic formations; and we understand the error of psychologism. The temptation was strong to leave these mythical beings to their nothingness (*néant*) and only take into account psychic contents. But Husserl restores to the centaur precisely its transcendence at the very heart of its nothingness (*néant*). As much nothingness (*néant*) as one wants, but by this very token it is not in consciousness.

Husserl does not say anything more about the very structure of the image, but one will easily measure the service that he renders to psychologists. The image, by becoming an intentional structure, moves from the state of an inert content of consciousness to that of a unified (*une*) and synthetic consciousness in relation with a transcendent object. The image of my friend Pierre is not a vague phosphorescence, a wake left in my consciousness by the perception of Pierre. It is a form of organized consciousness that relates, in its manner, to my friend Pierre. It is one of the possible ways of aiming at the real being, Pierre. Thus, in the act of imagination, consciousness relates directly to Pierre and not by the intermediary of a simulacrum, which would be in it. With a single blow all the difficulties that we evoked in the preceding chapter concerning the relation of this simulacrum with its real object and of pure thought with this simulacrum are going to disappear along with the immanentist metaphysics of the image. This 'Pierre in reduced format', this homunculus carried along by consciousness has never been of consciousness. It was an object of the material world lost among the psychic beings. By throwing it back outside of consciousness, by affirming that there is only a single and self-same Pierre, an object of perceptions and of images, Husserl has freed the psychic world from a heavy weight and eliminated almost all the difficulties that obscured the classical problem of the relations of the image with thought.

But Husserl does not limit his suggestion to this. Indeed, if the image is only a name for a certain way that consciousness aims at its object, nothing prevents us from putting material images (pictures, drawings, photos) together with images called psychic. Psychologism, curiously, ended up in radically separating the ones from the others, even though it would at bottom reduce the psychic images to being only material images in us. Finally, also, according to this doctrine, one could interpret a picture or a photograph only in reference to the mental image that it evokes by association. It was, practically, a postponement to infinity, since, the mental image being itself a photograph, it would require another image in order to understand it, and so on. On the contrary, if the image becomes a certain way of intentionally animating a hyletic content, we will well be able to assimilate the grasping of a picture *as image* to the intentional apprehension of a 'psychic' content. It will only be a matter of two different types of 'imaging' consciousnesses. The inception of this assimilation is found in a passage of the *Ideen* that deserves to remain classic, where Husserl analyses the intentional apprehension of an engraving of Dürer.

> Let us consider Dürer's etching, *The Knight, Death, and the Devil*. We will distinguish in the first place here the normal perception, of which the correlate is the 'engraving' *thing*, this page of the album.
>
> In the second place, we find the perceptual consciousness, in which, through these black lines, little uncoloured figures, 'Knight on horse', 'Death', 'Devil' appear to us. We are not, in aesthetic contemplation, directed to them as objects; we are directed toward the realities that are represented 'as imaged' ('*en image*'), more exactly to the 'imaged' realities (*abgebildet*), the knight of flesh and bone, etc.[14]

This text can be at the origin of an intrinsic distinction between image and perception.[15] Surely, the '*hylē*' that we apprehend in order to constitute the aesthetic appearance of the knight, of death and of the devil is indubitably the same as in the pure and simple perception of the page of the album. The difference is found in the intentional structure. What matters here to Husserl is that the 'thesis' or positing of existence has received a *neutrality modification*.[16] We do not have to occupy ourselves with that here. It suffices for us that the matter by itself cannot distinguish image from perception. Everything depends on the mode of animation of this matter, that is to say, on a form that is born in the most intimate structures of consciousness.

Such are the brief allusions that Husserl makes to a theory that he has probably elaborated in his courses and his unpublished works, but which, in the *Ideen*, remains still very fragmentary. And most likely, the service rendered to psychology is invaluable, but all of the obscurities are far from being dissipated. Certainly we can understand at present that image and perception are two intentional 'Erlebnisse' that differ foremost by their intentions. But of what nature is the intention of the image? In what does it differ from that of perception? It is here, evidently, that a description of essence is necessary. In the absence of further indication from Husserl, we are left to ourselves to perform this description.

Moreover, an essential problem remains without solution. After Husserl, we were able to sketch the general description of a large intentional class comprising the images called 'mental' ('*mentales*') and the images we will call external, for lack of a better term. We know that the consciousness of external images and the corresponding perceptual consciousness, while radically differing as to the intention, have an identical impressional matter. These black lines serve at once for the constitution of the image 'Knight' or for the perception 'black lines on a white page'. But does all this hold for the mental image? Does it have the same *hylē* as the external image, that is to say, finally, as the perception? Some passages of the *Logische Untersuchungen*[17] would seem to let us suppose this. Husserl there explains, indeed, that the image has for its function the 'filling' of empty cognitions (*savoirs*), just as *things* do for perception. For example, if I think about a lark, I can think about it emptily, that is to say, produce only a signifying intention fixed on the word 'lark'. But to fill this empty consciousness and transform it into an intuitive consciousness, it is indifferent whether I form an image of a lark or whether I look at a lark in flesh and bone. This filling of the signification by the image seems to indicate that the image possesses a concrete impressional matter and that it is itself a *fullness*, like a perception.[18] Moreover, in his *Phenomenology of Internal Time-Consciousness*,[19] Husserl carefully distinguishes retention, which is a non-positional way of keeping the past as past for consciousness, and *recollection*, which consists in making the things of the past reappear with their qualities. It is a matter in this second case of *presentification (Vergegenwärtigung)*, and it implies the reiteration, although in a modified consciousness, of all the original perceptual acts. For example, if I have perceived an illuminated theatre, I can reproduce indifferently in my memory the illuminated theatre or the perception of the illuminated theatre ('There was, that night, a party at the theatre. …' 'In passing, that night I saw the illuminated windows. …'), that is to say, in this latter case, *to reflect in memory*. This is because, for Husserl, the reproduction of the illuminated theatre implies the reproduction of the perception of the illuminated theatre. One sees that the image-memory is here nothing other than a modified perceptual consciousness, that is to say, affected with a coefficient of being past. It would seem thus that Husserl, while laying down the bases for a radical renewal of the question, has remained a prisoner of the old conception, at least as it concerns the *hylē* of the image, which would then remain, according to him, the re-emerging sensible impression.[20]

But if this is so, we will encounter difficulties analogous to those that stopped us in the preceding chapter.

First of all, on the phenomenological plane, that is to say once the reduction is effected, it seems to us, if their matter is the same, quite difficult to distinguish image and perception by their intentionality. The phenomenologist, indeed, having put the world 'in parentheses', has not lost it by doing so. The distinction consciousness-world has lost its sense. Now the cut is made differently; one distinguishes the set of *real* elements of the conscious synthesis (the *hylē* and the different intentional acts that animate it) and, on the other hand, the 'sense' that inhabits this consciousness. The concrete psychic reality will be named *noesis* and the sense that comes to inhabit it *noema*. For example 'perceived-blossoming-tree' is the noema of the perception I have at this moment.[21] But this 'noematic sense' that belongs to each real consciousness is not itself *anything real*.

> Each 'Erlebnis' is so made that there exists a possibility in principle of directing the gaze on it and on its real components or instead, in an opposite direction, on the noema, for example the perceived tree as such. What the gaze encounters in this latter direction is, in truth, an object in the logical sense but an object that could not exist by itself. Its 'esse' exclusively consists in its 'percipi'. But this formula must not be taken in the Berkeleyan sense since the 'percipi' does not contain here the 'esse' as a real element.[22]

Thus, the noema is a nothingness (*un néant*) that has only an ideal existence, a type of existence that is close to that of the Stoic λεκτόν [*lekton*]. It is only the necessary correlate of the noesis:

> The eidos of the noema refers back to the eidos of the noetic consciousness; they imply each other eidetically.[23]

But if this is so, how can one distinguish the Centaur that I imagine from the blossoming tree that I perceive once the reduction is made? The 'imagined-Centaur' is also the noema of a full noetic consciousness. It also is *nothing*. It also does not exist anywhere, as we have seen earlier. Though, before the reduction, we found in this nothingness (*néant*) a means for distinguishing fiction from perception: the blossoming tree existed somewhere outside of us, one could touch it, embrace it, turn away from it, and then, go back find it again at the same place. The centaur, on the contrary, was nowhere, neither in me nor outside of me. At present, the *thing*-tree has been put in parentheses, we only know it anymore as the noema of our current perception; and, as such, this noema is an irreal, exactly like the centaur.

> The pure and simple tree, the tree in nature, is nothing less than this 'tree-perceived-as-such', which belongs as 'that-which-is-perceived' to the sense of the perception, in an inalienable way. The pure and simple tree can burn, be dissolved into its chemical elements, etc. But the sense—the sense of *this* perception, an element that necessarily belongs to its sense—cannot burn, does not have chemical elements, does not have forces, does not have real properties.[24]

So, where is the difference? How is it that there are images and perceptions? How is it that when we make the barriers of the phenomenological reduction fall, we find again a real world and an imaginary world?

One will reply that everything comes from intentionality, that is to say, from the noetic act. Didn't you say yourself that Husserl laid the bases for an intrinsic distinction between the image and the perception by the intentions and not by the matters? Husserl himself distinguishes, by the way, in the *Ideen*, noemas of images, memories and things perceived.

It can be everywhere a matter of a blossoming tree and this tree can appear everywhere in such a way that in order to faithfully describe *that which appears* as such one will have to rigorously use the same expressions. But the noematic correlates are not any the less different by essence when it is a matter of perception, imagination, imaged presentifications, memory, etc. At times the appearing is characterized as 'reality in flesh and bone', at times as fiction, at times as presentification in memory, etc.[25]

But how must we understand this? Can I animate whatever impressional matter as perception or image at my whim? But what will 'image' or 'thing perceived' mean in this case? Will a refusal to put the noema 'blossoming tree' in relation with the preceding noemas suffice for constituting an image? Surely it is in this way that we proceed before Dürer's engraving, which we can, at our whim, perceive as object-thing or object-image. But this is precisely because it is an issue of two interpretations of the self-same impressional matter. Now, as soon as it is an issue of a mental image, everyone can verify that it is impossible to animate its *hylē* so as to make of it the matter of a perception. This hyletic ambivalence is only possible in a small number of privileged cases (pictures, photos, imitations, etc.). Were it even admissible, one would still have to explain why my consciousness intends a matter as imaged (*en image*) instead of as perceived (*en perception*). This problem concerns what Husserl calls *motivations*. And probably one sees rightly that the animation of the impressional matter of the engraving, so as to make an image with it, depends on extrinsic motives (because it is impossible that this man be there, etc.). In sum, we come back to the extrinsic criteria of Leibniz and of Spaier. But if the same goes for the mental image, here we are then, in a way, sent back to the difficulties of the preceding chapter. The insoluble problem then was: How do we find the characteristics of the true image? The present problem is this: how do we find motives for forming (*informer*) a matter into a mental image rather than into a perception? In the first case, we responded: if the psychic contents are equivalent, there is no way to determine the true image. In the second we must respond: if the matters are of the same nature, there cannot be any valid motives.

To tell the truth, there are, in Husserl, the beginnings of a response. The fiction 'Centaur playing the flute' is likened in the *Ideen* to the operation of *addition*. In both cases it has to do with a 'necessarily spontaneous' consciousness, whereas for the consciousness of sensible intuition, for empirical consciousness, spontaneity is out of the question. Later, in the *Cartesian Meditations*, he distinguishes the passive syntheses that are made by association, and the form of which is the temporal flow, from the active syntheses (judgements, fictions, etc.). Thus every fiction would be an active synthesis, a product of our free spontaneity. Every perception on the contrary is a purely passive synthesis. The difference between image-fiction and perception would then come from the deep structure of the intentional syntheses.

We subscribe entirely to this explanation. But it still remains very incomplete. First, does the fact that the image is an active synthesis entail a modification of the *hylē* or only a modification of the type of unification? One can quite well conceive of an active synthesis that operates by the composition of re-emerging sensible impressions. It is thus that Spinoza and Descartes explain fiction. The Centaur would be constituted by the spontaneous synthesis of a re-emerging perception of a horse and a re-emerging perception of a man. But one can also think[26] that the impressional matter of perception is incompatible with the intentional mode of the image-fiction. Husserl does not explain himself on this point. In any case, the result of this classification is to radically cut the memory-image from the image-fiction. We have seen above that the memory of the illuminated theatre was a presentification of the thing 'illuminated theatre' with the reproduction of perceptual operations. It is thus definitely a matter of a passive synthesis. But there exist so many intermediary forms between memory-image and image-fiction that we could not allow this radical separation. Either both are passive syntheses (that is, in sum, the classical thesis) or both are active syntheses. In the first case, we come back in a way to the classical theory. In the second, we must abandon the theory of 'presentification', at least in the form that Husserl gives to it in his *Phenomenology of Internal Time-Consciousness*. In every way, we are sent back to our initial observation: the distinction between mental image and perception could not come from intentionality alone. It is necessary but not sufficient that the intentions differ; it must also be that the matters are dissimilar. Perhaps it must even be that the matter of the image is itself spontaneity, but a spontaneity of an inferior type.

In any case, Husserl opens the way, and no study of the image can neglect the rich glimpses he gives us. We know at present that one must start again from zero, discard all the pre-phenomenological literature, and attempt before all to acquire an intuitive view of the intentional structure of the image. One will also have to pose the new and delicate question of the relations of the mental image with the material image (picture, photos, etc.). It will also be appropriate to compare the consciousness of the image with the consciousness of the sign, in order to definitively free psychology from this inadmissible error that makes of the image a sign and of the sign an image. Finally, and above all, it will be necessary to study the *hylē* proper to the mental image. It is possible that, along the way, we will have to leave the domain of eidetic psychology and have recourse to experiment and to inductive approaches. But it is by eidetic description that it is appropriate to begin. The way is free for a phenomenological psychology of the image.

NOTES

1 *Jahrbuch für Philosophie und phänomenologische Forschung*. Bd. I.

2 *Ideen zu einer reinen Phänomenologie und phänomenologischen Philosophie*. [Edmund Husserl, *Ideas Pertaining to a Pure Phenomenology and to a Phenomenological Philosophy, First Book*, F. Kersten, trans., Dordrecht: Kluwer, 1982.]
3 *Ibid.*, p. 53. [*Ideas*, p. 57.]
4 *Ibid.*, p. 56. [*Ideas*, p. 61.]
5 Eidetics in the sense of 'Sciences of essence'. Mathematics is an eidetic science.
6 *Ideen*, p. 132. [*Ideas*, p. 160.]
7 *Ideen*, p. 20. [*Ideas*, p. 19. Sartre's parentheses.]
8 *Ideen*, p. 64. [*Ideas*, p. 73.] *Erlebnis*, a term untranslatable into French, comes from the verb *erleben*. 'Etwas erleben' means 'to live something'. *Erlebnis* would have more or less the sense of 'vécu' in the sense in which the Bergsonians take it.
9 *Ideen*, p. 76. [*Ideas*, p. 89.]
10 *Farbenabschattung, Glätteabschattung*, etc.—untranslatable.
11 *Ideen*, p. 75. [*Ideas*, p. 88.]
12 'Beseelen', cf. *Ideen passim*.
13 *Ideen*, pp. 42–43. [*Ideas*, p. 43. Sartre's brackets.] Emphasis ours.
14 *Ideen*, p. 226. [*Ideas*, pp. 261–62. Second set of parentheses Sartre's.]
15 A distinction that Husserl, by the way, has not pushed further in his published works.
16 He wants above all to show that, in aesthetic contemplation, the object is not posited as existing. His descriptions refer rather to the *Critique of Judgement*.
17 In the revised post-war edition, which takes into account the progress accomplished by Husserl since the first edition of this work. [Edmund Husserl, *The Logical Investigations*, J.N. Findlay, trans., revised by Dermot Moran, London: Routledge, 2001.]
18 In any case, this thesis that we will seek to refute later has the great merit of making of the image something other than a *sign*, in contradistinction to contemporary English and French psychology.
19 [Edmund Husserl, *On the Phenomenology of the Consciousness of Internal Time (1893–1917)*, John Barnett Brough, trans., Dordrecht: Kluwer, 1991.]
20 We quite willingly recognize that this is a matter here of an interpretation, which the texts appeared to us to authorize but which they do not force us to adopt. It remains that they are ambiguous and that the question demands, on the contrary, that we sharply and clearly take a position.
21 We explain here very crudely a very nuanced theory, but its details do not concern us directly.

22 *Ideen*, p. 206. [*Ideas*, p. 241.]
23 *Ideen*, p. 206. [*Ideas*, p. 241.]
24 *Ideen*, p. 184. [*Ideas*, p. 216.]
25 *Ideen*, p. 188. [*Ideas*, p. 221.]
26 This is what we have tried to show in the preceding chapters.

CONCLUSION

Every psychic fact is synthesis, every psychic fact is form and possesses a structure. Such is the affirmation on which all contemporary psychologists are agreed. And certainly this affirmation is in a relation of full compliance with the data of reflection. Unfortunately, it draws its origin from *a priori* ideas. It *complies* with the data of the intimate sense (*sens intime*) but does not *arise* from it. It follows that the effort of psychologists has been similar to that of mathematicians who want to *recover* the continuum by means of discontinuous elements. They have wanted to *recover* psychic synthesis starting from elements provided by the *a priori* analysis of certain metaphysico-logical concepts. The image is one of these elements.[1] And it represents, in our opinion, the most complete failure of synthetic psychology. They have attempted to make it supple, to diminish it, to make it as vague and as transparent as possible, so that it would not *hinder* syntheses from happening. And when

DOI: 10.4324/9781003657408-6

certain authors realized that even thus disguised it necessarily had to break the continuity of the psychic stream, they have completely abandoned it as a pure scholastic entity. But they have not seen that their critiques were directed at a certain conception of the image, not at the image itself. All the bad is born from this: that they have *come to the image with the idea of synthesis*, instead of drawing a certain conception of synthesis from reflection on the image. They have posed the following problem for themselves: how to reconcile the existence of the image with the necessities of synthesis?—without noticing that the atomistic conception of the image was already contained in the very way of formulating the problem. In fact, we must respond sharply: the image cannot in any way be reconciled with the necessities of synthesis if it remains an inert psychic content. It can only enter into the stream of consciousness if it is itself a synthesis and not an element. There are no and there couldn't be any images in consciousness. But the image *is a certain type of consciousness*. The image is an act (*un acte*) and not a thing. The image is consciousness of something.

Our critical investigations cannot lead us further. At present, we would have to tackle the phenomenological description of the structure, 'image'. This is what we will attempt in another work.

NOTE

1 Cf., e.g., the conclusion of A. Burloud in *La pensée d'après Watt, Messeret Bühler*, Paris: F. Alcan, 1928, p. 174: '[One must] distinguish two things in a thought: its structure and its *content*. It has for content sensible elements and relational elements or the ones and the others at once. As for its structure, it is nothing other than the way in which we become conscious of this content.'

REVIEW OF *L'IMAGINATION*

Maurice Merleau-Ponty

J.-P. Sartre, *The Imagination*, 1 vol. in 16, 162 pp., from the *Nouvelle Encyclopédie philosophique*, Paris: Alcan, 1936.[1]

Descartes, Leibniz, Spinoza, and Hume may have differently conceived of the relations between the image and thought, but they nevertheless agree on an implicit definition of the image as a revived perception. It is in everything comparable to perception. It is a sensible content. As a modification of thought or a received impression, it is a real part of the thinking being. In a word, it is a thing within. Experimental psychology will never challenge that conception. It will never confront it with the data of the intimate sense (*sens intime*).

One may at times subordinate the order of images to its quasi-physical connections, but never will one contest its very existence. Taine's psychology is commanded by a certain idea of images that he formed not by direct analysis but introduced *a priori* beginning with the preface of *De l'Intelligence* in order to give himself the element that psychology needed if it wanted to resemble physics. In Ribot, it is from biology that psychology takes inspiration. He will thus never fail to stress the unity of psychic operations. But when Ribot wants to analyse the creative imagination, for example, the dissociations, associations, and synthetic factors he talks about are nothing but *constructions*. '… [T]his entire generative mechanism is pure hypothesis. Ribot is therefore concerned with describing the facts no more than Taine. He begins with the explanation' (41 [35]).

Must one at least say that with Bergson the notion of the image has been corrected according to the immediate givens of consciousness? Bergson did indeed expressly proclaim that between images and sensations there was a difference in nature. But in fact we shall see that his philosophy forces him to renounce this idea because he arrives at the problem of the image only after having established his conception of consciousness, of the object, and of the body. The examination of these metaphysical presuppositions and of their consequences concerning images occupies twenty very dense pages in J.-P. Sartre's opus that deserve reflection, but we can only bring out the general meaning of them here. Sartre's first criticism concerns the notion of the subject. The intention of Bergson is to break free from the conceptions that lock consciousness into its 'states', and to ensure that perception has a direct openness onto things. This is not what we blame him for here: we blame him for having, in a sense, sought less a solution than a compromise. For preparing the world to become representation in the subject, it is called pure perception; for preparing things to become thoughts, they are called 'images'. But either these terms are taken in an extremely vague sense: 'images' and 'pure perception' are nothing but other names for 'world', and then consciousness will truly remain to be deduced, the *esse* will not *a fortiori* imply the *percipi*; or else, in calling things 'images' one places into them a *diffuse* consciousness, *from which one will move, by degradation, to the personal mind*. But what is a consciousness without an I? '... [C]onsciousness appears as a quality, a given character, almost a kind of substantial form of reality ...' (44 [38]). If now one objects that it is the living body and the 'centre of indetermination' of which it is the envelope that account for becoming aware, '... then it would be an abuse of words to call the passive realities that consciousness can apprehend "consciousness", and one would be going back to a metaphysics that begins not from the world as conscious, but from consciousnesses facing a world' (47 [40]). It is also the passage from *matter to mind*, from pure perception to memory, and the Bergsonian concordism that are challenged in the author's second criticism. If, truly, for an image (in the Bergsonian sense), to be conscious is nothing but to be isolated, how can memories maintain an individual life in the Bergsonian unconscious, since, as soon as I stop perceiving an object, my body stops drawing these nascent actions that delimit, in the world, the objects I'm cognizant of, and thus, as soon as the perception is over, the conditions of knowledge cease to be given? How does the present maintain a durable psychic existence? How does it change into a past that I can evoke? '... [A] present that is pure action could not by any splitting produce an inactive past, a past that is *pure idea* ...' (51 [43]). It is true that one gives oneself the whole past at once by saying that the mind *is* memory, which amounts to refusing any explanation. Let us admit thus that the present continuously reduplicates itself into a memory. Brought back to consciousness by the reproduction of its motor framework, the memory reawakens: the old painting offers itself again to our eyes. But in what does it differ from perception? It is only evoked if it inserts itself into the corporeal attitude. But if it does, it is the present. How do we know that it refers to a past? There is the true problem of memory. It does not suffice that copies or photographs from the past be kept or even reproduced. What is essential is that they be understood as allusions to a past. But precisely, as long as one makes of memory a spectacle that maintains *itself*, albeit as a 'virtual' state, one prevents oneself from understanding how this present that subsists can ever take on the figure of a past and order itself in the perspectives of the past, which are deeper at each instant. In order to understand the *presentation of the past*, which indeed constitutes the essential of memory (*l'essentiel de la mémoire*), one would have to renounce the mythology of memories that maintain *themselves* in the manner of things, and substitute for it the rigorous analysis of the acts in which I know the past. These memories in third-person are nevertheless indeed the image-memories of Bergson. They want to 'push themselves into full light', they 'start moving' (55 [47]). We are quite close to the images of Associationism: fragments of the past endowed with their own causality. And indeed, even though Bergson superimposed intellectual effort onto the Associationist mechanism, he let the 'plane of images' subsist beneath that of the schema (*schéma*). Associationism remains a partial truth, the truth of moments of relaxation. But we ought to understand that it is not possible to give it any part, and that, if one admits images as it conceives of them, one will never be able to understand the intentional operation of thought. The materialism of images will contaminate it. One will speak of attraction and repulsion between schema (*schéma*) and images, and thought in turn will be conceived of in the third-person as a force that acts on things, and not as the apprehension of a meaning.

But let us consider the classical notion of the image in itself, and we will see that it excludes any valid solution to two essential problems: that of the 'characteristics of the true image' and that of the relations between thought and images. When they do not treat the image like a 'reduced' sensation (Taine), classical conceptions admit at least that perception and image are constituted on the basis of neutral representations by the activity of judgement. An image in isolation would not differ from a sensation in isolation. It is in accordance with whether or not it can be inserted into the logical context of the true world that the representation makes itself a perception or an image. But in fact, the perceptual field is at each instant crossed by accidents of light, strange noises, cracking sounds and apparitions, inexplicable at first, which we nevertheless never attribute to images. As astonishing as perception is, it is always its own proof. It appears as a 'primary source of knowledge' (107 [95]), and our judgement makes do with it as much as it can. Inversely, most of the time, there is nothing fantastic about our images, '… what we imagine precedes only by a little what will happen next or follows by a little what just happened'. If they were compared to the 'infinite system of reference' of the true world, they would be in good accordance with it. 'In these conditions, perception should at each instant be a conquest over dream; one would have to continually risk denying, based on sheer presumptions, the reality of such and such a figure, and risk affirming, without decisive reasons, the real existence of such and such another. The sensible universe, so painstakingly constructed, would be perpetually invaded by completely plausible visions that one would nonetheless have to set aside, as well as one could, without ever being absolutely sure of having the right to do so. We see that the world thus described—a world where one has never finished correcting the appearances, a world where all perception is conquest and judgement—does not correspond in any way to the world that surrounds us' (108–9 [97]). The classical conception of the image does not enable us to understand any further how the image could be useful to thought. If images are sensible contents that appear and disappear according to associative attractions, thought has no grasp on them. They are not at its disposal, no more than the things of the world of which the images are precisely only the 'inner' equivalent. If a relation can be established, if a judgement manages to form, it will be through an instantaneous act of thought immediately broken. At each moment the flux of images will escape from the 'directing theme' (116 [103]) of thought. This is why it will not suffice to maintain, as many authors do, that the image, which is a sensible content, possesses a meaning as well. As a sensible or quasisensible content, the image would still remain opaque to thought and would oppose its own inertia to it. Consciousness does not allow pure data into itself.

This proposition is obvious—if one is willing to reflect on the nature of consciousness, if one does not settle for a confused idea that would represent it as 'the world of psychic facts', parallel and similar to the world of physical things. In making the inventory of the existences we know, we realize that they amount to two types: spontaneous existence, which engenders itself and which is that of consciousness, and conditioned existence, which is independent of my will and which is that of the things in the world, and that of the sensible contents and classical images as well, since I must 'wait' for them, 'decipher' them, 'observe' them. To say that consciousness exists spontaneously is to say that it knows itself at the same time as it knows. If indeed it were only a cognizant power (*puissance connaissante*) unaware of itself, it would be given to itself as a fact and would thus fall into the second category of existences. One could allege that the acts of my consciousness are themselves conditioned, for example, by the state of my body, but these facts can do nothing against the given we started from. To renounce this giveness is to renounce knowing what one says. There is no fact that could establish that Euclid's propositions are not true in Euclidean space. It is starting from the spontaneous existence of consciousness, attested to by the *cogito*, that one will have to attempt to think about the action, in appearance transitive, of the body on the soul. In any case, it is quite clear that we can no longer allow without contradiction 'contents' such as the classical image 'in' consciousness: consciousness, even if it engenders itself, could not however evoke or select the images, as these opaque and inert contents can only be called to conscious existence or sent back to the unconscious by a *force* of the same nature as theirs; and consciousness is not a force (125–126 [110]). We are thus led to a reform of the notion of the image, and most of the notions that psychology uses without criticism would have to be revised in the same way, confronted with the effective operations of consciousness. Such would be the object of Husserl's eidetic psychology. And here one can surmise the reluctance of the psychologists. One knows indeed that, for Husserl, it is not even an eidetic psychology that would give us the truth concerning consciousness. This truth can only be achieved if one abandons the natural attitude, the realism of shared knowledge and of all sciences, for a transcendental attitude in which all *things* resolve themselves into *meanings* (*significations*). One understands that psychologists express little taste for (what they believe to be) a new metaphysical evasion. But first, neither eidetic psychology nor transcendental phenomenology pretends to *substitute itself* for experimental or inductive psychology. Husserl said more than once that the relation of the former to the latter is the same as the relation of mathematics to physics. Physics progressed when it started using this eidetics of space that was geometry, waiting for other eidetics that would complete the determination of the physical object. Likewise, 'Psychology is an empiricism that is still searching for its eidetic principles' (142 [128]), without which no experiment is univocal because one does not know *what one treats of*. It is thus clear that eidetic psychology is in no way a pretence for neglecting experience, but on the contrary it is the means by which to understand its sense. Moreover, such recourse to analyses of essence, even to a transcendental attitude, is nothing optional. The contradictions in classical conceptions of the image are what oblige us to at last pose the question, 'What is an image?' and to interrogate ourselves about the nature (or essence) of the image. And likewise, if one refuses to decompose consciousness into conscious events, to transfer into it a kind of causality that is comparable to physical causality, it is not arbitrarily that we thus pass to a transcendental attitude. It is because the very nature of consciousness is repugnant to the treatment that one makes it undergo, and because we are invited to build for psychology concepts and modes of explanation that are at last appropriate for its object.

For this new psychology, the image will thus no longer be an internal thing. It must not only be 'conscious', as one says in an obscure manner, but also 'consciousness'. The image of this sheet of paper that I have just perceived is not a simulacrum that I would take into me and through which I would seize again the object of my perception. Alain is quite right to say that I do not possess such a painting of the past (and anyway, if I had it, how would I recognize it, without the aid of a second image and so on to infinity?). But Alain is wrong to believe for all that that everything amounts to a false belief taking advantage of an ambiguous perception. If it were true, the imagination would always be affirmative, always an illusion. But precisely, it is peculiar to the imagination not to affirm the real presence of its object (136 [119]). My paper sheet that I imagine after seeing it is indeed the same paper sheet that I saw, but '… is it the sheet *in person?* Yes and no. Certainly I affirm that it is *the same* sheet with *the same* qualities, but I am not unaware that the sheet has remained *over there*. I do know that I am not enjoying its presence' (2 [2]). The so-called image is not *seen*, it does not impose itself to me as do the things of perception. When I think about my friend Pierre, I do not have under the 'gaze of the mind' a duplicate of my old perceptions. 'This "Pierre in reduced format", this homunculus carried along by consciousness has never been of *consciousness*. It was an object of the material world lost among the psychic beings' (148 [132]). What one calls an image is an act in which consciousness directly aims at the *same* object that was given to it in perception. '… [T]here is only a single and self-same Pierre, an object of perceptions and of images' and '… the image is only a name for a certain way that consciousness aims at its object', the image of Pierre is just 'one of the possible ways of aiming at the real being, Pierre' (148 [132]). It would remain to study the specific structure of these acts, which can only be done by an analysis of the acts of consciousness in general and then of their modalities. This task is only initiated in Husserl's published works. J.-P. Sartre proposes to pursue it regarding the imagination in a second book.

The one he has just published will certainly prepare quite an attentive readership for it. One would exaggerate by saying that J.-P. Sartre is always fair. It is possible, for example, to find a deeper sense to the 'images' of *Matière et Mémoire*. One could think that by presenting the world as an ensemble of 'images', Bergson wanted to suggest that the 'thing' should neither be resolved into 'states of consciousness' nor sought beyond what we see in a substantial reality. It would precisely be, in a much less precise language, an anticipation of Husserl's νόημα [noema]. Likewise, one may find that Sartre judges severely the distinction of matter and form in the image when he finds it in certain psychologists (89, 126–127 [69–70, 110]), and is too quick to grant Husserl (146 [132ff.]) his distinction between *hylē* and *morphē*, one of the points in his doctrine that has been contested in Germany itself and presents, in fact, the most difficulties.

But such injustices, if there be any, are covered by the rare merits of the work: the rigour and vigour of critical thought, and the constant felicity of expression.

NOTE

1 Page numbers in parentheses refer to the original edition of *L'Imagination*. Page numbers in brackets refer to this translation.

Bibliography

Ach, Narziß. *Über die Willenstätigkeit und das Denken. Eine experimentelle Untersuchung mit einem Anhange: Über das Hippsche Chronoskop*, Göttingen: Vandenhoeck & Ruprecht, 1905.

Ahrens, Heinrich. *Cours de psychologie, fait à Paris sous les auspices du gouvernement*, vol. 1, Paris: J.-A. Merklein, 1836; vol. 2, Paris: Brockhaus & Avenarius, 1838.

Alain (Émile Chartier). *Les Propos d'Alain*, vol. 1, Paris: Nouvelle Revue Française, 1920.

Alain (Émile Chartier). *Système des Beaux-Arts*, Paris: Gallimard, 1920.

Alain (Émile Chartier). *Quatre-vingt-un chapitres sur l'esprit et les passions*, Paris: Camille Bloch, 1921.

Aristotle. *Aristotle's Psychology; a Treatise on the Principles of Life (De anima and Parva naturalia)*, William Alexander Hammond, trans., New York: Macmillan, 1902.

Barnes, Hazel. *An Existentialist Ethics*, New York: Alfred A. Knopf, 1967.

Bayne, Tim and Montague, Michelle (eds). *Cognitive Phenomenology*, Oxford: Oxford University Press, 2011.

de Beauvoir, Simone. *The Prime of Life*, New York: Paragon, 1991.

Benjamin, Walter. *Benjamin on Hashish*, Cambridge, Massachusetts: Harvard University Press, 2006.

Bergson, Henri. *L'Énergie spirituelle*, 6th edn, Paris: Alcan, 1920. [*Mind-Energy: Lectures and Essays*, H. Wildon Carr, trans., London: Macmillan, 1920.]

Bergson, Henri. *L'intuition philosophique: Communication faite, au Congrès philosophique de Bologne le x avril M. CM. XI.*, Paris: Helleu & Sergent, 1927.

Bergson, Henri. *Time and Free Will*, New York: Harper, 1960, pp. 90–91.

Bergson, Henri. *Matière et Mémoire*, 26th edn, Paris: Alcan, 1929. [*Matter and Memory*, Nancy Margaret Paul and W. Scott Palmer, trans., New York: Zone Books, 1988.]

Bergson, Henri. *La Pensée et le mouvant: essais et conferences*, Paris: Alcan, 1934; 63rd edn, Paris: Presses Universitaires de France, 1966. [*The Creative Mind: An Introduction to Metaphysics*, Mabelle L. Andison, trans., New York: Citadel Press, 1992.]

Beringer, Kurt. *Der Meskalinrausch*, Berlin: Springer, 1927.

Binet, Alfred. *La psychologie du raisonnement; Recherches expérimentales par l'hypnotisme*, 1st edn, Paris: Alcan, 1886. [*The Psychology of Reasoning, Based on Experimental Researches in Hypnotism*, Adam Gowans Whyte, trans., Chicago: Open Court, 1899.]

Binet, Alfred. *Étude expérimentale de l'Intelligence*, Paris: Schleicher, 1903.

Binet, Alfred. *L'Ame et le corps*, Paris: Flammarion, 1905. [*The Mind and the Brain*, London: Kegan Paul, 1907.]

Brochard, Victor. *De l'erreur*, Paris: Berger Levrault, 1879.

Bühler, Karl. 'Tatsachen und Probleme zu einer Psychologie der Denkvorgänge: I. Über Gedanken', *Archiv für die gesamte Psychologie*, 9 (1907), 297–365.

Bühler, Karl. 'Tatsachen und Probleme zu einer Psychologie der Denkvorgänge: II. Über Gedankenzusammenhänge, III. Über Gedankenerinnerungen', *Archiv für die gesamte Psychologie*, 12 (1908), 1–92.

Burloud, Albert. *La Pensée d'après des recherches expérimentales de H.J. Watt, de Messeret de Bühler*, Paris: Alcan, 1928.

Butchvarov, Panayot. *Being qua Being*, Bloomington, Indiana: Indiana University Press, 1979.

Butchvarov, Panayot. *Skepticism in Ethics*, Bloomington, Indiana: University of Indiana Press, 1989.

Butchvarov, Panayot. *Skepticism about the External World*, Oxford: Oxford University Press, 1998.

Caeymaex, Florence and Cormann, Grégory. 'Sartre and Merleau-Ponty' in M. Eshleman and C. Mui (eds) *The Sartrean Mind*, London: Routledge, 2020, pp. 475–86.

Carlson, Sacha. 'Phantasia et imagination: perspectives phénoménologiques (Husserl, Sartre, Richir)'. *Eikasia: Revista de filsosofía*, 11 (2015), 17–58.

Chevalier, J. and Bouyer, H. 'De l'image à l'hallucination', *Journal de Psychologie normale et pathologique, 23* (1926), 439–55.
Chisholm, Roderick. 'On the observability of the self', *Philosophy and Phenomenological Research, 30* (1969).
Claparède, Édouard. *L'Association des idées,* Paris: Octave Doin, 1903.
Claude, Henri and Ey, Henri. 'La mescaline, substance hallucinogène', *Société de Biologie of Paris, 115* (1934), 838–41.
Coombes, Sam. *The Early Sartre and Marxism*, Bern: Peter Lang, 2008.
de Coorebyter, Vincent. *Sartre face à la phénoménologie,* Brussels: Ousia, 2000.
de Coorebyter, Vincent. 'De Husserl à Sartre: La structure intentionnelle de l'image dans *L'Imagination* et *L'Imaginaire*', *Methodos*, 12 (2012).
Dassonneville, Gautier. 'Mescaline, between Psychopathology and Phenomenology: Sartre and Experimentation in 1930s France', in E. Dyck and C. Elcock (eds) *Expanding Mindscapes: A Global History of Psychedelics, Cambridge*, Massachusetts: MIT Press, 2023, pp. 51–73.
Dennett, Daniel. *Elbow Room,* Cambridge, Massachusetts: MIT Press, 1984.
D'Jeranian, Olivier. 'Sartre, Stoicism, and the Problem of Moral Responsibility (from 1939 to 1948)', in K. Lampe and J. Sholtz (eds) *French and Italian Stoicisms: From Sartre to Agamben*, London: Bloomsbury, 2020, pp. 15–34.
Dufourcq, Annabelle. *Merleau-Ponty: An Ontology of the Imaginary*, Bryan Smyth, trans., Cham: Springer, 2024.
Elpidorou, Andreas. 'Imagination in Non-Representational Painting', in J. Webber (ed.) *Reading Sartre: On Phenomenology and Existentialism*, London: Routledge, 2020, pp. 15–30.
Ey, Henri. *Traité des hallucinations,* Paris: Masson, 1973.
Ferri, Louis. *La psychologie de l'association depuis Hobbes jusqu'à nos jours (histoire et critique)*, Paris: Germer Baillère, 1883.
Flajoliet, Alain. '*Analoga* and *Phantasmata*: On the Intuitiveness of Imagination in Husserl and Sartre.' *Research in Phenomenology*, 51 (2021), 221–45.
Galton, Sir Francis. 'Statistics of Mental Imagery', *Mind, 5* (1880), 301–18.
Galton, Sir Francis. *Inquiries into Human Faculty and its Development,* London: Macmillan, 1885.
Gerassi, John. *Conversations with Sartre,* New Haven, Connecticut: Yale University Press, 2009.
Giard, Alfred. *Controverses transformistes,* Paris: Masson, 1904.
Godelier, Maurice. *The Imagined, the Imaginary and the Symbolic,* Nora Scott, trans., London: Verso Books, 2020.
Gutting, Gary. *French Philosophy in the Twentieth Century,* Cambridge: Cambridge University Press, 2001.

Hallie, Philip P. *Maine de Biran: Reformer of Empiricism 1766–1824*, Cambridge, Massachusetts: Harvard University Press, 1959.

Hoernlé, R. F. Alfred. 'Image, Idea and Meaning', *Mind, 16* (1907), 70–100.

Holt, Edwin Bissell, Walter Taylor Marvin, William Pepperell Montague, Ralph Barton Perry, Walter B. Pitkin, and Edward Gleason Spaulding, *The New Realism: Cooperative Studies in Philosophy*, New York: Macmillan, 1912.

Hopkins, Robert. 'Imagining the Past: On the Nature of Episodic Memory', in F. Macpherson and F. Dorsch (eds) *Perceptual Imagination and Perceptual Memory*, Oxford: Oxford University Press, 2018, pp. 46–71.

Huang, Di. 'Accounting for Imaginary Presence: Husserl and Sartre on the Hyle of Pure Imagination', *Sartre Studies International*, 27 (2021), 1–22.

Husserl, Edmund. *The Phenomenology of Internal Time-Consciousness*, James S. Churchill, trans., Bloomington, Indiana: Indiana University Press, 1964.

Husserl, Edmund. *Ideas Pertaining to a Pure Phenomenology and to a Phenomenological Philosophy, First Book*, F. Kersten, trans., Dordrecht: Kluwer, 1982.

Husserl, Edmund. *On the Phenomenology of the Consciousness of Internal Time (1893–1917)*, John Barnett Brough, trans., Dordrecht: Kluwer, 1991.

Husserl, Edmund. *Méditations cartésiennes*, G. Peiffer and E. Lévinas, trans., Paris: A. Colin, 1931/Paris: Vrin, 2001. [*Cartesian Meditations*, Dorian Cairns, trans., Dordrecht: Kluwer, 1991.]

Husserl, Edmund. *The Logical Investigations*, J.N. Findlay, trans., revised by Dermot Moran, London: Routledge, 2001.

Husserl, Edmund. *Phantasy, Image Consciousness, and Memory (1898–1925)*, John Brough, trans., Dordrecht: Springer, 2005.

James, William. *Principles of Psychology*, New York: Henry Holt, 1890.

James, William. *Psychology: The Briefer Course*, New York: Henry Holt, 1892; Notre Dame, Indiana: University of Notre Dame Press, 1985.

James, William. *Précis de psychologie*, E. Baudin and G. Bertier, trans., Paris: Marcel Rivière, 1909.

Jay, Mike. *Mescaline: A Global History of the First Psychedelic*, New Haven, Connecticut: Yale University Press, 2019.

Kind, Amy. 'How Imagination Gives Rise to Knowledge', in F. Macpherson and F. Dorsch (eds) *Perceptual Imagination and Perceptual Memory*, Oxford: Oxford University Press, 2018, pp. 227–46.

Klüver, Heinrich. *Mescal and Mechanisms of Hallucinations*, Chicago: University of Chicago Press, 1928/1966.

Kremer, R. 'Le Néo-Réalisme américain et sa critique de l'Idéalisme', *Revue Philosophique de Louvain, 85* (1920), 71–106.

Kriegel, Uriah. 'Perception and Imagination: A Sartrean Account', in S. Miguens, G. Preyer, and C.B. Morando (eds) *Pre-Reflective Consciousness: Sartre and Contemporary Philosophy of Mind*, London: Routledge, 2016, pp. 245–76.

Lachelier, Jules. 'Psychologie et métaphysique', *Revue philosophique de la France et de l'étranger, 19* (1885), 481–516.

Lagache, Daniel. *Les Hallucinations verbales et la parole,* Paris: Alcan, 1934.

Lagache, Daniel. *Les hallucinations verbales et travaux cliniques: Oeuvres I (1932–1946),* Paris: Presses Universitaires de France, 1977.

Lagache, Daniel. 'L'imaginaire, de Jean-Paul Sartre', *Bulletin de la Faculté des lettres de Strasbourg, 8* (1941), 309–25.

Lalande, André (ed.) 2006. *Vocabulaire technique et critique de la philosophie.* 2nd (Quadrige) edn. Paris: Presses Universitaires de France.

Laporte, Jean. 'Le scepticisme de Hume', *Revue philosophique de la France et de l'étranger, 115* (1933), 61–127.

Lavisse, Ernest and Sagnac, Philippe. *Histoire de France contemporaine depuis la révolution jusqu'à la paix de 1919,* Paris: Hachette, 1920–22.

Leibniz. *New Essays on Human Understanding,* Peter Remnant and Jonathan Bennett, trans., Cambridge: Cambridge University Press, 1982.

Levine, Joseph. *Purple Haze: The Puzzle of Consciousness,* Oxford: Oxford University Press, 2001.

Levine, Joseph. 'A "quasi-Sartrean" theory of subjective awareness', in S. Miguens, G. Preyer, and C.B. Morando (eds) *Pre-Reflective Consciousness: Sartre and Contemporary Philosophy of Mind*, London: Routledge, 2016, pp. 342–62.

Lhermitte, Jacques Jean. *Le Sommeil,* Paris: Colin, 1931.

Long, A.A. and Sedley, D.N. *The Hellenistic Philosophers: Volume I, Translations of the Principle Sources with Philosophical Commentary,* Cambridge: Cambridge University Press, 1987.

Magee, Bryan. *The Great Philosophers,* Oxford: Oxford University Press, 1988.

Maldidier, Jules. 'Les Caractéristiques probables de l'image vraie', *Revue de Métaphysique et de morale, 16* (1908), 281–320.

Marbe, Karl. *Experimentell-psychologische Untersuchungen über das Urteil: eine Einleitung in die Logik,* Leipzig: Engelmann, 1901.

Marie, Pierre. 'Révision de la question de l'aphasie: La troisième circonvolution frontale gauche ne joue aucun rôle spécial dans la fonction du langage', *Semaine Médicale, 26* (1906), 241–47.

Marie, Pierre. 'Révision de la question de l'aphasie: Que faut-il penser des aphasies sous-corticales (Aphasies pures)?', *Semaine Médicale,* 26 (1906), 493–500.

Marie, Pierre. 'Révision de la question de l'aphasie: L'aphasie de 1861 à 1866: essai de critique historique sur la genèse de la doctrine de Broca?', *Semaine Médicale,* 26 (1906), 565–71.

Marie, Pierre. 'Sur la fonction du langage: Rectifications à propos de l'article de M. Grasset', *Revue de Philosophie,* 9 (1907), 207–29.

Marie, Pierre. *Pierre Marie's Papers on Speech Disorders,* Merritt Frindel Cole and Monroe Cole, trans., New York: Hafner, 1971.

Mates, Benson. *Stoic Logic,* Berkeley, California: University of California Press, 1961.

McGinn, Colin. *Mental Content,* Oxford: Blackwell, 1989.

McGinn, Colin. *The Making of a Philosopher,* New York: HarperCollins, 2002.

McGinn, Colin. *Mindsight: Image, Dream, Meaning,* Cambridge, Massachusetts: Harvard University Press, 2004.

Merleau-Ponty, Maurice. *The Phenomenology of Perception,* Donald A. Landes, trans., London: Routledge, 2012.

Messer, August. 'Experimentell-psychologische Untersuchungen über das Denken', *Archiv für die gesamte Psychologie, 8* (1906), 1–224.

Meyerson, Ignace. 'Les Images' in *Le Nouveau Traité de psychologie*, vol. 2, bk 4, Georges Dumas, ed., Paris: Alcan, 1932, pp. 541–606.

Moutier, François. *L'Aphasie de Broca,* Paris: G. Steinheil, 1908.

Nagel, Thomas. 'What is it like to be a bat?', *Philosophical Review, 83* (1974), 435–50.

Peillaube, Émile. *Les Images: Essai sur la mémoire et l'imagination,* Paris: Marcel Rivière, 1910.

Philippe, Jean. *L'Image mentale (evolution et dissolution),* Paris: Alcan, 1903.

Quercy, P. 'Remarques sur unethérie bergsonienne de l'hallucination', *Annales médico-psychologiques,* 2 (1925), 242–59.

Ribot, Théodule. *La Vie inconsciente et les mouvements,* Paris: Alcan, 1914.

Ribot, Théodule. *Essai sur l'Imagination créatrice,* Paris: Alcan, 1900. [Essay on the Creative Imagination, Albert H.N. Baron, trans., Chicago: Open Court, 1906.]

Ribot, Théodule. *La Logique des sentiments,* 4th edn, Paris: Alcan, 1912.

Ribot, Théodule. *La Psychologie des sentiments,* Paris: Alcan, 1896. [*The Psychology of the Emotions*, London: Walter Scott, 1897.]

Riedlinger, Thomas. 'Sartre's rite of passage', *The Journal of Trans-personal Psychology,* 14 (1982), 105–23.

Rosenberg, Jay. 'Apperception and Sartre's pre-reflective cogito', *American Philosophical Quarterly*, *18* (1981), 255–60.

Rouhier, Alexandre. *Le Peyotl: La plante qui fait les yeux émerveillés*, Paris: Gaston Doin.

Sandemeyer, Bob. *Husserl's Constitutive Phenomenology: Its Problem and Promise*, London: Routledge, 2009.

Saraiva, Maria. *L'Imagination selon Husserl*, The Hague: M. Nijhoff, 1970.

Sartre, Jean-Paul. *The Imagination: A Psychological Critique*, Forrest Williams, trans., Ann Arbor, Michigan: The University of Michigan Press, 1962.

Sartre, Jean-Paul. 'Intentionality: a fundamental idea of Husserl's phenomenology', Joseph P. Fell, trans., *Journal of the British Society for Phenomenology*, *1* (1970), 4–5.

Sartre, Jean-Paul. *Sketch for a Theory of the Emotions*, Philip Mairet, trans., London: Routledge, 2002.

Sartre, Jean-Paul. *The Imaginary: A Phenomenological Psychology of the Imagination*, Jonathan Webber, trans., London: Routledge, 2004.

Sartre, Jean-Paul. *The Transcendence of the Ego*, Andrew Brown, trans., London: Routledge, 2004.

Sartre, Jean-Paul. *L'Image dans la vie psychologique: rôle et nature*. In *Études Sartriennes, 22, Sartre inédit: le mémoire de fin d'études (1927)*, edited and annotated by G. Dassonneville, Paris: Classiques Garnier, 2018.

Schilpp, Paul Arthur (ed.). *The Philosophy of Jean-Paul Sartre*, La Salle, Illinois: Open Court, 1981.

Smith, Joel. *Experiencing Phenomenology: An Introduction*. London: Routledge, 2016.

Sokolowski, Robert. *The Formation of Husserl's Concept of Constitution*, The Hague: M. Nijhoff, 1964.

Spaier, Albert. 'L'image mentale d'après les experiences d'introspection', *Revue Philosophique de la France et de l'étranger*, *77* (1914), 283–304.

Spaier, Albert. *La Pensée concrète: Essai sur le symbolisme intellectuel*, Paris: Alcan, 1927.

Stawarska, Beata. 'Defining imagination: Sartre between Husserl and Janet', *Phenomenology and the Cognitive Sciences*, 4 (2005), 133–53.

Stawarska, Beata. 'Sartre and Husserl's *Ideen*: Phenomenology and Imagination', in S. Churchill and J. Reynolds (eds) *Jean-Paul Sartre: Key Concepts*, Durham: Acumen, 2013, pp. 12–31.

Stewart, Jon (ed.). *The Debate between Sartre and Merleau-Ponty*, Evanston, Illinois: Northwestern University Press, 1998.

Stubenberg, Leopold and Wishon, Donovan. 'Neutral monism', *The Stanford Encyclopedia of Philosophy* (Spring 2023 Edition), Edward N.

Zalta and Uri Nodelman (eds), https://plato.stanford.edu/archives/spr2023/entries/neutral-monism/.

Taine, Hippolyte. *De l'intelligence,* 6th edn, vols 1–2, Paris: Hachette & Co., 1892. [*On Intelligence*, T.D. Haye, trans., London: L. Reeve, 1871.]

Vachet, Pierre. *La Pensée qui guérit,* Paris: B. Grasset, 1926.

Valéry, Paul. *Oeuvres,* vol. 2, Paris: Gallimard, 1960.

Wahl, Jean. *Vers le Concret*, Paris: J. Vrin, 1932.

Wahl, Jean. *Transcendence and the Concrete: Selected Writings*, A.D. Schrift and I.A. Moore (eds), New York: Fordham University Press, 2017.

Warmbier, Adriana. 'Emotional affectivity and the question of appraisal, viewed in the light of a phenomenological account of pre-reflective affective consciousness', *Forum Philosophicum,* 27(2) (2022), 163–77.

Watson, John B. *Behavior: An Introduction to Comparative Psychology,* 1st edn, New York: Henry Holt, 1914.

Watson, John B. 'Image and affection in behavior', *Journal of Philosophy, Psychology, and Scientific Methods,* 10(16) (1913), 421–28.

Watt, Henry. 'Experimentelle Beiträge zu einer Theorie des Denkens', *Archiv für die gesamte Psychologie,* 4 (1905), 289–436.

Watt, Henry. 'Experimental contribution to a theory of thinking', *Journal of Anatomy and Physiology,* 40 (1906), 257–66.

Webber, Jonathan. 'Sartre's' phenomenological psychology of imagination, in M.C. Eshleman and C.L. Mui (eds) *The Sartrean Mind*. London: Routledge, 2020, pp. 104–16.

Williford, Kenneth. 'Headlessness without illusions: phenomenological undecidability and materialism', *Journal of Consciousness Studies,* 27(5–6) (2020), 190–200.

Windt, Jennifer M. *Dreaming: A Conceptual Framework for Philosophy of Mind and Empirical Research*. Cambridge, Massachusetts: MIT Press, 2015.

Witkiewicz, Stanisław Ignacy. *Narcotics*, S.A. Gauger, trans., Prague: Twisted Spoon Press, 2018.

Index

Note: Page numbers followed by "n" refer to endnotes.

For Product Safety Concerns and Information please contact our EU representative GPSR@taylorandfrancis.com
Taylor & Francis Verlag GmbH, Kaufingerstraße 24, 80331 München, Germany

www.ingramcontent.com/pod-product-compliance
Lightning Source LLC
LaVergne TN
LVHW010650110826
845149LV00014B/3022

* 9 7 8 1 0 3 2 9 3 3 3 0 6 *